THE COMPLETE HANDBOOK FOR CHILDREN'S MINISTRY

THE COMPLETE HANDBOOK FOR CHILDREN'S MINISTRY

How to Reach & Teach the Next Generation

From Birth to Age 12

Dr. Robert J. Choun
and
Dr. Michael S. Lawson

Foreword by Dr. Howard G. Hendricks

Publishers Since 1798

THOMAS NELSON PUBLISHERS
Nashville

Published in Nashville, Tennessee, by Thomas Nelson, Inc., Publishers, and distributed in Canada by Word Communications, Ltd., Richmond, British Columbia, and in the United Kingdom by Word (UK), Ltd., Milton Keynes, England.

Unless otherwise noted, Scripture quotations are from THE NEW KING JAMES VERSION. Copyright © 1979, 1980, 1982, Thomas Nelson, Inc., Publishers.

Scripture quotations noted NIV are from the HOLY BIBLE, NEW INTERNATIONAL VERSION®. Copyright © 1973, 1978, 1984 by International Bible Society. Used by permission of Zondervan Bible Publishing House. All rights reserved.

The "NIV" and "New International Version" trademarks are registered in the United States Patent and Trademark Office by International Bible Society. Use of either trademark requires the permission of International Bible Society.

Scripture quotations noted KJV are from The Holy Bible, KING JAMES VERSION.

Library of Congress information

Choun, Robert J.
    The complete handbook for children's ministry : how to reach and teach the next generation from birth through age twelve / Robert J. Choun and Michael S. Lawson. p.   cm.
    Includes bibliographical references.
    ISBN 0-8407-4898-1
    1. Church work with children.   2. Christian education of children.
I. Lawson, Michael S.   II. Title.
    BV639.C4C46   1993
    259'.22—dc20   93-23308
                                                                           CIP

Printed in the United States of America

1 2 3 4 5 6 7 — 98 97 96 95 94 93

To
Dr. Kenn Gangel
our encourager, guide, and friend

Table of Contents

Contents

Contents

Acknowledgments

We wish to acknowledge the help of:

Dr. Sara Lundsteen, professor of education, University of North Texas, Denton, Texas.
   Thank you, Dr. Lundsteen, for your constant encouragement, help and guidance in the area of children's education.

Mrs. Elsie Lippy, editor of *Evangelizing Today's Child* magazine, Child Evangelism Fellowship, Warrenton, Missouri.
   Thank you, Elsie Lippy, for your friendship and for many opportunities to serve children through the ministry of print.

The authors wish to thank the following contributors: Hank Angell, Andrew Beaty, Jane Choun, Doug Duerkson, Roy Fruits, Jerry and Cathy Hull, Dan Mitchum, and LaVerne Winn and Pat Zukeran, whose willingness to share their expertise and experience made this book possible.

The passage of years sharpens the outline of important things in one's life, and I see with increasing clarity why God made me a father and a grandfather as well as a teacher of young people for more than four decades. No basic resource is more critical to the future of the human race than children.

God clearly established this priority when He assigned Adam and Eve parental roles, but He brought it into bold relief when He contravened the Egyptian pharaoh's attempt at infanticide by causing one of the very babies marked for death to rise in opposition. Moses, ordained by God for life instead of death, not only led his nation to freedom but left his bequest for continuing life.

"Teach . . . your children and their children after them" what God has done, Moses instructed. Physical child care is for the present, but spiritual nurture is critical for the welfare of generations to come. In this spirit of transmitting the message of life to children, two of my cherished and seasoned colleagues have collaborated to leave their own superb testament for those adults who care enough about tomorrow to invest their efforts in training children.

"Let the little children come . . . do not hinder them," Jesus said (Mark 10:14 NIV). Children are naturally perceptive; they respond to love. Children willingly follow the Savior if they are skillfully led. Drs. Choun and Lawson, veterans of family life, have submerged themselves in the technical know-how of instructing children in order to inform and assist teachers and leaders of the body of Christ with this determinative task. *The Complete Handbook of Children's Ministry* is a constellation of helping hands for families and churches, a valuable and timeless guidebook based on biblical standards.

It is my deep conviction that no effort in Christian ministry is more enduring or more stabilizing to our Christian faith than outreach to children. Many homes in our confused society are neither equipped for nor concerned about obedience to the Lord's command that our children be reared "in the training and instruction of the Lord" (Eph. 6:4 NIV). Today's children must hear about the message of spiritual life, and because these men care so much, this volume greatly enhances that possibility.

Howard G. Hendricks
Distinguished Professor and Chairman
Center for Christian Leadership
Dallas Theological Seminary

Part 1

Why Minister to Children?

1

Why Minister to Children?

The Biblical Perspective

---

*T*he ill treatment of children has left an ugly smudge on the glittering twentieth century's closing days. An alarming number of American adults have forgotten where child-rearing fits into the scheme of their lives. Personal goals such as career advancement, adult relationships, and leisure activities have steadily moved ahead of raising children as a priority. While America searches for a reason to raise its children, Latin America, India, Africa, and most of the Third World search for the means. Staggering numbers of children worldwide are born into lifelong poverty each year. As strange as it seems, that might be considered the good news.

The bad news really gets scary: The numbers of unwanted pregnancies terminated through abortion on demand in the United States show how many American women consider children an inconvenience. But just because a child is born does not mean his or her safety is guaranteed. A frightening future could await the child who reaches full term. In fact, for many children, sexual, physical, and psychological abuse have become an increasingly common growing-up experience.

Even if a child manages to escape abortion or abuse, on the average he or she will have to cope with more than one family setting.[1] When that happens, the child who begins with his or her natural parents later must adjust to a single-

3

parent and then a stepparent home with various unrelated siblings. Some unfortunate youngsters have to make these adjustments several times in their childhood.

Even the child who lives with his or her natural parents throughout the growing years may face emotional neglect. The most caring mothers and fathers can face chronic weariness simply from the pace of their life and/or work. The necessity of labor and the conditions of modern living conspire to abbreviate a family's much-needed "together" times. The energy we all need to nurture our children simply gets siphoned off.

Unfortunately, parental presence does not guarantee quality child care either. Even in seemingly ideal homes, a child may become emotionally detached and starved for guidance and affection. Parents must *choose* to devote the necessary time and energy to their children. But children need more than that. The most conscientious parents can be misguided in their efforts; they need skill, understanding, and applied wisdom to perform the complex task of raising their children.

All of this may sound unique to our overpopulated, underpersonalized, technological age. But that is hardly the case!

Biblical and Modern Similarities

The Bible describes similar distresses in the lives of children. And in certain instances, children in ancient times faced conditions far worse. The lack of modern medicine, for example, made disease and famine a constant threat to life. Raiding parties from hostile peoples routinely slew children along with their families, and often victimized and enslaved those they did not kill (1 Sam. 22:19; Dan. 1). Herod's decree for infanticide throughout Bethlehem typified the kind of rampant brutality children faced. Child abuse was not invented in the age of Christ. Long before, Exodus 1:16 describes how Egypt's pharaoh commanded and persuaded Israelite parents to cast their male children out to die.

Children also felt the brunt of their parents' neglect of godly duty—often in horrifying terms. In Old Testament times, Israel was attacked by surrounding enemies each year as regularly as football season arrives today. But God promised Israel that as long as the people served Him, He would give them victory over their enemies. If they turned away to serve other gods, however, they would face horrible calamities.

In one shocking passage, God—foreseeing the sinfulness of the people's hearts—prophesied how idolatrous parents would eat their own children during an enemy siege (Deut. 28:53–57). Israel did indeed turn to other gods—and, unfortunately, their children paid dearly for their parents' sinful practices.

God hates idolatry in any form, but He gave an especially scathing denunciation when Israel offered its children's blood to idols (Ezek. 16:36–38). Israel was not the only nation, however, that practiced such horrors; 2 Kings 17:31 describes similar practices by refugee settlers in Samaria. They offered their children to their gods by burning them alive as sacrifices.

Perhaps the strain we see on families today reflects our aptitude for abusing the most important relationships we have. In any case, whether through outright sinful rebellion against God or latent sinful neglect of His Word, we have strayed a long way from God's original plan.

God's Plan for Children

God's plan for humankind always included children. Young ones were neither postscript nor the result of the curse on Adam and Eve. Rather, God's command to "be fruitful and multiply" in Genesis 1:28 came prior to the Fall in Genesis 3.

As a person involved in children's ministry, you probably have wondered at times what life would be like for children had the Fall not occurred. Think about it: With neither child nor parent possessing a sin nature, how would child-rearing and Christian education have been affected?

We certainly could expect differences in the confrontational nature of discipline. Without a sin nature, a child would not be pushed at every turn by the innate desire to act independently or rebelliously. Parents, on the other hand, would not routinely overreact, control, or mistreat their children.

What about learning? No one can really say how much sin has affected our mental capacity. But research tells us we use only between 5 and 10 percent of our brain's capacity.[2] If a child's memory or learning speed were enhanced, the educational process at home (and at church) might change dramatically. Parental training undoubtedly would follow a totally different path. Regardless of the sin issue, God originally intended—and still intends—children to grow and thrive in families with loving parents who attend to their needs, give them appropriate information at opportune times, and explain the wonders of God on a daily basis.

We can only speculate as to why God intended children to develop so slowly. Their slow spiritual development seems to parallel their slow but steady physical and mental progress. They need repetitive reinforcement and constant increases in information. Perhaps God created them this way to solidify the faith of their parents. It is true that as Christian mothers and fathers teach their children about God, they simultaneously reinforce their own faith through their insights and explanations. (Imagine the impact of multiple generations living together and sharing their experience with God!)

Or, perhaps God intends parents and children to contemplate Him together—slowly, continually, and repetitively. A growing awareness of God takes time. And practicing truth resembles practicing the piano: Both take incalculable repetition to achieve proficiency. Children bring qualities with them into life that require that kind of attention and repetition.

Maybe God invented children simply because of the wonder and hilarity children bring to life as they grow and develop. Who can resist the laughter of children? Art Linkletter made a living from interviewing children for the joy and amusement of adults. The childish explanations of life revealed on his show were refreshing fun for everyone. And if you ask any grandparents how much they enjoy talking to their grandchildren, be prepared for a lengthy discourse— and perhaps a few dozen pictures!

The Bible simply does not give us much information about God's original intention in making children. However, one passage offers a fascinating hint at one such purpose.

In Zechariah 8, God reassured Israel of His determination to fulfill His promises in a future kingdom. He described how He would personally rebuild Jerusalem and return to live with His people there. The city would have a new name, "the City of Truth" (Zech. 8:3). God also offered a vision of how Jerusalem would look in that glorious time. He did not speak of great parks, cheap public transportation, or affordable housing; no, his urban renewal plan included special places and activities for children. He said, "The streets of the city shall be full of boys and girls playing in its streets" (Zech. 8:5). That's quite a statement from God! When He spoke of rebuilding Jerusalem, He specifically mentioned child's play! Might there be a lesson here for those of us in the church who plan children's activities?[3]

God's "New Jerusalem plan" for children obviously includes features very different from what we see today. For example, in some parts of our world today, surviving childhood is a youngster's first order of business. During the Iran-Iraq war, one Iranian mother began to weep as she saw American children roller skating; she had not seen children play for so long. But God's ultimate plan for children is so safe that His agenda for them reads simply, "Play!"

Indeed, Scripture says, the streets of Jerusalem will be *full* of children playing. Such imagery makes frolicking, laughing children the very center of attention in this passage. That must have been a happy thought for God as He contemplated with Zechariah the abysmal condition of His beloved Israel and foresaw the tragedy and sin in our present world. Thank God, He has given us hopes, dreams, and a promise of a better future for children.

Such a picture seems so far in the future, though. What is God's plan for children today given the reality of our present circumstances? To answer this, we need to understand how the Bible describes children after the Fall. Then God's plan for parents and the church will make much more sense.

God's Description of Children

The Bible provides a rather lively description of children. A thorough concordance search of "child," "children," "boys," "girls," "sons," "daughters," "little ones," and "fatherless" reveals hundreds of references. Here are just a few that are pertinent to our purposes:

- Proverbs 20:11 shows how life choices define a child. Children cannot escape the fact that others perceive them by their behavior. Ultimately, individual acts form patterns which reveal their character.
- 2 Chronicles 13:7 marks a time in Rehoboam's development when he was tenderhearted ("young and inexperienced"), that is, sometime before he became an adult. Is it possible that any child who does not pass through a tenderhearted stage should be considered abnormal or exceptional?
- Psalm 34:11 invites children to learn to fear the Lord, a major theme in the Old Testament. Neither children nor adults do this naturally. They must learn it as a part of their educational curriculum.
- Proverbs 22:15 declares how "foolishness" is one of a child's characteristics. Perhaps the quantity of "foolishness" varies from child to child, but no amount is desirable since the writer suggests the "rod of correction" be used to temper its influence.
- Ezekiel 2:4 (KJV) finds God speaking metaphorically of Israel as "impudent children and stiffhearted." Although these qualities are present in many children—notably younger children—they obviously do not be-

long exclusively to children. Impudence and stiff-heartedness are equally unpleasant among children and adults.

- Daniel 1:4 distinguishes Daniel and several other Israelite young men from their peers. This verse says they were men with "no blemish, but good-looking, gifted in all wisdom, possessing knowledge and quick to understand, who had ability to serve in the king's palace." When combined with Daniel's tenacious commitment to God, these superior qualities bore great fruit. While many children may share Daniel's commitment, not all share his personal qualities. Children differ greatly from one another and require different treatment.
- Mark 9:20–21 describes a child with deep spiritual problems. This demonized boy lived in the worst possible spiritual condition a human could know. Adults frequently underestimate the depth of spiritual needs among children. No child can develop fully who does not develop spiritually. Yet there may be barriers to that development which require immediate attention.
- Romans 9:11 alerts us that children can and do choose between evil and good. This does not deny some sense of innocence present in children—but it does confront us with the reality of evil in their experience.
- Hebrews 5:11–14 compares new believers with children of early ages—neither can distinguish between good and evil. Both apparently need constant repetitive training in this area. Children require time and opportunities to practice making choices and coping with the consequences.
- 1 Corinthians 14:20 (KJV) encourages adults to resemble children when it comes to "malice." Perhaps Paul means malice emerges after a child becomes an adult; in any case, we see that children possess an innocence that adults need in their relationships.
- Ephesians 4:14 pictures some adult Christians as children victimized by "cunning," "crafty," "deceitful"

false teachers. This reveals that both children and immature adults constantly shift in their thinking. We can expect such evil "teachers" to take advantage of the naïve condition of children—but adults should know better. Children naturally require protection because of their inexperience in life and limited perspective.

- Titus 1:6 requires the children of church leaders to be believers and not to embarrass their parents or the congregation with wild and disobedient behavior. Yet children can and do contradict their faith with unacceptable behavior. Paul warns that if leaders do not give attention to their children's spiritual development, they must forfeit their opportunity to lead the Christian community. This verse emphasizes, among other things, the reality and importance of the Christian faith as belonging to children as well as to adults.

- 1 Corinthians 13:11 distinguishes children from adults in three categories. Paul said he once spoke, thought, and reasoned as a child. In his early years his verbal descriptions, understanding, and logic were childish. All of that changed, however, when he became an adult.

  Indeed, years may pass before children clearly understand logical cause-and-effect relationships. Their ability to decipher life remains hampered for a long time by their limited comprehension and vocabulary. Children rarely generalize one experience to form a principle for similar experiences. We can tell them, "You just didn't learn from your mistake"—but they couldn't!

  Perhaps we should temper our expectations of children and develop a more patient attitude concerning their limitations. Teachers of spiritual truth must realize that the world of a child only vaguely resembles the world of an adult.

- Luke 2:40 covers some eight to ten years of Jesus' life with these few words: "And the Child grew and became strong in spirit, filled with wisdom; and the grace of God was upon Him."

Jesus' development as a child must have followed normal patterns. And if He modeled life for adults, certainly He modeled life for children as well. Unfortunately, this verse and the twelve that follow recounting His time in the temple reveal all we know about His early life. Yet there is enough here to distinguish between His childhood and adult experiences. The section concludes with this summarizing verse: "And Jesus increased in wisdom and stature, and in favor with God and men" (verse 52). This verse gives a threefold description of Jesus' development: He grew mentally (in wisdom), physically (in stature), and spiritually (in favor with God) in an orderly fashion.

These verses paint a fairly complex picture of children with a full range of qualities both good and bad. This wide variety of descriptions show us that there can be no simplistic explanation of a child's nature.

God's Plan for Parents

Parents face a complex task in child-rearing with no guarantees about the outcome. Even the best job of careful parenting can be frustrated by a child's strong will, physical or emotional handicap, or unpredictable life experiences. Without question, the challenge with which the Bible charges parents is great.

Parents should monitor all aspects of their child's development. But there is one the Bible emphasizes above all others: Over and over, God commands, exhorts, and reminds parents to supervise their children's spiritual development.

For example, when God reorganized Israel from a tribal-family base into a national power, He included a formal charge to parents. Deuteronomy 6:4–9 records the preeminent commandment to love God—and God glues to that commandment clear instructions about teaching children to love God. For adults, loving God included teaching their children! This teaching was to take place informally. Parents were to use every occasion in their normal routine to teach their young ones about loving God.

The integrated nature of this teaching reveals how significantly God views spiritual development. Unlike modern education, in which religion must take its place among other subjects, God made religion the central subject around which the rest of life should revolve. And a parent's love for God in practical, everyday situations provides many living illustrations for ongoing discussion with children about God.

Unfortunately, the Bible does not provide many explicit examples of families who followed this procedure. Without question many families loved God; but, for reasons unknown to us, we have no history of their family life. The apostle Paul, however, mentions one example in which a child received clear, consistent instruction in his family. Paul commends to Timothy the young man's grandmother and mother, Lois and Eunice, for teaching him God's ways (2 Tim. 3:14–15; 1:5). Note how certain phrases in Paul's commendation fulfill the Deuteronomy mandate:

- They began their instruction when Timothy was still an infant, "from [his] childhood."
- They taught Timothy to love God through "the Holy Scriptures," centering on God's commandments.
- Their lives backed up their words; Paul said, "Knowing [those] from whom you have learned [it]."

Since Paul does not include Timothy's Greek father in the commendation, we can assume these faithful women taught Timothy without his support. We don't know whether Timothy's father was dead or simply missing from the picture. Yet we do know that Lois's and Eunice's training provided the foundation for Timothy's godly life and theology. Their early teaching laid a solid foundation for Paul's enriching instruction to form a powerful influence on and through this prominent New Testament pastor.

If, in fact, Timothy's Greek father failed to take spiritual leadership over his family, then this passage has important implications for religiously mixed marriages. In a day when it was common for marriages to be arranged, Timothy's mother may have had no choice in the selection of her husband. What should she do if her husband failed to take spiritual leadership? Apparently, she took a spiritual initiative which Paul later commends.

In 1 Corinthians 7:14 Paul stated that children in religiously mixed families have special "sanctified" advantages. For one, the believing parent has a great opportunity to influence his or her children for God through both word and example. Timothy's success through the witness of the Scriptures should encourage any parent in similar circumstances today.

The verses we have examined so far focus on the instructive side of children's spiritual development. But the Bible gives a corrective side as well. When parents neglect their duty to correct their children, often the results are rebellious children and spiritual disaster. In contrast to Timothy, for example, the sons of the high priest Eli developed reprehensible behavior. These young men did not respect their father and they did not fear God (1 Sam. 2:12–36). But God held Eli responsible, and eventually the Lord replaced Eli with Samuel and brought judgment on Eli's entire household.

Other passages of Scripture describe parental tasks in different ways. But the same goal always emerges—the spiritual development of the child. Ephesians 6:4 contrasts the admonition to parents to rear their children in the "training and admonition of the Lord" with warnings against doing things that would "provoke" them. First Thessalonians 2:11 uses the words "exhorted," "comforted," and "charged" to describe the normal activity of parents.

Clearly, parents must take the lead in giving spiritual direction to their child's development. However, some parents are ill-equipped to begin or sustain this responsibility. Some have never started their own spiritual journeys. Some have only just begun or perhaps "plateaued" early in their development. Others face debilitating emotional or life struggles. Still others find that remarriage and blending a new family saps energy from the task of parenting. Yet all the while children keep growing physically and mentally without essential spiritual input.

While parents must bear primary responsibility for their child's spiritual development, the Bible shows other agencies to bear responsibility also. In the Old Testament, God used the temple, the sacrificial system, and the feasts of Israel to enhance children's spiritual understanding:

- The tabernacle-temple itself was the most complete kind of visual aid a teacher could ever have. Alfred Edersheim's monumental work on the subject reveals how each detail provided a different insight into the character of God.[4] The color, shape, mystery, and activity surrounding the temple appealed to the senses and minds of children as well as adults.
- The sacrificial system graphically demonstrated the horror of sin with its consequences of blood atonement. Seeing an animal sacrifice made an indelible stamp on everyone who witnessed it.
- The feast days held throughout the year broke the daily, weekly, and seasonal routine. Each feast focused on a different aspect of Israel's life with God. All children look forward to times of celebration when the family ceases work, comes together, and prepares special foods. Exodus 12:26 implies that the Passover in particular was expected to stimulate curiosity in children.

Also, to reaffirm God's wonderful acts on their behalf, Israel erected monuments (Josh. 4:5–6). These monuments sparked special curiosity in children as well. God seems to have had children in mind very specifically when He gave Israel these instructions.

In the Old Testament, the temple system reinforced the

teaching and values children were supposed to receive at home. And in the New Testament up to the present, God uses the church's educational program to serve a similar but expanded purpose.

God's Plan for the Church

Opinions vary on the precise role the church should play in children's Christian education. The Roman church historically assumed full responsibility for children's spiritual development, while parents had little or no input. Parochial schools became the educational arm of the church.[5]

In reaction to some abuses in the Roman church and the abdication of responsibility by parents, some Protestants formed the belief that the church should have very little direct involvement in the Christian education of their children. The church should teach adults how to be good Christians, they have reasoned, and Christian education should "trickle down" to children.

Even today such thinking prevails. For instance, church-growth expert Carl George focuses almost exclusively on adults in his strategies. When solving child-care problems for adult care groups, he ignores kindergarten through sixth-grade children altogether. For smaller children, he wonders: "Should this nursery time contain spiritual education? If possible, fine, but its main purpose is to enable adults to grow in Christ so that, as one of many results, they learn to talk with their own children about the gospel."[6] Of course, his approach contains a kernel of truth. Churches should teach parents how to be better Christians, which in turn will impact the children of their families. But is it reasonable to assume that when adult needs are taken care of, somehow the needs of children and young adults will take care of themselves?

George's church-growth material for the most part ignores the place of children's ministries and children's workers. Our question is, when and where are children's needs supposed to be met? George's diagrams never show what children are supposed to do while adults attend meetings.

George does affirm (albeit weakly) some need for children's ministry. He states: "I affirm all the advantages of our current models of Sunday school, as well as the indispensableness of churches providing something on premises for children during adult worship."[7] Yet he almost immediately withdraws his affection by saying, "I believe that the care system to supplement and eventually supersede Sunday school in priority will be the lay-pastor-led nurture group."[8]

The failure to fully address the needs of children in church-growth or renewal programs greatly restricts the helpfulness of such strategies. Moreover, this underemphasis is inexcusable—not to mention impractical—because we believe the number-one concern among Christian parents in seeking a church remains the well-being of their children. Yet, most important of all, failing to provide a comprehensive plan that specifically meets the needs of children ignores New Testament teaching.

What, indeed, does the Scripture teach? First of all, the church had to instruct parents when cultural norms for child care differed from God's standard. Paul encouraged church leaders to help parents assume their rightful roles. For instance, in Titus 2:4 Paul says the church must "admonish the young women to . . . love their children." At first, that instruction may appear needless. Today we think of a mother's love as being natural, intuitive, and instinctive. But cultural conditions can break down natural instincts, as examples from the Old Testament have shown. Women in the New Testament also lived in cultures where children were not always valued. (Doesn't this sound much like the conditions already described as existing in modern-day America?)

Similar passages apply to fathers as well, whom Paul instructed to administer discipline in a more caring and nurturing way than existed in the community around them (Col. 3:21). On the positive side, fathers were instructed to raise their children in the "nurture and admonition of the Lord" (Eph. 6:4 KJV). This injunction would not have been necessary if fathers had been carrying out their duties properly.

Yet the church's work with parents is only one side of the

equation. *The church has to work directly with the children as well.* Some churches and pastors affirm the church's responsibility to contribute to the spiritual development of children. Often, however, they fail to back up their affirmation with time, money, and planning. Indeed, the pastor who spends all of his time with adults or planning adult events neglects a significant portion of his flock!

For a moment, though, let us put aside modern realities and take a fresh look at the church, children, and several key passages of Scripture. A good place to start is with Matthew 28:16-20—the Great Commission. Jesus' command to "make disciples" contains no restrictions. Nothing in the context of this passage leads us to believe that discipling was a uniquely adult experience. If anything, the broad nature of the commission would cause any hearer or reader to think beyond his or her conventional boundaries and take the command far beyond his or her political and geographical horizons. The passage contains no racial, gender, or age-group limitation. Thus, children must become disciples too—and the church must help them if it expects to fulfill the command of our Lord!

In Luke's description of the vibrant early church in Acts 2:42-47, four categories of discipling are identified: worship, instruction, fellowship, and expression. All of these identify components that are essential to a discipling ministry for children. And any church today can evaluate itself by asking the following questions about those categories:

- *Does our church provide opportunities for children to worship?* Are worship services meaningful to children, rather than just being adult experiences in which children must conform to adult standards? Does anyone talk to the children—before, during, or after church—about their worship experience?
- *Does the church provide instruction at the child's level in the things of God?* Do teachers recognize the divinely designed limits of children and organize their instruction accordingly? Are the teachings systematic

17

enough for children to get a consistent notion about God, or do teachers merely bob and weave through the Bible, picking and choosing things of interest to themselves?[9]

- *Does the church provide and encourage fellowship among children?* Do leaders and parents recognize that children, as much as adults, need deep, abiding friendships that focus on the things of God? Are children encouraged to visit, talk, or play together at church? Are such activities respected as the foundations for relationships that build true fellowship? Does the church organize specific times and places for fellowship in the life of a child?[10]
- *Does the church provide encouragement for children to express their spiritual gifts for the benefit of the body of Christ?* Do we give enough attention to helping children who know Christ to find a role in ministry? Have we taken the time to break ministry tasks into child-sized portions?[11]

Let's look at each of these four areas as applied in the life of Samuel:

- 1 Samuel 2:11—Samuel *ministered* to the Lord before Eli (*expression*).
- 1 Samuel 2:21—Samuel *grew* before the Lord (*worship*).
- 1 Samuel 2:26—Samuel grew in *favor* with God and men (*fellowship*).
- 1 Samuel 3:8—God spoke directly to the child Samuel (*instruction*).

Do you find it disconcerting to think that God spoke directly to the child Samuel, bypassing both his parents and the high priest? Indeed, God speaks primarily through His Word today—but do we really believe God speaks directly to our children—or any children—through His Word?

The ministry of Jesus uniquely included children. Granted,

He spent most of His time with adults according to the proportion represented in the biblical record. But the Gospels point out as significant that Jesus did *not* spend all of His precious time with adults. And neither should we!

Children were present in most cases whenever Jesus taught. Matthew 14:21 and 15:28 mention children specifically.[12] And Jesus' teaching had (and still has) intergenerational appeal. He told short, simple, easily remembered, profound stories. If we in the church today cannot communicate effectively to such a wide range in ages, then we must plan special messages and times to teach those we normally exclude (i.e., children!).

As Jesus uniquely reached out to common people, included in this group were children! Mark 9:36–37 and other passages record that He took a child in his arms, looked at his disciples and said, "Whoever receives one of these little children in My name receives Me. . . ." If that doesn't commission the future founders of the church to give special attention to children, what does? Remember, these children were not the disciples' own family members. They simply belonged to the community of people who gathered to hear Jesus teach. Jesus' invitation remains open today to anyone —yes, even to modern church leaders—who wish to welcome Him.

Jesus also worked with individual children who had special spiritual problems (Mark 9:20–21). In one dramatic situation He intervened and ministered directly to the child. He bypassed the father, even though He could have given the man instructions and been on His way, as He did on other occasions. But Jesus' approach here, as in *every* instance, should serve as our model: The church also should minister directly to the spiritual needs of children.

Finally, James brought to the church's attention an underemphasized concept from right out of the Old Testament. The test of true religion, he said, requires active caring for widows and orphans. Fatherlessness here implies a deficiency in spiritual instruction as well as other areas.[13] Who would see to it, the apostle asked, that these children received much-needed fatherly input about God?

The Old Testament raised this issue over and over as Israel consistently neglected its duties to the fatherless. Might the church today have also neglected its duties in this regard? In a society filled with increasing numbers of single mothers, James's concern ought to echo in our ears. What is our response?

Summary

We have seen the precarious condition of children, from their plight in biblical history and prophecy to our present-day situation. Children are, have been, and will continue to be extremely vulnerable. Yet God has always included children in His plan of creation and redemption.

We have noted as well the complex nature of children, with testimony from several passages in Scripture. The Bible focuses primarily on spiritual formation in children, and therefore we do not have a comprehensive profile for child-rearing. However, the Scriptures do indicate the individuality of children (Prov. 20:11), requiring parents, teachers, and spiritual leaders to plan accordingly for the development of the young ones in their charge.

We believe that the Bible places primary, but not exclusive, responsibility for children's spiritual formation on parents. The temple system in the Old Testament and the church's educational program in the New Testament were meant to supplement and reinforce what children receive at home. In some cases, however, the church must carry more of the responsibility for children's spiritual development while simultaneously helping parents learn how to assume their rightful roles. Whatever the church does to "make disciples" should include a specific plan for all age groups, including children. Moreover, the church body needs to reach out in special ways to children who lack spiritual input from their homes.

The church has been given a wonderful opportunity to

show the love of Christ to the world through its care of children. And that is reason enough for every church to be encouraged to give children's ministry its proper place among its priorities.

2

Why Minister to Children?

The Historical Perspective

At various times throughout history the church has been at the head and heart of all education. In such times curricula was Bible-centered and value systems were in accord with God's laws. There also have been times when education has rejected Christianity, promoting instead a humanistic philosophy and a morality stripped of absolutes. It may be surprising (and, hopefully, reassuring) to many Christians, then, to know that today's public school system, although steeped in humanism, pursues a biblical methodology.

Life-Related Lessons

Today's teachers are trained to promote active involvement in the learning process and to teach students to relate lessons to life. What could be more life-related than the approach recommended by Moses? "And these words which I command you today shall be in your heart. You shall teach them diligently to your children, and shall talk of them when you sit in your house, when you walk by the way, when you lie down, and when you rise up" (Deut. 6:6–7). For the children of Israel, each day was filled with ritual, each year with celebrations, and each landscape with monuments that told of God's special relationship with His people.

Early Childhood Education

Solomon understood the importance of early child-training and its impact on adult life: "Train up a child in the way he should go, and when he is old he will not depart from it" (Prov. 22:6). The Hebrew term used to describe the training process suggests a picture of a newborn baby, whose palate is rubbed with honey to stimulate sucking and feeding. Solomon used this image to show that early education can stimulate a child's interest in spiritual matters. This very tender image also suggests that we should not wean infants prematurely and force-feed them the spiritual equivalent of a steak-and-lobster dinner in our eagerness to instruct and evangelize!

Developmentally Appropriate Practice

Both Scripture and modern educational theory emphasize the importance of developmentally appropriate practices. Lesson contents and teaching methods must be geared to the student's level of understanding. Paul speaks to this in his letter to the Corinthians, using as an example an infant who is not yet ready for solid food. In evaluating the church's spiritual growth, Paul said, "I fed you with milk and not with solid food; for until now you were not able to receive it" (1 Cor. 3:2).

The journey from the use of biblical teaching methods centuries ago to their "rediscovery" today has been long and convoluted. Like the disbelieving Israelites who wandered in the desert, education lost valuable mileage when it failed to listen to God's Word.

A Look Back

In Old Testament times, prophets taught adults, and parents taught children. By the time of Jesus' birth, the Jewish home-schooling system was supplemented by childhood and adolescent instruction in the synagogue and school. The home, the synagogue, and the school were partners in education. Academic and vocational instruction were integrated with the study of the Torah, the final authority in all matters.

One of the things that motivated the Jews to open their own schools was the encroachment of Hellenistic culture. To combat the man-centered philosophy and heretical cults of the Greeks and Romans, many Jews (and some Christians) sent their children to private schools. Most Christians, however, sent their children to public schools and did their best at home to deal with the influence of teachings about the gods and heroes. At one point, Roman government administrators made worship of the gods a job requirement for teachers in an effort to limit the number of Christians involved in public schools.

Christian education continued to gain ground eventually to the point that institutions of higher learning were established, such as the one headed by Clement in Alexandria. A two-year training period called "the catechumate" was required of all new believers before they could be baptized. Under Constantine, the catechumate system flourished, but it floundered when infant baptism became popular in the fifth century.

With the collapse of the Roman Empire came the end of secular schooling. The responsibility for preserving and spreading knowledge fell on the shoulders of the church, and missionaries began taking the gospel throughout Europe. Monks living in monasteries offered formal instruction to children of royalty and to those who chose to pursue a religious life. The largely illiterate population began to be educated through sermons, frescoes, stained-glass windows, art, and dramas. Eventually, however, ritual obscured the original, heartfelt meanings of verses, prayers, and creeds. (A magician's "hocus pocus," for instance, has its origins in words corrupted from the mass.)

Teaching guides were distributed among clerics to help them explain doctrine to the unlettered, but few of the guides were written in the common language, and many of the clerics themselves were uneducated. By the thirteenth century, penitents who didn't understand the nature of sin were being required to confess to priests who couldn't explain it to them. In the spirit of reform, the church began to urge clerics to preach sermons in the common language. Aelfric, the monk, preached in Old English, and Thomas Aquinas, the scholastic, preached in Italian.

During the Renaissance there was an explosion of learning throughout Europe. Schools of art and science sprouted up in every major city. The church, although a political power and a patron of the arts, was no longer the only source of education. Learning itself was worshiped. New philosophies of learning improved methodology but diminished the importance of the gospel in the curriculum. Reformers such as Erasmus began to speak out against corruption in the church, and outspoken critics such as Savonarola, Hus, and Tyndale went to the stake as the church struggled to tighten its grip on knowledge.

In northern Europe, Luther urged that the state provide education for each child and that it also restore a Bible-centered course of study. Calvin and others joined the movement, and Reformation education became a blend of Scripture and innovative methodology. Printing presses and the translation of Scripture into common languages made Bibles available to many, promoting both Bible knowledge and literacy.

Henry VIII, who destroyed the power of the Roman Catholic Church in England for personal as well as political reasons, paved the way for public education and dissension among religious factions. Every sect felt driven to open its own schools, or risk the indoctrination of its young believers by an opposing creed. Believers in some sects felt driven even to leave the country. Some remaining groups still were dissatisfied, but, overall, the educational system improved dramatically during the post-Reformation era.

Better organization, new catechisms, and vernacular Scripture translations promoted understanding. In the seventeenth century, Comenius boosted methodology and student morale by introducing picture books that paired illustrations with vocabulary. Religion and morality remained part of the curriculum in both private and public schools. In Boston, textbooks were printed, placing the alphabet side-by-side with the Lord's prayer.

More and more attention, however, began to be centered on the child and the process of learning. Influential educators such as Pestalozzi and Rousseau recommended learning in a natural way, through observation and experience. Theories of child development were tested in laboratory schools. Due largely to the efforts of Froebel, the kindergarten movement was begun, and its popularity spread quickly on both sides of the Atlantic. Researchers such as John Dewey designed ways to assess learning, and teacher preparation became more formalized. Education achieved status as an art and a science.

As the public school system became more secularized, educational philosophy and religious instruction went their separate ways. Churches needed new agencies to promote religious training. Parochial schools served some needs, but the major impetus to Christian education came in 1780 with Robert Raikes's establishment of the first Sunday schools. As the years passed, camps, conferences, youth groups, vacation schools, and national and international organizations shaped Christian education. Comprehensive curricula were designed, teacher training was formalized, and Christian education courses were taught on the Bible college and seminary level.

Today, many Christian educators draw from the behavioral sciences to design and implement the teaching of God's Word. Sociology, anthropology, and psychology all contribute to our understanding of the teaching and learning process. From Montessori we learned that children are natural learners and that the role of the teacher should be mostly that of facilitator. Gesell and others in the child development movement emphasized the importance of play and of understanding the characteristics of each stage of growth. Piaget and his colleagues emphasized the importance of applying learning to life experiences. Maslow, Erikson, and other proponents of humanism pointed out the type and sequence of the needs of the child. (Note: Humanism, as it is used here, is a technical term meaning a child-centered focus of education. It does not mean "godless" or "atheistic.")

Sadly, the preeminent view of the needs of the child disregarded any need whatsoever for a relationship with God. Skinner, in his theories of behaviorism, so mechanized the responses of human beings to stimulus that they might have been considered no more than animals or automatons. In the Christian perspective, on the other hand, each child is an individual who can be expected (but not required) to follow norms for development. Each believer has special gifts to be nurtured and directed into service; each person is drawn to a relationship with his Creator by the working of not a clock or calendar but the Holy Spirit of God.

Christian education owes a debt to the educators and researchers who have measured norms, explained stages of development, unlocked the workings of the brain, and recognized the role of the environment, but their findings must be accepted and utilized by Christian educators only with an equal measure of discernment.

Conclusion

It would be poor stewardship of our knowledge to neglect new ideas simply because they are new—but neither are we to act in blind awe of new ideas. Let us not burn books, as the church has done in the past, but study and measure them against God's truth. We must never doubt that the methods that work and are profitable will be in accord with those of the prophets and the Master Teacher, Jesus Himself. We may never fear that the teaching of the Word of God could ever be fruitless. And may we never lose sight of the goal of bringing each child to a saving knowledge of his Lord.

"If I have the gift of prophecy and can fathom all mysteries and all knowledge . . . but have not love, I am nothing" (1 Cor.13:2 NIV).

Part 2

Who Ministers to Children?

3

Who Ministers to Children?

The Role of the Christian Education Specialist

*O*ur God is an orderly and organized God. Not only does He keep the galaxies in line, but He pays attention to details like the lives and deaths of sparrows and the number of hairs on our individual heads. Scripture also reveals Him as the Lord of long-range planning. In Paul's first letter to the church at Corinth, we are instructed, "Let all things be done decently and in order" (1 Cor. 14:40). Thus, to honor God, the education ministry of the church should reflect the order and deliberation so evident in God's creation. How can that order be achieved?

Churches must first realize the importance of the education ministry. It is only after acknowledging this ministry's place in the church that a congregation can confer proper status upon those who minister to children's education needs. When seen in the proper perspective, that need for quality organization and administration of an education ministry becomes a priority. The education ministry deserves finances, facilities, willing workers, and a leader with special training and abilities—a Christian Education Specialist (CES).

Although job descriptions vary from church to church, the CES acts primarily as an organizer, administrator, recruiter-trainer, and planner. Specific duties depend on the individual church and the division of responsibilities among other staff. In a small- or medium-sized church, for example, the CES is often a part-time staff person who has direct responsibility for everything from keeping the nursery supplied with disposable diapers to teaching a Sunday school class. Yet, as a church grows in numbers, its CES will be pressured to spend more time in offices and conference rooms and less time in classrooms.

One of the CES's first duties in a church is the development of a biblical philosophy of ministry. This means, simply, answering the questions: "Why minister to children?" and "What do we aim to accomplish?" When those questions are answered, the CES and a team of key people can decide goals and objectives for the education ministry. Armed with those goals, programs can be planned to meet the specific needs of the church. When progress toward each goal has been measured and evaluated, new goals can be set and the CES can lead the team through a recycling of the process.

If managerial science were the only requirement for the task, the CES's job description would be titled "business administrator." The CES needs not only the skills of an administrator but also the knowledge of an educator. The CES must understand not only what must be taught and why, but how God's truth should be presented in order to be best understood and applied by learners. An understanding of the teaching and learning process is an absolute necessity.

Most church leaders, such as a CES, start out managing a single program. When it proves successful, they add another. With each added program, their control over direction and quality is stretched further and further. Like a juggler with too many balls in the air, eventually they will drop the ball and mismanage a program. One of the CES's tasks is to discover and develop leaders among the church's mature Christians. Workers who are thoughtfully recruited and carefully trained can share in the ownership of and responsibility for the ministry. By delegating both responsibility and authority, the CES guarantees that programs will continue, even if he or she leaves.

Management is required not just for people, but for things as well. The CES serves as purchasing agent for the curriculum, supplies, and furnishings used by the education ministry. Good stewardship of funds and facilities is a must. Tact and diplomacy are necessary skills because the available funds and facilities are seldom equal to the requirements of each ministry. To further the goals of the church as a whole, the CES must be able to work in harmony with other members of the church staff and make the best possible investments of available resources.

The church that is about to add a Christian Education Specialist to its staff would be well advised to develop a specific, detailed job description. If the CES candidate, the church staff, and the congregation can arrive at similar expectations, then most major problems can be avoided. Specifics might include: curriculum development, leadership of midweek programs, marriage counseling, and music or youth ministries. Responsibilities may involve anything from computers to camp-outs, but each one should be clarified in writing.

As a church reaches out to serve its community, the roles of its staff members inevitably change. A CES originally hired to administrate the Sunday school program, for example, may later be expected to be headmaster of the day school or to direct the child day-care center. As more and more children with mental, emotional, or physical impairments arrive at the church's door, education specialists have to be prepared to welcome them. The CES must be aware of cultural differences, technological developments, and other changes that affect the ministry.

The CES should have special training in education and leadership as well as in biblical studies. Personal characteristics should include: the ability to work with people (even difficult ones), attention to small details that can make a big difference, the flexibility to try another way, the tact to say either the right thing or nothing, the objectivity to recognize what just doesn't work, the enthusiasm to excite others, the patience to wait for change, and the energy to move ahead when the time is right.

4

Who Ministers to Children?

The Role of the Teacher

*I*magine the thrill of discovery felt by Christopher Columbus when he first sighted the New World. How much more thrilled might he have been if Native Americans had come to Spain, picked him up in their boat, and taken him to their own shores, offering him endless travelogues about all he was seeing for the first time? That, in a nutshell, is the role of the teacher—he or she is a student's compass, chart, wind, current, and ship. The teacher enables a person to learn.

Remember the times when Jesus took His listeners on voyages of discovery—telling them parables and guiding them to the meaning behind the symbols? He taught with stories, guided conversations, and learning activities. The Master Teacher provided all the resources and guidance His learners needed to discover the truths in His teachings.

We begin to see the role of the teacher by first answering the question: What does the teacher do to fulfill the role of enabler?

The teacher's first step is to know the learner. To teach effectively, the teacher must know how the learner processes information. Only when the needs and abilities of the learner's age group are understood can the teacher select lesson aims and the most appropriate methods and materials with which to teach them.

If the lesson aim, teaching methods, and materials are all suited to the mental, physical, emotional, social, and spiritual needs and characteristics of the learner, then an important part of the teacher's work is already done before the classroom door flies open. Ready and waiting, the teacher can step into the most vital aspect of his or her role as the first learner enters the room.

"Hello, Mark—I'm glad you're here. Is your grandfather better? Did you get my birthday card in the mail? You'll find your name above the hook for your coat. Tell me what you did this week."

There is truth to the adage that learners don't care what you know until they know that you care. When a godly adult establishes a caring relationship with a child, he or she already possesses the ultimate teaching tool. If asked, most Christians probably couldn't recall from whom they first heard Christ's teachings on the subject of loving-kindness—but most likely they will smile at the memory of teachers who exemplified those words!

The teacher who is not only loving but wise resists the temptation to give learners too much assistance. When a learner persists in doing things on his or her own, the child should be allowed to do so. The object of a child's painting exercise is not for him or her to produce a masterpiece, but rather to experience the joy of line, color, and creativity. The object of a Sunday school lesson is not for a child to fill all the blanks before parents arrive, but to understand a concept that can be applied to daily life.

One task of the teacher is often lost among the chores of cutting out flannel-graph figures, pouring juice, and then mopping it up. That task is to step back from the business of the moment and gain some perspective on the overall purpose. If the aim of the teacher is to bring learners into a lifelong relationship with God and to motivate them to serve Him and their fellow human beings, then that aim must be in the forefront of the teacher's mind at all times. If the children are old enough and mature enough, they can be allowed to serve each other the juice and cookies. This may require more time and towels than if the teacher did the serving, but how else can children experience what the disciples did when Jesus washed their feet and encouraged them to serve each other?

Another task of the teacher is to limit class size. We don't know how many listeners Jesus had when He addressed the multitudes, but we do know he spent most of His time with a small group of twelve learners. On the adult learner level, one teacher to twelve students is about the right ratio. With younger learners, however, the fewer of them the better to be assigned to a single teacher. Experienced teachers of any grade level should take on trainees while classes are still small. In this way, young teachers can observe veterans in action before accepting a class of their own.

With too many learners per teacher, it is impossible to give each child the attention he or she deserves. Each learner should be greeted warmly, motivated, and encouraged in his or her efforts, praised for his or her accomplishments, and treated in a way that reveals a sympathetic understanding of the child's unique characteristics and needs. An alert teacher with a small group of learners will learn what to expect from each child and perhaps recognize a child who exhibits characteristics outside the normal range of his or her peers.

To be an enabler, the teacher must understand each learner's ability and to place goals just within that child's reach. With each goal achieved, the teacher nudges the child a little farther toward the ultimate aim. The sensitive teacher, however, will be aware of individual abilities and not compare the efforts of one child to another. Each learner may require a different measure of assistance, but none should receive more than he or she needs.

Here are some examples of ways teachers can enable their students to discover Bible truth and apply it to their lives:

"In this Bible dictionary you'll find the answer to your question about idols. Just look under the first letter in the word *idol*. When we come to that word in our lesson, would you like to explain it to us?"

"God made each of us special. Use this stamp pad and paper to make thumbprints of your group. Use the magnifying glasses to examine them. Tell us about what you discover."

"Our Bible story today told how David was kind to his friend. Show me that you know how to be a kind helper. Here are sponges to clean off our table."

Teaching children about God is not a job to be accepted out of a grudging sense of obligation or arm-twisting persuasion. On the contrary, Scripture warns that teachers will receive a stricter judgment than others (James 3:1) and that a millstone awaits the person who causes a child to stumble and sin (Matt. 18:6).

Teaching is a privilege and a responsibility awarded to those willing to work hard for a high calling and low status. It is perhaps the most important, and yet least respected, job in the church. Ironically, teachers of the young have more long-lasting impact on their charges but are accorded less status than those who instruct adults. Above all, teachers need and deserve encouragement and support. "Let us fix our eyes on Jesus . . ." the Hebrew church was told, "so that you will not grow weary and lose heart" (Heb. 12:2-3 NIV).

Part 3

Who Are the Children to Whom We Minister?

5

Who Are the Children to Whom We Minister?

A Child Development Overview

7o some, the following chapter on the findings of researchers in the field of child development will seem to approach blasphemy. To imply, for instance, that a child cannot make an authentic profession of faith at a young age is to cast doubt on the conversion experiences of many Christians —some of whom have given their lives to God's service!

It is not our intention, and neither is it within our ability, to look into the hearts of individuals and decide which ones have a relationship with their Savior and when it began. It is, however, the responsibility of anyone trained in how a child thinks and learns to share the observation that the child's thinking process develops in predictable stages. Those stages can be linked to stages in physical growth.

Spiritual maturity is the hardest of all areas of growth to measure, but it can be cued to a child's mental ability to understand the concepts associated with salvation and sanctification. Without question, God accepts the trust of a child. In fact, Scripture says that we adults must be childlike in our trust in order to enter the kingdom (Matt. 18:3). There is a quality to a child's awe of God and trust in His protection that is difficult to find in adult conversions, but there is also a mature understanding of situations and the human condition that is absent from a young child's experience. Teachers must never discount a young child's conversion experience as invalid—but they should reinforce it with follow-up study and perhaps a rededication at a later age.

Anyone who has observed children knows that as they grow they change in ways that are both obvious and subtle. A clinging infant, for instance, grows to be a toddler struggling for a measure of independence. He squirms to be set down on the floor, and then runs from his parents' arms as fast as his unsure legs can carry him. Why then does the same child wail like a banshee when turned over to the babysitter's care?

Over the years, researchers have observed children systematically and have come up with a set of standards by which to measure their development. When children reveal abilities or disabilities beyond or below those standards, they require special attention. Arguably, some of these methods of assessment are inadequate or inaccurate; but we believe we have arrived at a set of standards that are workable for our purposes in this book.

How are these standards to be used? Let's approach the question in a practical way: When an educator designs a curriculum, he determines first what the learners *can* learn and, second, what the learners *need* to learn. Once a lesson aim is established, methods and materials must be determined by the learners' ability to process information and their manual dexterity.

Physical Development

An infant quickly outgrows the church nursery and tears around the early childhood rooms, which afford him more space than he will need later on as an adult learner. He learns to take care of his personal needs, develops control of his large and small muscles, and survives the trauma of losing baby teeth. Periods of slow development alternate with spurts of growth. Girls shoot ahead of him stature-wise, but eventually he will catch up. As he leaves childhood behind and enters the challenging years of adolescence, his body once again survives major changes.

Social and Emotional Development

The dependent infant grows in his or her need for independence. The child wants the approval of adults but later prefers the plaudits of peers. He or she plays alone, then alongside a companion, and, finally, cooperates with a group. The child's initial self-centeredness expands to a concern for the welfare of others and an appreciation of how his or her actions affect them. The young child who didn't care whether playmates were boys or girls soon refuses to sit next to the opposite sex, only to change his or her mind in later years and decide that the other kind isn't so bad after all.

Mental and Spiritual Development

These two aspects are linked and yet they are not. A child too young to grasp the concept of guilt, for example, is not ready to accept forgiveness for it. On the other hand, many individuals who can understand guilt and desperately need forgiveness may refuse to acknowledge either the guilt or the need. An important factor in determining an individual child's need is in discerning his or her ability to associate the result of an action with an intent.

A famous experiment by Jean Piaget involving broken dishes showed that a group of young children were incapable of seeing the difference between a single plate broken by a child who was told not to touch it, and a pile of dishes unintentionally broken by a child. The children interviewed selected as most guilty the child who broke the most dishes, regardless of his good intentions. Only the test subjects nine to twelve years of age were able to distinguish guilt based on intention. At that point in their mental development, they were able to see beyond the obvious result of an action and to deal with the abstract concepts behind it.[1]

Researchers tell us (as any experienced teacher or parent can) that young children have a tough time understanding symbols and unfamiliar terms. A child naturally associates any newly learned word with one that sounds similar. "Hallowed be thy name," for instance, can become "Halloween be thy name." Unfamiliar terms, especially religious ones that are unlikely to be encountered in daily life outside the church, must be replaced by ones with meaning. If the teacher does not perform this service, the child will do it with embarrassing results.

Whenever a teacher uses symbolic words with children, he or she should remember to think of the child as an alien from another planet who needs everything explained in clear terms (or, better yet, actions). Children seem to depend most heavily on sight and sound for learning—perhaps because adults depend too heavily on these two stimuli for teaching methods. The more of a child's senses that can be involved in learning, the more likely the lesson aim will be solidly grounded in his or her experience and understanding.

At some stages in child development one area of growth can take precedence over the others. The individual whose mental development may not proceed beyond childhood may grow into a physical giant, and the one whose emotional maturity leaves his peers in the dust may remain small in stature. Likewise, the boy who can repeat every memory verse may be the same one who shakes down his classmates for lunch money!

There are exceptions to every rule, and teachers need to be familiar with the standards for child development. Our God is an orderly God—and even though each of His individual creations is unique, they all fall into sets and patterns. Each stage of an individual's growth will take place according to a God-ordained timetable unique to that person, and never haphazardly. Educators must be prepared to cooperate with God's plan, regardless of whether God chooses to adhere to the rules as we perceive them.

(For a detailed discussion of age-group standards, see the chapter entitled "Age-Group Characteristics and Needs," under Section V, Children's Ministry, A to Z.)

Part 4

What Is Children's Ministry?

6

What Is Children's Ministry?

Goals and Objectives
of the Ministry

*T*he education ministry's goals and objectives must be based on two criteria: the needs of the children it serves, and the church's philosophy of ministry. The overall goal of Christian education, of course, is to lead individuals to a personal relationship with their Savior, Jesus Christ, and a life of service to Him.

Any attempt to reach that ultimate goal without first determining intermediate goals along the way is like driving across the country without a map. We need landmarks along the way to tell us if we're going in the right direction, how far we've traveled, and how many miles we have yet to go.

Education Goals

Because children have different needs at various stages of their lives, separate goals must be set for each age level. Programs must address each learner's physical, emotional, social, intellectual, and spiritual development. Curriculum must be both educationally and biblically sound.

Here are some of the primary needs in any children's education ministry:

- a Bible-centered, learner-focused curriculum that involves children in an active process of learning and encourages their application of all lessons.

- clear presentations of God's plan of salvation at age-appropriate levels.
- a balance of worship, instruction, fellowship, and expression.
- unified curricula from nursery through sixth grade, to ensure coverage of Bible themes and continuity of teaching and learning styles.
- established policies and procedures that are clearly communicated to parents, teachers, and children.
- Bible memorization.
- outreach programs.
- discipleship of believers to a life of service.

Facility Goals

Realistic and workable goals should be set for obtaining a ministry facility and furnishings that will meet the physical needs of the church's young learners. Safety and security are crucial, and steps should be taken to maximize the potential of the learning environment, both indoors and outdoors.

A children's education facility should include:

- adequate floor space per learner, according to age group.
- furnishings of a correct scale.
- comfortable temperatures.
- nearby toilet facilities of a correct scale.
- light to work by.
- clean, safe, and stimulating surroundings.

Personnel Goals

Goals must be set to provide for recruitment, training, and retention of an education team and teaching staff. Parents and teachers must be able to work in an environment of partnership.

Some needs in this area are:

- long-term service commitments to build teacher-learner relationships.

- pre-service and in-service training on a continuing basis.
- required attendance at planning-training meetings.
- commitment to personal spiritual growth.
- staff numbers to ensure an acceptable teacher-to-learner ratio in each class.
- qualified administrative team to supervise, plan, and evaluate the department.
- clearly defined job descriptions.
- continual recruitment of workers prior to need of them.

Teaching would be simple if children brought only their intellect and spiritual nature to church, leaving home their loose teeth, untied shoelaces, and temper tantrums. Teaching is necessarily complex, because each learner is a package of needs and characteristics—like his peers in most ways but unique in others. Each area of growth is like a single gear in the workings of a clock—all moving ahead, but not at the same speed. A child is not an adult in miniature, but simply a child—charmingly simple and amazingly complicated.

The child and his need for Christ must be the keystone of the children's ministry. This goal must keep all programs, plans, and procedures in their proper place. The child's development as a whole person and as a disciple must be the vision of every committee, team, and board involved in this ministry.

7

What Is Children's Ministry?

The Future of Children's Ministry

*A*t present, children's ministry suffers from an unfortunate combination of vital importance and low status. The pressures of life today make the need for ministry to children greater than ever before. Millions are in danger of imminent starvation—emotionally, spiritually, or physically. The pressing question for us is: What should the role of the church be in a society that considers children disposable?

Churches that are willing and able to devote their resources to children's ministry are hiring specialists and designing programs and facilities to meet the special, desperate needs of children. In many cases, churches provide a vital service by identifying children in need and securing social services for them and their families. Many homeless or transient families shy away from any official agency, including a public school, but will come to a church for assistance. Churches and parachurch organizations already are straining to funnel those in need into the social service system and to catch the ones who fall through the cracks.

What about other families, with other needs? Church leaders who have catered exclusively to adults are discovering, to their surprise, that most parents of young children choose a church according to its educational environment for their youngsters. Like quantum particles, families can suddenly disappear and show up somewhere else—and nobody saw them go! Churchgoers are looking for a "full service" church with less regard to its denominational ties than to a healthy menu of age-group programs.

Children who are forced to grow up too fast need to see the relevance of their lessons. Those accustomed to being entertained need to discover the excitement of exploring God's Word for themselves. Young ones in need of caring relationships need to find friendship and fellowship at church.

A children's ministry needs to respond to cultural differences in order to minister effectively. A major consideration is the growing cultural diversity in America. Teaching methods and materials based strictly on an Anglo culture will need to be adapted to a variety of ethnically related learning styles. Teachers must be flexible to meet the needs of a multicultural class and to guide their learners to an appreciation of each other's uniqueness.

Increasing numbers of disabled children who previously have been housebound or institutionalized are being introduced into the public school system. More and more of these children will appear at the doors of our churches. Education must be prepared with the special knowledge, skills, and facilities necessary to accommodate them. (In many cases, such needs may be mandated by law.)

Parents in the work force often require care for their preschool-age children and before- and after-school care for their school-age youngsters. Many churches provide such services, and many more will be asked to provide them as the next century approaches. The establishment and administration of child care and private schools are serious issues and should be undertaken only by qualified individuals and churches committed to excellence. Corporations are beginning to provide on-site child care for their workers, and many observers predict a proliferation of government-run centers in the future. The opportunity that the church has now to impact young children with the message of God's love today must not be lost.

The traditional two-parent family is on the decline in

America. As the number of single-parent families and other nontraditional arrangements increase, children will need adults to whom they can go for attention and guidance. In many cases, teachers may be called on to fulfill the expectations children normally place on their own parents. Churches will find it helpful to have a children's counselor on staff. Record numbers of youngsters are currently being treated for depression and other emotional problems, and most likely that number will continue to rise. The church's ministry to single parents and their children will continue to grow in importance—because a parent raising children alone will always need support.

The explosion in electronic entertainment has made it possible for children to spend entire days in front of VCRs, TVs, and computers, which have become substitutes for flesh-and-blood friends. The children's ministry can provide children with a place where they can find caring adults and fellowship with other children in a godly atmosphere. A church with a recreation center will draw in both children and their families.

The church should avoid rejecting technology as some plug-in tool of the devil. It should explore the possibilities of adapting it for use in the education ministry. As the children who grew up with computers become church leaders, they naturally will find application for such tools in the Sunday school classroom. Computers in Christian education may soon become as common as our flannel-graph cutouts.

Yet, the best the ministry has to offer has been—and always will be—the love of God as revealed through the care and concern of adults committed to children. In the technology-glutted, relationship-hungry future that is projected for us, the personal touch of Christ through one of His own will serve as the church's best drawing card.

Part 5

Children's Ministry, A to Z

Abuse and Advocacy

Statistics now tell us that more than two million cases of child abuse are reported annually in the United States, and reports increase each year.[1] It is possible that among the youngsters in your church are some who have been abused. Officials estimate some two-thirds of sexual abuse cases remain unreported.[2] The question that concerns us is: How can the church prevent such abuse, and what steps should be taken when it is suspected?

What Constitutes Abuse?

Abuse is any action that causes injury to a child. When an injury is due to a lack of proper care or supervision, that constitutes neglect. Abuse can be emotional or physical. Sexual abuse can range from non-touching to touching to violent advances. When a sexual touch involves an imbalance in age, size, or knowledge, it can be considered abuse.

Who Are the Abusers?

Many children are victimized by strangers, but most are abused by family members and friends of the family. Abusers include men and women from all economic and social groups. Some actually seek employment in professions that put them close to children, especially in a position of trust.

The church constantly needs to be aware of the threat to the children in its care.

Abusers can build a shield of secrecy around their crime by threatening their victims, promising gifts, or accusing them of willing complicity. An abuser can manipulate a child's emotional state so that the youngster assumes the guilt and protects the attacker.

There are several actions the church can take to break down the abuser's shield of secrecy:

The Ministry of Advocacy

The first step in this area is education. Children must be educated to know when they are being victimized and how to report abuse. Children's workers must know how to recognize signs of abuse and whom to notify. Church leaders must know how to prevent abuse in the church and what steps to take when they receive reports of suspected incidents.

Teach the Children

1. Teach them to trust. If abuse of a child is parental and the youngster is a preschooler, the children's worker may be the victim's only trusted adult contact. Teachers must build a trusting, friendly relationship with their learners so that a victimized child can come to his teacher without threat of rejection. If abuse comes from a source outside the home, a good parent-child relationship will facilitate communication. Only about 2 percent of children who are sexually assaulted report the crime.[3]

2. Teach them awareness. With the cooperation of parents, a children's ministry can help youngsters learn the difference between "good touches" and "bad touches" and what to do in the case of trouble.

3. Teach them to be prepared. Children, parents, and church workers must know whom to tell and when to tell. Parents should have ready fingerprints and recent photos of their children in case of an emergency. In the case of rape, a physical examination will be needed for evidence.

Children should know their address, phone number, and how to use a phone. Parents should rehearse the procedures necessary if a child were to get lost.

Teach the Workers

1. Avoid compromising situations. Instruct workers to avoid being alone with a child. Insist on additional adult supervision for field trips. At church, be sure parents always have access to their children. Train workers in discipline techniques that do not involve corporal punishment.

2. Work with parents. Encourage workers to talk to parents and help them clearly understand the workers' motivation behind special attention, notes, or small gifts given to their children. Parents need to be wary of any unfamiliar adult who wants to lavish attention on their child.

3. Be security-conscious. Churches are favorite targets for child molesters.[4] Children under fourth grade should not be allowed to go to the bathroom or on errands alone. Classroom doors should be kept locked (but first check restrictions for fire safety). Young children should not be dismissed from class without an accompanying parent or adult designated by the parent.

Special care must be given to nursery security. Many churches use identification card checks when babies are picked up. Even though most abuse victims are eight to twelve years old, even infants can be victims.[5] A rising number of kidnappings, cases of abuse, and murders among infants and children are the result of satanic rituals.[6] Teachers should be alert to any reference by youngsters to occult practices.

Take Preventive Measures

1. Screen workers. Carefully screen all vocational and volunteer workers in the children's ministry. Check references and for possible criminal records. Most abusers are repeat offenders and simply change locations instead of their behavior.[7] (The average offender has had more than sixty victims.)[8]

2. Be security-conscious. Make frequent checks of empty offices, closets, or closed classrooms. Put fences around playground areas. Be especially wary of gates and doors near roads and highways. Encourage ushers to note adults who leave for part of a worship service. Require teachers to keep careful attendance records. Provide hallway and parking lot security for children's programs.

3. Have a plan ready. Have written policies ready regarding security and what to do in cases of suspected abuse. Train all workers to recognize the signs of abuse and neglect. Keep written records of all reports from workers and all subsequent reports made to the law enforcement agency.

Know the Signs

1. Unexplained injuries. Be alert for injuries that are in various stages of healing, bruises covered by clothing, burns (especially in patterns), and welts that show the imprint of a strap or buckle. Victims of sexual abuse may show discomfort in walking or sitting, pain in urinating or defecating, persistent throat infections and gagging, or blood spotting in underwear. Nursery and early childhood workers who tend to the toilet needs of children should be trained to recognize signs of abuse.

2. Behavior changes. Abused children may show excessive violence while at play with dolls or animals. They may regress into younger behavior patterns and experience relapses in toilet training. Sexually abused children may exhibit fear of certain individuals or places. They may also exhibit sexual knowledge, language, or actions inappropriate for their age level. Children who have been coerced into sexual acts may also possess gifts or money from an unexplained source. A family member who is an abuser usually wants to limit his or her victim's social contacts, so a child may be isolated somewhat from his or her friends.

3. Signs of neglect. Neglected children may be inappropriately or inadequately dressed. Their nutrition and hygiene needs may have gone unattended. They may fall asleep in class from lack of rest. Neglected children may be the first to show up and the last to go home. Church workers need to be alert for signs of hunger or for clues that a child has been left unsupervised by parents for a lengthy period. Unsupervised children often become the victims of accidents and/or attackers.

When Abuse Is Suspected

1. Report. In most states, health and education professionals are required to report suspicions of child abuse. In some locations, clergy are also required to do so. Failure to report such cases can be punishable by fines, jail terms, or both. Know your state's laws, and report suspected cases within the required time period.

Everyone has heard horror stories of the system's failures to protect children even when suspicions have been reported, but unreported suspicions leave a child without hope. Reporting suspected abuse starts the investigation that can lead to a victim's protection, treatment, and recovery.

Reports should be made to local law enforcement offices, the Child Protective Agency, or the Department of Social Services. Additional information can come from local hotlines listed in telephone books.

Any information is helpful in reporting abuses, but those reporting must provide the victim's name and address, the names and addresses of the victim's parents or custodians, and (in some states) the identity of the suspected abuser. Federal law protects any reporter with immunity from prosecution, and some states excuse them from participation in court proceedings.

If a suspected abuser is on the church staff, the church will need to contact a lawyer. A lawsuit may be involved if the church was negligent in hiring, supervising the worker's practices, or failing to report abuses. A parent's suspicions of church workers must not go uninvestigated.

2. Support. An abused child needs professional care for physical and emotional healing. Concerned adults can be part of the treatment by reassuring the child that he or she was the *victim*. A circle of caring, sensitive adults can help restore a child's trust. A church should be sure that any counseling provided is competent in the area of abused children's needs.

How long did it take you to read this section? If it took ten minutes, then five children were molested while you were reading.[9] Christians need to speak out on behalf of children. Churches and individuals can protest pornographic publications and films and reject playthings that promote violence. Legislation to benefit children needs support from voters, including the church. We can both pray for and actively protect children against the crimes of which they are helpless victims.

The following resources include training and educational materials, and/or information concerning child abuse:

For Kid's Sake, Inc.
31676 Railroad Canyon Road
Canyon Lake, CA 92380

"Child Abuse and Neglect: State Reporting Laws"
DHHS Publication No: (OHDS) 80-30265
Write: National Center on Child Abuse and Neglect
    Children's Bureau
    Administration for Children, Youth, and Families
    U.S. Dept. of Health and Human Services
    P.O. Box 1182
    Washington, DC 20013
CHILD HELP National Child Abuse Hotline
1 (800) 422-4453

Active Learning

Children will not actively apply what they have been passively taught. Learning that leads to changed perceptions, and behavior must actively involve the student. By participating in the learning process, a child owns, appropriates, or internalizes Bible truth for application in daily life. How can the teacher provide such learning opportunities?

Purposeful activities can be designed to promote the aim of the lesson while meeting the age-group characteristics and needs of the learners. The more of the five senses that an activity utilizes, the greater the learner's involvement and rate of retention. Research has proven that learners remember only 10 percent of what they hear and only 20 percent of what they read.[1] Since lecture and reading are the two most common teaching methods in educational ministries, these percentages are somewhat depressing. Research shows, however, that the use of visuals boosts learning by an additional 10 percent. The combination of both seeing and hearing pushes the percentage all the way to 50 percent!

Teachers don't have to settle for sending their learners home remembering only half of what they've seen and heard. If a learner has comprehended enough of a lesson to verbalize the concept in his own age-level vocabulary, he will be able to remember 70 percent of the information. The learner who not only can talk about a concept in his own words but can also be actively involved in learning it will retain a whopping 90 percent!

What would happen if swimming instructors sent their students to the beach after only a series of lectures on swimming? Students who had never before even gotten their feet wet would soon be in over their heads—literally! Why should we expect our learners to apply God's Word to their lives solely on the basis of lectures? To equip them, we must provide teaching that promotes not only the understanding of Bible truth, but the know-how and desire to apply it to daily life.

Activities that teach Bible truth can involve art, creative writing, drama, discussion, games, research, books, music, nature—the possibilities are endless. The successful use of such an activity depends on whether the teacher chooses an appropriate one and follows these guidelines for implementation:

- The activity must be appropriate to age level.

    Research is a good activity for upper elementary children, but not for those in early childhood. On the other hand, art activities provide projects appropriate for all age levels. Teachers must be familiar with the abilities and interests of their learners in order to make a wise selection.
- The activity must be lesson-related.

    All segments of a lesson must focus on its theme. Any song, project, or game that does not direct the learner to the lesson aim distracts him from it! Young children enjoy familiar melodies, so if the lyrics don't fit the lesson aim, resourceful teachers should feel free to rewrite them and use the melodies anyway.
- Activities must be varied.

    Children have different learning styles and preferences. Aural-oriented learners manage well with lectures, storytelling and recorded resources. They enjoy discussions, debates, and panels. Visual learners enjoy pictures, time lines, maps, and charts. Some children learn best when they can be physically active. Using a variety of activities guarantees each type of learner an opportunity to succeed. Even the most avid learner will become bored with the same activity week after week —so teachers need to maintain a vast repertoire of selections.

Once a teacher has a stock of activities—and a criteria for appropriate selection—the question remains: "When and how do we implement activities?"

Use Learning Activities

You can use learning activities to:

- Demonstrate abstract concepts.
    "Today's lesson is about sharing. On this plate there are enough cookies for everyone at our table. What is the fairest way to hand them out?"
- Develop social, conversational, and decision-making skills.
    "You three boys have chosen the research project. Let's talk about how you're going to divide the work among you to complete it on time."
- Focus learner attention on the lesson theme.
    "When you first came into the room, I had you hunt for this toy lamb. Today's story is about a shepherd who had to search for his lost lamb. How do you think he felt when he finally found it?"
- Provide a purposeful outlet for creative energy.
    "Now that you have heard the story of the Good Samaritan, you may do one of two things: Join the drama group and make up a modern-day version of the story; or, you may go to the art center and illustrate it."

Using Activities Effectively

For effective implementation, the teacher must:

- Give clear, sequential directions.

  Older children can follow a list of written directions if the instructions are clearly expressed. Younger children need to be directed through an activity one step at a time.
- Direct the activity to the lesson aim through guided conversation.

  Teachers should plan questions that will focus learners' attention on the lesson aim. Guided conversation can direct the learners toward self-discovery of a concept—a positive step toward retention!
- Encourage learner creativity.

  Learners are highly motivated when they can contribute their own ideas to an activity. Teachers should always remember: The process of learning a concept is more important than the maintenance of an immaculate classroom. When a teacher gives directions for an activity, he or she should provide as many choices as possible for the learner's involvement.
- Adapt activities to the special needs of the class.

  Professionally prepared resources and guides always consider the abilities and interests typical of an age group. Individual teachers need to adapt these activities to meet the unique needs of their own learners.

If the curriculum guide for a class or club does not provide activities for reinforcing the aims of each lesson, teachers may need to go to a Christian bookstore or educational supply store for activity handbooks. Some activities require supplies and equipment. In this case, a resource-room system in the church—used for organization and storage—can reduce waste and loss while saving money through bulk purchasing. Some activities require special teaching skills. Teachers should be able to receive training for these at regular training-planning meetings.

Active learning requires a little more effort from teachers than other learning programs. Activities take time to plan, set up, and implement. It may take less time and effort to simply arrange learners in rows and read to them from the teacher's guide, but a teacher's investment of time and effort will pay off richly, because the learner's job is made easier when he or she can actively participate in the discovery of God's truth.

Age-Group Characteristics and Needs

The charts that follow will help children's leaders develop a sensitivity to learners at each level of their development. Teachers must not label a child "slow," "behind," or "abnormal" if he is not in exact sync with typical stages. Wide variance may indicate a need for intervention. The following charts provide a sequence of human development that allows us to estimate when various abilities or readiness can be expected to appear in a child's growth.

You will find listed here mental, social, emotional, spiritual, and physical areas. Familiarity with each of these areas can help children's leaders prepare and teach their charges on an appropriate level of comprehension.

The concepts children can grasp at each level of development are also indicated. Our teaching of God's Word must be presented on the level of the child.

Age Group: Two and Three Year Olds			
Development	**Their Characteristics**	**Their Needs**	**What They Can Learn**
Mental	Poor memory Literal, concrete thinking Learns through play and exploration Limited vocabulary Interest span two to four minutes Learns through senses	Repetition No abstract concepts or symbolism Freedom and stimulating environment Labeling of objects and behaviors Freedom to move from	The Bible is a book that has stories about God and Jesus.

Development	Their Characteristics	Their Needs	What They Can Learn
	One focus at a time	activitiy to activity Sensory activities One direction at a time	
Social	Plays alone Trusting and affectionate Dependent and wants independence Fearful and insecure	Room for solitary play and opportunities to interact Love and support Activities geared for success Security of routine	Church is a happy place.
Emotional	Self-centered and craves attention Wants to please	Small teacher to learner ratio Specific praise	I can talk to God; Jesus is my friend.
Spiritual	Sense of awe and wonder Trusting	Examples of God's creation Adult models of God's loving care	God made the world. God made me. God loves me.
Physical	Little endurance, tires easily Developing large muscle control No small muscle control	Alternating periods of activity and rest Room and opportunity to move around Toys that encourage coordination	

Age Group: Four and Five Year Olds

Development	Their Characteristics	Their Needs	What They Can Learn
Mental	Beginning to separate reality from fantasy Learns through senses Interest span five to ten minutes Limited understanding of time and space Literal, concrete thinker Imaginative Curious Imitative Expanding vocabulary	Emphasis on reality of Bible stories Sensory activities Frequent change of activity No references to chronology or geography No abstract concepts of symbolism Settings that encourage imaginative play Opportunities to learn by doing Adults who model God's love Adults who label objects and behaviors	God's book is true. God helps me every day.
Social	Wants to please Dependent and wants independence Enjoys group play	Responsibilities to perform Freedom within safe limits Social interaction with adult guidance	I am a part of my church family.
Emotional	Fearful, emotional Talkative, wants attention Forming self-image	Security of routine and rules Small teacher to learner ratio Activities geared for success	I can trust God.
Spiritual	Understands disobedience Capable of worship	Forgiveness Spontaneous worship encouraged	God loves me, even when I disobey. God is wise and powerful.
Physical	Developing small muscle control	Opportunities to practice new skills	

	Little endurance, tires easily	Alternating periods of activity
	Large muscles need exercise	and rest
		Room and opportunity to
		move around

Age Group: First Through Third Graders

Development	Their Characteristics	Their Needs	What They Can Learn
Mental	Enjoys dramatic play Creative Limited grasp of time and space Reasoning skills developing Literal concrete thinking Attention span 10 to 15 minutes Good memory Writing/speaking/reading skills	Drama activities to teach Bible truth Varied forms of expression Few references to chronology and geography Opportunities to learn by doing No abstract concepts or symbolism Frequent changes of activity Directions in series, Scripture memory Independent work using new skills	The Bible has answers to my questions.
Social	Interested in peer group Learning cooperation Wants independence	Club activities Group-based activities Ability-level tasks	I can share God's love with others.
Emotional	Talkative, craves attention Forming self-image Developing self-control Seeks approval	Small teacher to learner ratio Activities geared for success Fair and consistent discipline Chances to handle responsibilities	God helps me do what is right.
Spiritual	Can understand forgiveness Developing personal values Questions about God and heaven	Models of forgiveness, reconciliation Biblical standards for life-style choices Guided Bible study	God forgives. Jesus is the Savior.
Physical	Active Control of small muscles Voice control and rhythm developing	Frequent changes of pace Opportunities to practice new skills Active songs	

Age Group: Fourth Through Sixth Graders

Development	Their Characteristics	Their Needs	What They Can Learn
Mental	Beginning to grasp abstract concepts Reasoning ability Academic skills Longer attention span Grasp of time and space	Introduction to abstract concepts Opportunity to learn by discovery Writing, speaking, research activities More complex activities References to chronology and geography	God's plan is seen in history.
Social	Craves peer acceptance Less need for adult approval Enjoys competition	Guided social interaction Guidance leading to self-direction	I can bring friends to church.

		Limited competition as motivation	
Emotional	Wants adult status	Challenging responsibilities	Jesus is my
	Unsteady emotions	Love, support, consistency	hero.
	Hero worship	Models of godly lifestyle	
Spiritual	Can understand salvation	Clear presentation of gospel	Jesus is my
	Developing a sense of morality	Guidance in decision-making	Lord. God has a plan for my life.
Physical	Large and small muscle control	Varied activities and skills	
	Healthy, active	Frequent changes of pace	

Art Activities: Busywork or Bible Learning?

It's almost time to go home. The lesson has been completed, but there are still ten minutes of class time before parents come to pick up the children. What now? Should we sing a song? Tell a story? Aha! The coloring books at the bottom of the storage closet will save the day!

Lured to their seats by books and crayons, your students work quietly and the crisis passes. The time was filled—but was it used? Those same ten minutes could have been devoted to a meaningful art activity.

It's easy to overlook the true potential of art activities in the classroom, resorting to them only as "busywork," but that doesn't develop either the lesson theme or the creativity of the learners.

Children love art. The process of making something does several things for them. It stimulates their imagination, releases energy, relaxes tension, provides an outlet for their own ideas and feelings, and reinforces the lesson aim. Those benefits alone would justify devoting part of each teaching session to art activities, but there's more: *Art projects can help teach the lesson by illustrating a concept.*

In our age of ready-made everything, weaving a bit of cloth or paper can help a child appreciate some of the skill and dedication that went into the adornment of the tabernacle. Molding a clay jar could bring home the meaning of Isaiah's reference to "the Potter." Making a gift for a family member or a sick friend could start a young Dorcas on a lifetime of loving actions.

Such projects present many opportunities for sharing, being kind, and speaking in love. Learners who dutifully memorize "Be kind to one another" will internalize the meaning as they put the concept into practice by sharing materials. Artwork can serve to reinforce a lesson and can be a resource for parents who want to discuss the lesson at home. Group cooperation skills can be developed through work on art projects, such as a mural. Confidence and self-image can be given a boost through the display of learners' efforts.

Art and craft materials do not have to be expensive. For example, a class can campaign for donations of throwaway items, such as baby food jars and fabric scraps. Teachers can raid post-Christmas sales at discount craft stores. The minister of education should know that paint, construction paper, clay, etc., are learning materials that should be included in the budget. The church should have a resource center for supplies, or at least a cabinet for storage of materials. If necessary, teachers can carry items to and from home in a box. Whatever system you employ, keep supplies organized to prevent loss or waste. Children can help keep everything in its place—if there is a place for everything.

Part of the privilege of working with art materials includes responsibility for cleanup. Cleanup takes less time if you plan ahead. Newspaper or plastic sheeting can protect tables and floors. Box lids make good trays for finger painting. Garbage bags with holes for heads and arms make good aprons. Stand paint jars in tubs or plates to catch spills. Wash brushes as soon as possible, and don't leave them standing in water. Keep a piece of paper under glitter applications to catch fallout. (Make notes on your own tricks of the trade to share at teacher training meetings.) Take care not to annoy one of the most powerful members of the church hierarchy—the janitor!

Ideas can be found everywhere, but most curricula offer good suggestions for projects. Find those that carry out your theme, appeal to the age group of your learners, and do not exceed their young abilities. Survey craft fairs, ask for resources at bookstores, and recruit friends to help. Ask art teachers for input and suggestions.

Beauty, it has been said, is in the eye of the beholder, and teachers must be careful to resist the temptation to "fix" a young artist's creation. Once touched by an adult, the project (and lesson!) is no longer the child's.

Certain craft projects may need a display sample to show how the pieces go together. For a project to remain the child's own expression, room should be left for individuality, and one child's work should never be compared unfavorably with another's.

The joy a child experiences in creating his or her own work of art helps a young person understand the love that God has for that child as his special and unique creation.

Here are some tips for implementing art activities:

- Keep within the ability and interest range of the learners.
- Distribute materials as they are needed.
- Make directions clear and simple.
- Take steps to simplify cleanup.
- Relate the activity to the lesson.
- Praise each child's efforts.
- Be prepared with extra supplies.
- Provide choices.
- Try a dry run at home with identical supplies.
- Vary projects from week to week.

Beginning a Children's Education Ministry: Solid Ground or Shifting Sands?

The phrase "beginning a ministry" can mean any number of things. It can mean initiating a children's program at a newly planted church. It can mean that an established program run by volunteers has grown so that it now requires the direction of a part-time or full-time professional. "Beginning a ministry" can also imply that a new leader is stepping into the shoes of a predecessor. In any case—and in every case—"beginning a ministry" calls for careful planning, thoughtful decision-making, and change.

Evaluation

Whether a program is starting from scratch or starting over, the first step needed is evaluation. Here are some factors that should be weighed when considering a children's ministry:

- How does this ministry fit into the church's statement of purpose?

- What are the needs in this area of ministry?
- What resources are available?
- What kind of program will fit the purpose and invest the resources to meet the needs?

A common mistake churches make is to create a clone of a program that was successful elsewhere, without considering the special needs of the new situation. The best way to proceed is to invest time in observing the existing situation, learning about the workers, and becoming familiar with the history (i.e., the successes and failures) of the program. A "new" idea may be one that has been tried and abandoned before; and the new leader may be doomed to repeat the failure unless he or she does the necessary homework.

Any evaluation must include an honest look at the church's need for a paid Christian Education Specialist (CES —see chapter 3). A church must ask itself: Are there enough people in the church and enough potential attenders in the community to financially support a CES? Do our plans for growth include expanding the children's ministry? Will a CES need to handle other ministries or perhaps divide his or her time (and salary) with other churches?

The needs of the church family also must be identified. A children's program should include opportunities for worship, instruction, fellowship, and evangelism for young learners. Sunday school is usually heavy on instruction—thus, a children's church program may need to emphasize worship. Club programs, retreats, and camps can be included for extra fellowship time.

Resources must be inventoried, including facilities, finances, supplies, and workers. Additional questions need to be asked: What are the needs for space, materials, and leaders? How can the ministry make the most of what it has? What are the projected needs based on attendance records from past years?

Goal-Setting

Goals must be set on the solid base of biblical directives and sound education philosophy. The goals of the children's ministry must coordinate with the church's overall purpose—thus, goal-setting and decision-making must be team efforts. If volunteers do not understand the purpose of a program and do not have a voice in its planning, they will be less likely to feel "ownership" and responsibility for its success. Long-range and short-range goals should be set, along with a time frame for the necessary steps in-between. Goals must be prioritized so that major needs are met first. (In children's ministry, a good place to start is with those who can do the least for themselves—the nursery.)

Programming

Once the ministry team agrees on what it wants to do and determines the resources it needs to accomplish those goals, it is time to design (or redesign) the program.

Let's look at an example: One church offers Sunday school 9:30-10:30 A.M. but has no children's alternative to the adult worship held from 11:00 to noon. Most of the children in the church are between ages five and eight. They are left unsupervised for a half-hour and may disrupt the adult worship.

Evaluate, Plan, and Program

The following aspects need to be weighed:

- *Consider the purpose of the ministry*—to provide opportunities for children to worship, receive instruction, have fellowship, and become members of God's family. Adult worship is not meeting these goals.
- *Consider the needs of the children.* They require activity and learning opportunities on their own level. They need the security of supervision.
- *Consider the resources.* Sunday school classrooms are empty during the adult worship time. Willing recruits

are available to be trained to lead children in worship. Money is available for supplies.

As a result, a new program, "Welcome to God's House," is publicized—but it is not initiated until workers have been recruited and trained. The program is designed to serve a group of children from first through third grades, beginning with a minimum of eight to ten children. It requires two workers. (A maximum number of learners and teachers must be decided on, not to exceed the space available and the required student-to-teacher ratio.)

In this new program, all Sunday school attenders and early arrivals are involved in supervised activities until (a) they are picked up by parents or (b) they go directly to children's worship. Children's worship themes are related to Sunday school learning aims. After six weeks, the program is reevaluated and improvements are made. As leaders are trained, more children and rooms are added to expand the program. Periodic evaluations ensure that the program continues to meet changing needs.

Sound effective? Of course it does, but sometimes the only way to improve the ministry is to scrap an old program. Such change must be brought about by tact, diplomacy, and a general consensus; otherwise, feelings will be hurt. Suppose a church that has sponsored a Vacation Bible School (VBS) for many years experiences reduced attendance, difficulty in recruiting volunteers, and rising expenses. A little digging shows several reasons for the decline: Many ex-volunteers have joined the work force, working parents need all-day care for their children, and other churches offer competing VBS programs. What should this church do?

Working as a team, key people must consider alternatives. Will a schedule change from morning to evening classes help? How about backyard Bible clubs or day camps?

A joint decision is made to cancel VBS and replace it with a 9 A.M.-to-4 P.M. day camp at a local site, with extended care for children of working parents. All of this will be made available at a reasonable fee that pays for counselor salaries and supplies.

The program must serve the needs!

The Role of the Specialist

Whether he or she is a professional or a volunteer, the person in charge of the children's ministry has a heavy and varied responsibility. If this position is filled for the first time by a paid professional, there may be confusion about the leader's role. If the children's ministry has been progressing smoothly, some will ask, "Why do we need him (or her)?" Yet if the ministry has a history of confusion and frustration, some will say, "Now that this person's here, let him (or her) handle it!"

A detailed job description is the first requirement for a position of leadership. It should be updated annually. Whenever the position is vacated, an "exit interview" should be held with the departing staff member and new information added to the description.

An addition or change of such a leadership position may be interpreted by some workers as a dismissal bell. Loyalty to an individual leader rather than to the goals of the ministry can mean desertions when an individual moves on. Whether a leader is beginning a new ministry or developing an existing one, a major goal of that leader must be to share the vision and responsibility of the ministry with the church family. A ministry built on the solid ground of shared vision and participation will not fall victim to the shifting sands of confusion and indifference when its leader departs.

The Bible and Children

Children need to know what the Bible says, understand what it means, and apply it to their daily lives. Their progress depends on how firm their footing has become on the preceding step, and the fewer obstacles between each step, the better.

A wise teacher will teach Bible concepts that are age-appropriate. Such a teacher will also seek out the clearest Bible version for a text that's chosen for reading and memorization. If a child reads a Bible verse and finds its meaning obscured by unfamiliar words, word order, symbolism, or cultural context, he or she will find it hard to apply the meaning to experience (and, ultimately, to his or her behavior).

Centuries ago, it was considered blasphemy to translate the Word of God into common languages. It wasn't until the Reformation that the Bible became widely available in languages other than Hebrew, Greek, and Latin. Translators were hunted down and burned at the stake for their work. Many died for the mission of making the Word of God available in a language the common man could read and understand.

Today's Bible teachers need just as much enthusiasm for expressing the clarity of God's truth! Paul urged Timothy to be a teacher who "rightly [divides] the word of truth" (2 Tim. 2:15). Teachers must consider the ages of their learners. The best translation to use with children is one that carries out the original meaning of the text using an age-appropriate vocabulary.

Paul goes on to remind young Timothy that "all Scripture is given by inspiration of God, and is profitable for doctrine, for reproof, for correction, for instruction in righteousness, that the man of God may be complete, thoroughly equipped for every good work" (2 Tim. 3:16–17). All Scripture is indeed useful for teaching, but Paul himself knew and used the technique of developmentally appropriate concepts. In dealing with spiritually immature Corinthians, for instance, he commented, "I fed you with milk and not with solid food; for until now you were not able to receive it" (1 Cor. 3:2).

Teachers should encourage children toward Bible memory, but only with verses that can be easily understood. (Comprehension of meaning is just as important as memorization of the words!) Memorization of a power-packed verse with important theological implications may simply have to wait a few years if it is incomprehensible to a learner at his or her present state of development.

For classroom reading, use children's Bibles (one version) that feature not only a clear interpretation, but also large print, illustrations, and possibly study helps. If Bibles do not include maps and other resources, be sure to have the materials available in class. If difficult words are encountered during the Bible lesson, design an activity that will send learners to the Bible dictionary. Encourage children to read their personal Bibles at home.

For very young children, publishers provide Bible storybooks that feature summaries of the familiar Bible stories and lots of colorful illustrations. These are often useful in class and make good gifts for families to use at home.

As learners approach the third- and fourth-grade level, they have enough grasp of history and geography to understand a little about biblical archaeology. An interesting study for children at this age is the exploration of how the Bible came down to us through the ages. Missions agencies can often supply a teacher with teaching resources on how God's

Word is translated into other languages. The history of the Bible is filled with adventure, intrigue, and exploration. A child who takes his Bible for granted may learn new respect for it when he discovers its wonderful heritage.

Bible Memory: Hiding God's Word in Their Hearts

Consider the following interaction:

David and Barry are busy playing a table game along with a small group of other first-graders. At one point, David slips below the table to hide. Barry takes advantage of the situation to give David, a bigger boy, a kick in the teeth. David is dragged from beneath the table, crying and screaming, by his teacher while Barry retreats to a neutral corner, whimpering. David turns and advances on his assailant, grabs him by the arm and says, to everyone's amazement, "I forgive you."

Dabbing cold water on David's swollen lips, the teacher asks David what made him forgive Barry instead of hitting him back. "Do not repay anyone evil for evil," he replies. "It says so in my Bible."

This incident is an illustration of the value of teaching Bible memorization to children. David had not just memorized the words of the verse, but had internalized the verse's meaning and made it part of his behavior. David's teacher had obviously taught the verse in ways that helped him grasp its significance.

Here are a few suggestions regarding Bible memorization for children:

- *Be certain the memory verse relates to the lesson aim.* When all the learning activities of the day relate to a single concept, that concept will be easily grasped.
- *Use visuals.* Pictures can help students visualize a difficult concept. Let students draw their own illustrations. Avoid symbols.
- *Use a simply worded translation of the verse.* Unfamiliar words that have no meaning for a child will be misunderstood and soon forgotten.
- *Repeat the verse throughout the class session.* Apply it to appropriate situations.
- *Use music to teach the verse and aid memorization.* Many songbooks include Scripture set to music.
- *Write the verse on the blackboard and send home copies for review.* Most school-age children have some reading skills. Use games in which learners can put the words of a verse in correct order or match Bible references to verses.
- *Show the children the verse in the Bible.* Mark the verse in a large-print or children's edition of the Bible and set it in a place where learners can easily read it for themselves.
- *Use drama.* Role plays and skits can help learners understand verses containing concepts that may be vague or general. For example, "Love one another" can be illustrated in a skit in which one child helps another to push home a damaged bike. Puppets can also be used to dramatize verses or to make a lesson review more fun.

Listening to children's recitations privately and individually is also a good practice. This reduces tension for slow or nervous children and provides opportunities for one-on-one discussions. Several verses a week may be expected from a bright child whose parents drill him every day; but to expect the same from a child whose reading skills are deficient or who receives no help at home is unrealistic.

One word of caution: Do not overemphasize prizes or

competition in memory work. Rewards for effort are always good motivators, but children should not be dazzled or enticed with gimmicks and gadgets. Teachers should emphasize comprehension of a verse's meaning.

Memorization is a skill that seems never again to be as sharp as it was in childhood. Now is the primary time to get the child into the Word—and the Word into the child!

Budgeting the Ministry: Money Matters

The children's ministry is the wrong budget area for penny-pinching. You can patch the choir robes, but if the walls in the nursery are peeling, repaint them. You can limit the use of the church copier, but buy the primary ages reams of drawing paper. A carillon tower would be very nice—but build a playground first!

The first step in budgeting the children's ministry is goal-setting. What education goals are appropriate? What are each age group's spiritual, emotional, social, physical, and intellectual characteristics? What resources will enable the children to learn the way they learn best?

Often stacked against lofty goals are the cold, hard facts of inadequate funding. The reality for most churches is that there is simply not enough money to do everything necessary. Discretion must be applied to all spending.

Establish priorities. Find out what the critical needs are. The true nature of needs may not be apparent, however, without some insightful, long-range plans. Many churches devote time and money to classroom remodeling based on immediate needs but without considering future needs. Often those churches find themselves tearing out walls a year later. Attendance records and projected growth statistics are some of the tools a budget designer must employ.

The System

Those in charge of the nursery, early childhood, and children's ministries should come up with an estimated cost for the upcoming year and submit the figures to a Christian Education (CE) board or committee. Then, with considerable prayer and prioritizing behind it, the church budget—including CE needs—should be presented to the congregation. Even if the budget is readily accepted without change, unexpected setbacks during the year can mean a return to plan B. (Some churches permit fund-raisers for special projects to aid short-changed programs.)

Blueprint for the Budget

The general fund of the average church includes items such as salaries, missions, worship, evangelism, and maintenance of property. Christian Education falls under the category of "programming."

You might find listed under the auspices of C.E.:

Nursery (birth to two years)
Early childhood (two to five years)
Children (first through sixth grade)
Youth (junior and senior high)
Adult (college to senior adult)
Audiovisual equipment/ supplies

Summer ministries/camping

Club programs

Support groups
Puppet/drama/clown ministry
Teacher Training/ recruitment/recognition
Office supplies/postage/ printing

Listed under each of the age-group headings should be the individual needs of that ministry—including curriculum, supplies, outreach, and other concerns. For example:

Nursery:
educational equipment/ toys

laundry and supplies

furnishings   parent outreach materi-
                                     als
snacks   curriculum for cradle
                                     roll/toddlers

Early childhood:
    curriculum   supplies
    children's church   furnishings
    educational equipment/   snacks
    books/toys
    outreach   special events

Children:
    curriculum   supplies
    children's church   furnishings
    educational equipment/   snacks
    books/toys
    outreach   special events

Many churches have found that a resource room stocked with supplies and equipment (and manned by a detail-oriented volunteer) saves money through bulk buying and reduces waste. A small amount of money could be provided for each department leader or teacher to spend at his or her discretion. Reasonable limits can be set as to what unauthorized expenses will be reimbursed.

The administrator of the children's ministry needs to know how the budget is being maintained as the year progresses. Regular updates should show how current funding and expenses match up to budget figures for both the year in progress and the preceding year. Let's suppose unexpected growth in the children's Sunday school has necessitated extra spending for the spring curriculum; yet, at the same time, the new growth has not resulted in a significant increase in giving. A review of the budget's current state may turn up a program that came in under budget, thus making funds available. It also may show that an unplanned fund-raiser will be needed to supplement day camp fees if the administrator has to dip into the summer ministry account to pay for the curriculum.

Some churches find that special-occasion fund-raising is effective if it is not overused. Many congregations receive a weekly update of the budget balance on the Sunday bulletin or in the church newsletter.

Attendance figures can be used to estimate the cost per person of certain aspects of the program. Babies and toddlers are the most expensive members of the Sunday school. They take up the most space, require the most specialized equipment, use up the most supplies, require the highest teacher-to-learner ratio—and are well worth it! The CE administrator needs to know that a surge in births at the church will mean higher expenses in the nursery ministry.

The value of a program needs to be weighed not only by the cost per person, but by whether the program has measured up to its goals for the individuals involved. Simply put, a program that does not meet needs is not worth the time, effort, and expense involved. But a program that provides age-appropriate opportunities for worship, instruction, evangelism, and fellowship, resulting in changed lives, is worth its weight in gold.

Guidelines

Here are some guidelines to follow in budgeting:

- When preparing a budget to be submitted for approval, do not inflate costs because you expect items to be slashed. Instead, designate the realistic cost of each item listed. That way, if a cut is proposed, planners can see exactly how it will affect the ministry.
- When purchasing equipment and supplies, buy in bulk from institutional suppliers. Buy durable, institutional furnishings, toys, and sports equipment that will last, even if the initial investment seems high.
- When previewing a curriculum or club program, determine the equipment that would be unusable if the curriculum or club were to be discontinued.

- Give careful thought before purchasing equipment that is so complicated it can only be operated by highly trained workers.
- Give priority to expenses related to the safety and security of children.
- Preview campsites, interview guest speakers, and check caterer references before signing contracts or making verbal obligations.
- Be skeptical of bargains. As the saying goes, you get what you pay for! Comparison-shop, evaluate, reduce waste, and be resourceful. Be the best possible steward of the resources with which you are entrusted.

Bulletin Boards and Posters

Most churches use bulletin boards and posters on their walls, and most often the people who decorate those bulletin boards and make those posters got the job not because they were graphic artists—but because they were out of the room when these jobs were assigned!

As a result, there are a great many unattractive bulletin boards and illegible posters lining church walls and halls these days. Here are a few simple guidelines for improving the look of those in your church:

Bulletin Boards

- Keep bulletin boards updated. Those in the classroom should be kept current with lesson themes. Hallway and lobby bulletin boards should be changed frequently to maintain the interest of passersby.
- Decorate your bulletin board with background paper, border strips, letters, and ready-made visuals in a wide range of seasonal and thematic designs. You can find these at art supply or teacher supply stores. The cost is worth it.
- Keep your design bold and simple. Study billboards to get ideas for layouts. The best ones will be uncluttered and readable from a distance. Do thumbnail sketches

of designs and possible layouts before marking or punching holes in the materials.

- Keep the color scheme simple—and limit the number of colors used. Bright, complementary colors (red+green, blue+orange, yellow+purple) will seem to vibrate when placed side by side. If the design is to be used for a long period of time, use non-fading paper.
- Post headlines in large, bold letters, and use smaller print for subheadings. Use computer-generated type, cutout letters or dry-transfer type. Use hand-lettering only as a last resort.
- During setup, consider the distance from which most passersby will view the board. Step back several times to check the effect.
- If the bulletin board is to be used on a classroom wall within reach of infants or toddlers, avoid using thumbtacks or pushpins.
- Photocopy both sides of two-sided items, such as missionary letters. The copies can be mounted side by side, flat against the board, instead of having the two-sided original left dangling by one corner.
- Bulletin boards at main entrances should be devoted to visitor information and announcements of special events.

Posters

- Keep it bold and simple. Most people who read a poster will do so from a distance of six feet or more and while moving. Information on a poster is like theater scenery: What can't be seen from the back row might as well not be there.
- Categorize information and put it into groups. What is the event being held? When and where will it be held? Who can attend? Is there an entrance fee? Who is sponsoring or holding the event?
- As with your bulletin boards, make the main heading of your poster big and bold, with less important information in descending size type.

- For lettering, use computer-generated graphics, dry-transfer type, stencils, or legible hand-lettering. Large brushes or jumbo felt-tip markers should be used for large letters. Tall letters made with thin lines are often unreadable.
- Do not print letters in a vertical column. Too often they can't easily be read.
- If artwork is used on the poster, do not let it overpower the message. The artwork should complement it.
- If you plan to use several posters to advertise the same event in different parts of the building, make sure the posters are similar in both color and layout for easy recognition.
- Use only one color for all the letters in a single word.
- Consider color choices carefully. Black on yellow provides the greatest visual impact, yellow on white the least. Day-Glo or fluorescent colors are eye-catching but often can be difficult to read.
- Remove posters as soon as they are outdated.
- Consider using cork backgrounds, or perhaps mounting strips to post signs. Tape and tacks can damage walls (and they can irritate the committee in charge of maintaining the facility!).
- Do not post signs on glass doors. The posters can be read from only one side, and blocked vision can cause accidents. In addition, tape is notoriously hard to remove from glass.
- Choose poster locations that will maximize reader impact. Avoid posting signs at the top or bottom of stairways, to prevent missteps and backups.

Keep in mind that bulletin boards and posters become a part of your facility's overall appearance. An attractively designed and decorated entryway can be marred by a single ugly poster. A cluttered, outdated bulletin board can promote an unappealing image of an otherwise excellent ministry, and an important special event can suffer poor attendance due to unreadable advertising. Attractive bulletin boards and posters are well worth the time it takes to produce them.

If there are talented artists in your church, ask them if they would be willing to design or produce the bulletin boards and promotional pieces for children's ministry programs. If they do not have access to the proper tools at home, perhaps an office in the church can be equipped with an inexpensive drafting table and a few basic items. (To save money, buy poster boards in bulk from institutional suppliers, rather than one at a time at a premium price, and bulletin board paper in rolls.) For the best results with outdoor signs and large banners, contact a professional sign painter.

Children and the Church: "Our Teacher Lives at Sunday School," and Other Childhood Myths

In ancient times people made up myths to explain the mysteries of the world's origins and workings. Even today children tell outlandish tales to explain what they don't fully understand. If you were to ask some young child where babies come from, or why the sky is blue, you might get a reply of, "I dunno." On the other hand, you might get a mind-boggling explanation that more than makes up for in imagination what it lacks in accuracy.

What do children think about the church? Go ahead, ask them. You may get answers such as: "The offering pays my Sunday school teacher." (She collects it, doesn't she?) "The minister has no legs." (Under his robes, who can tell?) Or, "The big church has a swimming pool in it."

Maybe it's time to get the facts straight. Here are some activities that will familiarize your class with the workings of your church (but results aren't guaranteed!):

- Take a tour of the building. Be prepared to give short explanations of special-purpose rooms or symbolic artwork you may see along the way. This is also a good time to point out to children the fire exit and perhaps the classroom they'll be using next year.
- Introduce the children to the leaders in your church. Ask these people to visit your class and talk about their responsibilities. Take their photos for the bulletin board. If possible, introduce next year's teacher.
- An older child may be willing to take a tape recorder and some prepared questions to interview a church leader. His or her interview can be shared with the class.
- Ask the church treasurer to talk to the children about some of the special projects and routine expenses of the church. It may help them become better stewards of their supplies and equipment when they realize their offerings help to buy them, and their care for them saves money. The meaning behind missionary offerings can be illustrated with photos of missionary projects the church has helped to finance.
- Let the children aid in service projects—folding bulletins, planting flowers, singing for the senior adults class, etc. Help your learners understand that for a church to function in the right way, people of all ages and abilities must pitch in and help.
- Let the children work together to prepare a scrapbook or a bulletin board on the subject, "My Church." Use photos and drawings of the people and characteristics of your church.
- Lead your learners in prayer for the people who serve in your church, whether they are on staff or volunteers.
- Explain why we gather together as a church. Help your learners discover that the church is a place to worship, to learn, to serve, and to enjoy the fellowship of Christian brothers and sisters.

The problem of recruiting willing workers won't be so difficult if you start early to teach young members that the church is not just a building. You can make sure they understand—*they are the church!*

Club
Programs

If a children's ministry is interested only in developing children spiritually, then it fails to minister to them as it should. To evaluate your church's ministry to children, make a list of the programs—Sunday school, children's church, children's choir, etc.—and write down each one's emphasis. Determine how these programs provide opportunities for the four vital elements of worship, instruction, fellowship, and evangelism. Sunday school and children's church usually score high in the worship, instruction, and evangelism categories, but fellowship is often a neglected aspect—yet it is one of the most vital in a children's ministry!

Many churches try to balance this with a midweek club program. Unfortunately, some churches use midweek children's programs for little more than baby-sitting while parents are busy with adult programs. When a well-designed midweek or other special program is carried out by trained workers, it can exceed a church's Sunday school in attendance and impact!

There are two basic types of midweek programs. The first is a program provided by a parachurch organization, such as AWANA, Christian Service Brigade, or Pioneer Clubs. Handbooks, uniforms, awards, and leader training materials are available, but the local church must provide the site and the leaders. The second type of midweek program is one that is designed by the church itself to meet its specific needs. Which approach is best?

In trying to determine the type of program your church needs, you must first answer the question, "What are the needs?"

After that question is answered, your church can move on to the following considerations:

1. Is there an existing program that has been designed to meet needs like ours?
2. Is the program biblically and educationally sound?
3. Can we meet the program's requirements of funds and facilities?
4. Do we have volunteers who can staff the program? Is training for them available? Are program materials user-friendly?
5. Does the program fit into our church's overall ministry? Do we foresee overlaps or conflicts? Are we already overprogrammed in this area?

If a satisfactory program cannot be found, a church may have to resort to designing its own. But many churches have done so only to find they have reinvented the wheel. A committee should be appointed to survey the programs already on the market. Here are just a few:

Adventure Club

Adventure Club is a coeducational program for four-year-olds through sixth grade. Competition is involved but is kept low key, and awards are available for attendance and Bible study. There is a charge for workbooks and leaders' guides. Each meeting includes a songfest, Bible lesson, small-group time for activity pages and memorization, and a time slot for suggested games, crafts, or projects.

AWANA Clubs International

AWANA Club programs are for ages three through high school. Some levels are coeducational while others are separate. Leaders are supported by plenty of programming material, training aids, and local staff. There is a yearly fee and a charge for handbooks, uniforms, awards, etc. One-third of each meeting is devoted to competitive games. The rest of the meeting includes a large-group "Council Time" and handbook work in small groups. The emphasis of the program is Bible memorization. AWANA programs have been adapted for use by the mentally retarded, the blind, and non-English-speaking groups. Camping opportunities are also available.

Christian Education Publishers (Space Cubs, Whirlybirds, Jet Cadets. CEP is a division of Success With Youth)

The program serves four-year-olds through high school. There is a yearly charge and a fee for take-home papers, award books, and resource books for leaders. Leaders' guides provide instructions for weekly meetings. Club members can win awards that are to be worn on beanies or sashes. Meetings include a large-group time followed by small groups for work on a variety of activities. Bible memorization is emphasized.

Christian Service Brigade

Brigade is a boys' program serving grades one through twelve. Leader training material and local representatives are available. There is a yearly fee and a charge for handbooks, leaders' resources, uniforms, and awards. Each meeting includes large- and small-group times devoted to Bible study and a wide range of activities. Camping opportunities are available. Brigade emphasizes the father-son relationship.

Pioneer Clubs

At one time a girls' program, Pioneer Clubs now provide programs for both girls and boys in grades one through twelve. Meetings can be separate or coeducational. Programs and leadership training materials are extensive. There is a yearly charge and fees for handbooks, leader resources, awards, and uniforms. The program emphasizes Bible exploration and memorization. Meetings also include games, crafts, and songs. Camping opportunities are available as well.

A club program that is fun and interesting can attract unchurched children, provide service opportunities for adults, and offer activities that otherwise may be inappropriate for Sunday school or children's church. The church that wants to consider beginning a club program should contact the offices of the various groups listed above and request literature or a visit from a local representative. If midweek programs are being held at nearby churches, visit and observe them. Think about which aspects of such programs can be tailored to fit your church's special needs. For those churches that have examined ready-to-use programs and choose to develop their own, Christian bookstores can provide many helpful resources.

No choice should be tackled by the children's minister or any individual alone. If the congregation is to support a program, they must take part in both goal-setting and decision-making.

Children's Ministry Programs

Adventure Club
David C. Cook
850 North Grove Avenue
Elgin, IL 60120
(800)323-7543

AWANA
1 East Bode Road
Streamwood, IL 60107
(708)213-2000

Christian Education Publishers
A Division of Success With Youth Publications
P. O. Box 261129
San Diego, CA 92126
(800)854-1531

Christian Service Brigade
Box 150
Wheaton, IL 60189
(708)665-0630

Pioneer Clubs
Box 788
Wheaton, IL 60189
(708)293-1600

Computers in the Classroom

When pocket calculators first appeared on the market, most people thought they were just a high-tech, expensive luxury item used only by scientists, engineers, or top executives. Today we would not be surprised to discover one in our cereal box.

When personal computers (PCs) became available, they too were considered costly and intimidating. In fact, most adults of my generation were intimidated by PCs for so long that the phrase "user-friendly" had to be invented to coax us to the keyboard. Now many offices, schools, and private homes have PCs. They are used for everything from charting next year's business profits to making out a grocery shopping list.

One of the most practical and profitable applications of personal computers has been in the area of education. Children seem to be immune to computer phobia. Drawn perhaps by the lure of hands-on activity and instant feedback, youngsters seem to commune with computers. They play with them and learn from them. We believe it is long past time for children's ministries to get in on the action!

New kinds of computers and varieties of software appear on the market so quickly that any we could describe here would be obsolete by the time this book is published. Every day, it seems, the neighborhood computer store restocks its shelves with new forms of technology. The best way for a church to buy a computer for its children's ministry is to determine the possible uses and then research the market for a model that meets its needs. Here are some possible uses for computers in a children's ministry:

In the Office

- Record-keeping: names & addresses, attendance records, inventories, purchases, names of suppliers.
- Long-range planning: data storage, graphics to display data.
- Promotion: attractive brochures, posters.

For the Teacher

- Classroom visual aids: maps, charts, banners.
- Handouts: teacher-generated worksheets, notes, instructions, patterns.
- Study aids: Bible study programs to help the teacher prepare.

For the Learner

- Research aids: information available on software.
- Games: learning exercises and games that are professionally prepared or teacher-programmed.
- Writing: creative writing projects, including making a newspaper with graphics.

The use of a computer in children's ministry does not mean there must be a computer for each child, or even a computer for each classroom. Mounted securely to a rolling cart, a PC could be shared between several classes.

Computer use does require minimal basic training for teachers who can then instruct their students. Equipment includes a display monitor that looks like a small TV set with no knobs; a keyboard similar to a typewriter's; and a printer on which to make copies of the material seen on the screen. Disks are loaded into the computer, containing the text and graphics that you see on the screen. Some of the disks (or "programs") are designed for interactive games, writing, graphics, record-keeping, and other purposes. Some monitors display colors, others only black and white. Printers come in a wide range of reproduction quality.

Computer Applications

Consider the following example of how a computer might be used in a church or a children's ministry during a typical week:

On Monday morning, the church secretary enters Sunday's attendance reports, offering amounts, and visitor data into the computer. Later in the week, the computer will be used to make a bar chart of attendance and financial records, to be given to the long-range planning committee. In addition, a printout of visitor data will be sent to the visitation and follow-up committee.

On Tuesday, the midweek club leader drops by the office to create a flyer announcing an upcoming event. The Sunday school superintendent comes in to check the curriculum inventory disk to help her prepare an order for the following semester. By simply calling up attendance records from last year, she can calculate future needs.

On Wednesday, the children's minister uses the computer to prepare worksheets and flyers for a teacher-training event. On Thursday, the church secretary uses it to consult the church member directory, separate the names of teachers, and print mailing labels for their flyers. On Friday, the children's minister uses the computer for correspondence and files copies of letters on disk for future reference. On Saturday, a Sunday school teacher drops in to use the computer to research information for a lesson.

On Sunday morning, the computer is wheeled over to the fourth-grade classroom. A group of students uses a special program to create a "word search" game of terms used during that day's lesson. As soon as their activity is completed, the computer is wheeled to the fifth-grade classroom, where a review game programmed by the teacher measures learners' ability to apply the Bible to a simulated situation. Next, in children's church, the computer is used to help youngsters write poetry, songs, and stories that express worship. Additional computers will be purchased for a summer "computer camp," at which the children can combine computer skills with fellowship and learning about God's love.

Computers can serve a church in a variety of ways. The wider a church's range of ministry, the more demanding and complex the need for programs becomes—and the greater the need for record-keeping and communication. Computers can be a great help in each of these areas. The busier the church office becomes, the greater the need for efficiency. Here again, a computer can streamline virtually any effort. As busy volunteers' time becomes more and more limited, the more the church needs to ease the burden with time-saving devices—and a computer is just such a device.

As technology makes educational aids increasingly available, the ministry needs to incorporate them. The closer the time comes to our Lord's return, the more urgent our efforts should be to reach children by whatever means are available —that we may "by all means . . . save some" (1 Cor. 9:22).

Conferences and Conventions: Playing a Role in Teacher Training and Staff Development

On any given day, the mail stacked on a minister's desk usually includes a brochure or two on an upcoming conference or convention. These events can be local, regional, national, or international. They can be designed for teachers, Christian education specialists, or senior pastors. Whatever the case, it is worth the time it takes to sort through such brochures—because conferences and conventions can be a valuable resource in teacher training and staff development that can help a church for years to come.

The staff of a large church may already have a Christian education specialist qualified to train teachers. Smaller churches may have access to a specialist through their denominational offices. A church of any size can take advantage of specialists who are available through local seminaries and Bible colleges, or use one of the many training resources prepared by curriculum publishers. All these training approaches are valid—and annual attendance at a large-scale conference or convention can supplement such training and offer additional benefits. Here are some of the ways:

- Teachers become encouraged when a church considers their ministry important enough to sponsor their attendance at such an event.
- Teachers become motivated by interaction with trainers and other teachers.
- Teachers grow excited and are encouraged by the displays of helpful resources.

Away from the distractions of work or the church office, a staff member can devote his or her attention to the seminars and informal discussions with colleagues that are an important part of such an event.

The terms *conference* and *convention* are sometimes used interchangeably. On the one hand, a convention is usually an annual meeting of a group that convenes for business meetings along with resource-oriented workshops. On the other hand, a conference may have a few meetings led by a guest speaker, along with workshops offering information on a variety of topics. (A seminar is an in-depth meeting or series of meetings on a single theme.) Promoters of conventions and conferences usually make arrangements with local hotels for discounted accommodations. Some even arrange special activities for children and spouses.

Christian education specialists who want their teachers to take advantage of these training opportunities should be discerning in their selection of the event and the particular workshops they wish their teachers to attend. Often, printed information for an event will spell out the content of each workshop, the qualifications of speakers, and the age level to which the information pertains. Not all workshops are equally helpful. At quality events, sponsors will solicit evaluations from those attending for help in planning the following year's event. The Christian education specialist who brings a van full of teachers to such an event should poll them for responses—and plan now to take advantage of the best events in their area.

Cultural Diversity

The Census Bureau predicts that by 2050 our population will be 46 percent Hispanic, African-American, Asian-American, and Native American. These groups already are more than half the population in fifty-one of our largest cities.[1] The world's population is two-thirds nonwhite and America's demographics will soon match that statistic. By the end of the twentieth century, one out of every three American children will belong to a minority group.

Any teacher who does not have minority children in a class today can expect to see them tomorrow. The best preparation for ministry in a multicultural setting is the elimination of bias and the nurturing of awareness. In our steadily shrinking world, what myths do we still hold about people of other races and cultures? Are we truly ready to love our neighbor?

Before teachers can lead their young students in lessons of acceptance and mutual respect, they must examine their own attitudes toward other races and traditions. Bias has too many victims.

The first step is *awareness* of differences. All people are created equal by God—but certainly not identical. The Lord is too creative for that. By the time children are three years old, even they are aware of racial and gender differences. By the time they are five years old, they have already formed what probably will be lifelong attitudes toward their and others' racial identity. Parents and teachers cannot begin too soon to teach children to respect their own group and others.

The second step is *appreciation* of those differences. Students of various cultures must approach their study with sincerity and humility. Books, films, and museums all can be helpful in learning about a certain culture—but the best way to learn is through friendship with an individual. Daily life offers a far more accurate picture of a culture than exotic costumes and holiday celebrations. One's anglicized image of a culture may be way out of focus.

Teachers should be aware of ways they might inadvertently offend a child or adult from an unfamiliar culture. Hand gestures common in Anglo-America are often offensive in other traditions. Casual physical contact, such as shaking hands or an affectionate pat on the head or back, can be an insult. Expressive displays of emotion that seem so much a part of some cultures are considered bad taste by others. Even nodding or shaking one's head to indicate "yes" or "no" is reversed in some cultures. Gifts can speak a language of their own too. Even an innocent basket of fruit or flowers can communicate something other than good intentions. It's best to use restraint in physical contact and gestures until you've had a chance to observe cultural preferences.

To be prepared to minister to children who have little or no English proficiency, teachers can start beforehand by practicing teaching methods that depend less on reading and writing. The best way to teach anything, in fact, is by providing hands-on, active involvement for learners. Children can develop their vocabulary by labeling objects. Teachers must avoid "church language" and concentrate on communicating important concepts in clear terms. Imagine the confusion that the simple phrase "Jesus in my heart" can cause when, in the hearer's culture, love comes from the liver, stomach, or kidneys. Churches wishing to minister to recent arrivals from other countries can set up centers to teach English to families and acquaint them with the social services available to them.

Children from other backgrounds come to class with their own distinctive learning styles. Experienced teachers know that children may be primarily aural or visual learners, but may profit more from either group or individual experiences, or may respond positively to a different form of discipline. A cultural group may show similarities among its members, but each child must be approached as an individual. Contests and competitions that motivate some American children might immobilize children of Third World cultures, who have been taught to value cooperation. Teachers who praise a student's efforts may confuse that child, who has been taught to value group cohesiveness over individual achievement. We're not recommending that you never praise children, only that you should be aware that individual praise can be a problem in some cultures.

An awareness of other faiths is also a valuable resource for teachers. Children of recent immigrants may or may not be Christians. Their parents may be interested in Christianity, or they may only be interested in exposing their children to English and American culture. Parents who have raised their children as Christians in another culture may view some American church traditions as unbiblical and unacceptable. A Christian from Zaire may wonder about the biblical origins of Easter eggs, for example. A Christian Native American may be reticent about celebrating Thanksgiving.

Poverty spares no culture. Impoverished children may be illiterate, malnourished, and homeless. Their families may be recent immigrants who have left everything behind in their country of origin. Not all churches are equipped to provide for the desperate needs of such families, but teachers can at least provide opportunities for the children to experience joyful social interaction and acceptance.

Teachers who want to minister to children of diverse cultures can begin with these five steps:

1. Discuss racial differences in your classroom. Guide students to an appreciation of differences. (Keep a mirror handy!)
2. Check your classroom for visuals, books, or toys that promote racial stereotypes. For example, are all the dolls white?
3. Examine visual aids for prejudice. Are all the missionary heroes Anglo? Is the color black ever equated with sin?
4. Use songs, games, crafts, and other activities from a variety of cultures.
5. Correct children who express prejudice, and support any child who has been the target of a racial slur.

Teachers are significant adults in the lives of children who come from another culture. Consider a teacher's impact on the life of a young child who is suddenly in unfamiliar surroundings, hearing a foreign language, and realizing he is different from his classmates. If a teacher warmly accepts that child just as he is, the child may someday believe that the teacher's God can also accept him just as he is.

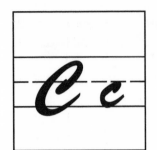

Curriculum

In spite of the vast number of well-written curricula available to teachers today, some teachers choose to use a program they prepare themselves. While it is possible for a teacher to design and develop a biblically correct, educationally sound program, most individuals lack the necessary training and resources. Hours that could have been spent developing teacher-learner relationships or adapting an existing curriculum to meet the learners' specific needs are instead spent reinventing the wheel. Some churches end up implementing an inferior curriculum simply because a committee has not taken the time to review what is available—or because they are reluctant to try something different, even though they are unsatisfied with what they have!

The first step in choosing a curriculum, of course, is to evaluate the needs of the ministry. You must first establish the ministry's doctrinal position, its philosophy of education, and its goals and objectives for each age group. Are there special needs to consider? What should the emphasis be? How does the curriculum fit into the overall aim of the church?

Once these factors have been established, a qualified committee should sit down and discuss the following criteria for curriculum selection:

- *Biblical content.* Every lesson should be based on the Word of God. Lessons should present age-appropriate life issues to which Scripture is applied. Evangelism should be emphasized. Bible memory should be featured.
- *Design.* Lessons should be separated into thematic units. Typically, four units complete a year. To be appropriate for age and grade groups, lessons should be designed for a span of no more than two or three years.

  If a child studies the same publisher's curriculum from early childhood through sixth grade, he or she should be exposed to all the major themes of the Bible three or four times. Continuity is one of the many reasons that the education ministry should, if possible, systematically use a single curriculum throughout those years rather than a potpourri of publishers' products.
- *Education philosophy.* All concepts, methods, and materials should be age-appropriate. Methods should vary from week to week and should address all areas of a learner's development. Learning must be child-directed rather than teacher-oriented. Lessons should feature hands-on, active involvement in learning. All material and activities in a single lesson should reinforce a single lesson theme. And the session schedule should reflect the physical needs and attention span of the age group.
- *Teacher appeal.* Materials should be attractive and easy to use. Each lesson must be simple to prepare and include a variety of teaching resources such as maps, posters, songs, and games. Teaching aims must be clearly presented—what the learners should know, how they should feel about what they have learned, and what action they should want to take based on their learning. Extra activities should be offered for extended classtime. (Many education ministries that have a second hour of Sunday school make the mistake of

introducing a new topic at that time, rather than reinforcing the one taught earlier.)

- *Student appeal.* All materials should be attractive. Activities should be interesting and fun. Life situations presented in the lessons should reflect universal childhood experience and a variety of cultures.
- *Church/home relations.* The curriculum should include material to reinforce lesson aims at home. Take-home papers support the teacher-parent relationship.

Major publishing houses can supply review kits of lessons for parents and perhaps the services of a consultant. Some also are able to offer training resources to teachers, in the form of books, tapes, or seminars.

Curriculum must be a priority budget item. And remember—excellence is worth the investment.

Day Care and Private Schools

Every weekday morning, thousands of churches open their doors as Christian schools or child-care centers. And parents who bring their children to them expect quality care and skilled teaching of a curriculum that integrates the Word of God with life experience. Usually, that is what they get. More often than the Christian community would like to admit, church-affiliated programs are inferior to other public and private offerings. No church opens a school or center with the intention of providing substandard service, but why do some church-affiliated programs fall short, while others honor God through excellence?

Purpose

The church that is considering opening a school or child-care center must first examine its purpose. Is the proposed school meant to provide a Christian alternative to the humanist philosophy promoted in local public schools—or is it merely to provide upwardly mobile parents with the status of sending their youngsters to a private school? Can the proposed center offer services such as counseling or therapy unavailable to children elsewhere, or is it meant primarily as an income-producer for the church building fund? Is there a need for the new school in the community, or does the church want a school simply because most other churches have their own?

In the 1840s, when public and parochial schools began to go their separate ways, public schools were still basically Christian in their values and curriculum. Roman Catholic, Lutheran, Reformed, Adventist, Episcopal, and other churches opened schools of their own, and some offered after-school instruction for public school children. Today, in response to restrictions on prayer and Bible reading in public schools, conservative Protestant groups comprise the largest category of Christian schools.

The motivation for creation of a school or child-care center must be that the church believes these things about a Christian education:

1. It teaches a child about his or her heavenly Father and His world.
2. It ministers to the whole family through partnership with parents.
3. It follows the biblical mandates for education set down in Deuteronomy, by teaching God's laws at teachable moments throughout the day. (This philosophy is no less applicable to high school seniors than it is to youngsters in early childhood. What might be thought of as simply "babysitting" is, rather, an opportunity to mold a young child's attitudes while he is most impressionable.)

If a church understands the purposes behind opening such facilities, perceives a need in the community, and is willing to commit the necessary time, effort, and finances to it, then the church can move on to the next consideration:

It Takes Money

Many facilities that are run by private organizations eventually fail for lack of funds. A school or center cannot open its doors without meeting government standards for staff, facilities, and policy. There are sizable start-up costs to consider. Rooms, equipment, and furnishings that satisfy Sunday morning requirements may not measure up to local and state requirements for a Monday-through-Friday classroom or lab without costly adjustments. Even a program destined to become self-supporting will need backing to get started.

When starting a school, a church would be wise to begin with a preschool and build on the original group of children by adding one grade each year. As major grade divisions develop, administrators would need to evaluate community needs, staff requirements, and the stability of the existing program before proceeding.

The tuition paid by each family for their child usually does not cover the cost incurred in his or her education. Fund-raising events, endowments, scholarships, and donations are needed in order to provide services at prices families can afford. Occasionally, an association of churches can pool its resources to develop a program. This arrangement can ease financial burdens but sometimes cause and complicate administrative problems. At the very least, associated churches should have compatible doctrinal statements.

It Takes People

A Christian school or child-care facility must be staffed by adults who not only are loving and spiritually mature Christians, but are trained professionals who meet the qualifications for state or local certification and licensing. Headmasters and directors must be skilled leaders and organizers who have received specialized training in education administration. These are not part-time jobs for a pastor's brother-in-law. Leadership of a school or child-care facility is a full-time profession that encompasses both career and ministry. Salaries and benefit programs should be generous enough to encourage long-term commitments from good prospects. Choosing the field of ministry in Christian education may be sacrificial, but it should not have to be terminal!

The church should recruit a trained administrator at the very outset of planning, to help during the school's development. This is a must—it can help your school's ministry to avoid implementing amateur methods which over time can become set in the cement of tradition. How many pastors or even Christian Education Specialists would know:

- What playground adaptations will be needed by disabled students?
- What nutritional requirements are included in a toddler's lunch?
- What is more beneficial, closed classroom or an open concept approach?
- Where can one find a high school science text that teaches creationism?

What about the other people who make up the school or center? What about enrollment? Administrators have to set admittance and expulsion policies, along with standards for dress, discipline, and academic achievement. How will the school handle applications from AIDS-infected children, handicapped students, and those with limited English proficiency?

It Takes Buildings

Few church nurseries or Sunday schools are prepared for immediate occupancy by weekday school or child-care programs. Provision must be made not only for indoor comfort and security, but also for outdoor recreation. Facilities for weekday care and schooling must pass stringent health and safety regulations. If meals are to be prepared on the premises, kitchens also must meet legal requirements. Classrooms, bathrooms, and playgrounds should be accessible to the handicapped, even if that is not a legal requirement in your area. Office space and record storage areas are needed.

In small facilities, a room that serves first-graders on Sunday may have to serve double duty as a sixth-grade classroom during the week. This brings up the complications of sharing facilities. The needs of a weekday classroom and a Sunday school room are uniquely different. On the positive side, sharing can mean improved classrooms and divided expenses. On the negative side, conflicts are inevitable whenever two drivers buy a car. Where are you going? How long will you need the car? Where are the keys? Who's responsible for this dent in the fender?

A spirit of teamwork modeled by school administrators and the pastoral staff can set the tone for workers who must share rooms. The school or center will eventually bring families into the church, and promotion from the pulpit can help the congregation appreciate a school or center as an important part of ministry rather than as a budget-draining nuisance.

It Takes Time

A school or center should be in the planning stages for years before its opening day. It takes time to evaluate need, recruit staff, develop facilities, and build a financial base. Planners must find out what state, local, and federal regulations govern staffing and facilities. Organization must be designed and job descriptions must be written for each position, and all of the following questions must be answered:

Can the school achieve accreditation? Who will control the school or center? What are the qualifications for a trustee or board member? To what agencies is the school accountable? Is the financial vision for the program self-sufficiency or continued dependence on the church? What will be the role of the church if the program becomes financially independent? What is the policy toward parents' roles, and does it address the situation of unchurched parents?

Plans must include preparation not only for opening day but for what can evolve in years to come. Can the child-care center respond to a need for a preschool and kindergarten? Can the elementary school develop into a junior and senior high school in the future?

Planning includes both short- and long-range goals. The crib room designed to hold the first year's registration day may be overcrowded the next year, resulting in a drop in registration the third year. The school chapel whose lovingly donated pews are bolted securely to the floor may need to be converted into a lunchroom. In the parlance of carpenters: "Measure twice—cut once!"

The Good News

The prospectus for schools and centers, however, is not all unreachable goals and impossible standards. Children who attend quality Christian schools and child-care programs enjoy the security and consistency that comes when home and school are partners. Such children can be taught from the same (biblical) perspective, no matter what the day of the week, and when pressured parents must turn over child-care responsibilities to another adult, they can be assured the care-giver will model God's love to their youngsters. When parents ask, "What did you learn in school today?" they can expect a reply that will not conflict with God's Word.

It must be said in defense of the public school system that public school teachers are not exclusively mantra-chanting worshipers of nature deities. Nursery and day-care centers are not manned by fanged child abusers. On the contrary, most professionals who work with children choose to because they are caring, dedicated individuals. Among them are Christians who daily salt the earth in public schools and day-care centers. Quality is not assured by a sign that identifies a facility as Christian. Parents must assess the needs of their children and evaluate the staff, facilities, and program of any school or center they are considering. A church-affiliated program that truly wishes to honor God will exceed what is required, and will display the distinctives that characterize a godly, effective ministry to children.

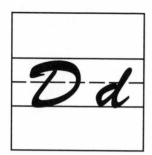

Discipline:
Five Keys

Discipline can be a problem for teachers in clubs, classes, or camps. Teachers often ask themselves: "How much obedience should I demand? How permissive should I be?" Sometimes a situation with a student can get out of control and almost beyond endurance. An undisciplined class is demoralizing to the child, teacher, and other children alike.

Here are five preventive keys to ensure productive class time:

Key One: The teacher's attitude toward the learners

Be genuine. Show a sincere interest in the children. Be accepting of them and love them unconditionally, just as God loves and accepts you. Develop a positive attitude toward the students and try to make positive comments on their behavior. Always be in control of your temper and your tone of voice; never allow anger to flare up in the heat of the moment—no matter how hot it gets! Pray for yourself and your children. If you are too busy to pray for your Bible teaching ministry, then you are just too busy.

Key Two: The teacher's responsibility toward children

Prepare in advance—and adequately. Preparation will give you confidence and develop the children's trust in you as their leader. A warm, caring environment helps children know they are loved and accepted. Understand how God has designed your learners—physically, mentally, socially, emotionally, and spiritually—and equip your surroundings to meet their needs. Many teachers have to expend most of their time and patience struggling to keep learners seated in chairs that were not designed to hold children their size. Know your learners' home situations. Insight in this area will help you understand their backgrounds and perhaps their negative behavior. Learn the names of all your students—not just the ones of those who get into trouble.

Key Three: Following an age-appropriate schedule

A child is not a miniature adult. He or she is a child with specific needs. So allow children plenty of time to move from one activity to another, to avoid feelings of pressure. Provide them with choices to motivate their interest. Encourage those who are reluctant to join in. Provide movement that engages both large and small muscles. Variety in the type and pace of activities helps to eliminate boredom and restlessness. And involving learners in activities as soon as they arrive is especially crucial in averting any likely trouble. *Always* be ready and waiting for the first arrival.

Key Four: The teacher's behavior

Be a model in all you say and do. Direct learners by statements rather than by questions. A child may answer the question, "Don't you want to sit down?" with a resounding, "No!" A better way to phrase the directive is, "You may sit down here or over there." Make good use of nonverbal communication—eye contact, a smile, a touch on the shoulder, a stern look. Take time to listen to your learners. For many of them, negative attention is better than no attention at all, and they'll do what they have to in order to get it. Encourage your learners through praise of specific positive behavior. Be aware that your class may be growing beyond the recommended teacher-to-learner ratio and the size of the room.

When discipline problems arise, take remedial action immediately. This is actually a fifth key to discipline:

Key Five: Having a ready plan for discipline problems

1. Deal with the child individually. Scolding a child in front of classmates may lead them to side with their friend against you.
2. Ask the child to describe his or her actions. Sometimes the teacher witnesses only the effect and not the cause of misbehavior. A child may not be able to articulate why he or she misbehaved, but should be able to describe what he or she did. If two children are involved, be sure to get both sides of the story.
3. Define limits. Post rules in the classroom. Make it clear why certain kinds of behavior are unacceptable. Sometimes discipline problems arise simply because children have stumbled over invisible limits. Be consistent.
4. Redirect the child into positive behavior. Once a child has been corrected, allow the youngster to rejoin the class. Make a note if the same misbehavior is repeated. A pattern of disobedience is worth discussing with parents.
5. Allow the child to experience the consequences of misbehavior. This might mean making the youngster clean up the mess made as the result of rowdy play, or having the child apologize to the offended party in a fight. The punishment should fit the crime. Usually, a delay in correction or a non-fitting punishment keeps the offender from connecting it with the misbehavior. Don't threaten what you can't deliver.

Sometimes a child behaves in a manner so defiant or violent that it exceeds normal misbehavior and the average teacher's ability to cope. Often the answer is to employ an adult helper who can work individually with the child. A teacher who takes the time to check up on a problem may find the child has a history of emotional disturbance or abuse, or a tendency to forget to take doses of prescribed behavior-modifying medication. Any teacher faced by unusually defiant behavior, however, should get help from the Christian education specialist or the pastor. The problem may call for pastoral counseling, referral to a Christian counseling center, or intervention by social services.

At all times, remember God's dealings with Moses, David, and Peter. Moses whined and complained. David fell into spectacular disobedience. Peter denied Christ. Despite their behavior, God used them all. Every Sunday school curriculum features these three as heroes of faith—but few teachers would have wanted them in their class!

Discussion Skills: Can We Talk?

The words "group discussion" have been used to describe anything from a verbal free-for-all to what is actually a monologue by the teacher. There are many types of discussion activities that can be used with children.

Getting Them Started

Children who are reluctant to join in discussions may need particular encouragement. This encouragement can come through an accepting atmosphere, or simply the opportunity to speak uninterrupted. "Brainstorming" is a nonthreatening form of discussion in which each participant can make his contribution without immediate criticism from his listeners. In this instance, the teacher first compiles opinions, ideas, or suggestions from individuals without commentary, then guides learners in their open consideration of what has been presented.

Learners who don't enjoy speaking in front of the class might prefer the "neighbor nudge" method of discussing a topic with their nearest neighbor. "Buzz groups" involve several learners in a group small enough to ensure that each member has his or her say. The "agree-disagree" discussion opener begins with a statement with which each learner must simply agree or disagree. The ensuing discussion can be guided to exploration of both perspectives.

Learners who love to voice their own opinions may have to be restrained so others will have a chance to speak. An indicator of "speaking rights," such as a book or a ball, can be handed from speaker to speaker for a specific length of time, guaranteeing that turns will be taken fairly.

Keeping Them on Track

The role of the leader in class discussions should be that of moderator and guide. Each contribution must be acknowledged, even if it needs to be tactfully corrected. When a discussion veers off course, the leader must decide if the change is valid. As the gatekeeper of the activity, the leader may constantly have to redirect discussion to the lesson aims.

By using prepared questions in a "can of worms" activity, a teacher can be sure that each slip of paper pulled from a can will focus on one theme. (To keep the discussion going, questions should be subjective rather than requiring simple "yes" or "no" answers.)

Visuals are great for focusing discussions on a topic. A photograph, poster, or teaching picture from a curriculum packet can be used to keep eyes and thoughts on the lesson theme. A sustained discussion can be held through a panel format, with participants having a chance to do some preparation on the topic.

Too often, "discussions" consist of children rebounding answers to teachers' questions with very little child-to-child interaction. Instead, teachers should use stimulating questions to draw learners into exchanges with one another.

Here are some examples of the use of discussion activities:

- *Brainstorm.* "In what different ways can Daniel respond to the king's edict against worship of God? I'll write all your ideas on the board."
- *Neighbor nudge.* "Ask the person sitting next to you which of these ideas seems best."
- *Buzz groups.* "Form your chairs into two groups and

pick out the best suggestion from among your answers."

- *Agree-disagree.* "Your most popular answer is written on the board. Who agrees and disagrees with it, and why?"
- *Can of worms.* "Here are some situations like Daniel's that we are faced with today. Pick one to discuss."
- *Panel discussion.* "Three people in our class spent time last week reading what the Bible has to say about obeying God's laws. What questions would you like to ask them?"
- *Visuals.* "Look at these photos from newsmagazines. Can it sometimes be easy to do the wrong thing and hard to do right? What would God want us to do in these situations?"

Teachers can use up an awfully large amount of time trying to silence learners. It is much more productive to guide their conversation in a lesson-focused direction, and to encourage their development of thinking, listening, and problem-solving.

Drama: The Play's the Thing

Shakespeare's Hamlet knew that the king was involved in his father's murder. To make the king betray his guilt, Hamlet forced him to watch a troupe of players reenact the crime. "The play's the thing," Hamlet hoped, "wherein I'll catch the conscience of the king."

As Hamlet said, "The play's the thing"—for children's ministry as well. Classroom drama can set the stage for children to understand God's Word in a unique way. As we have said, students learn best when they are actively involved—and what better way to involve them in the lives of the Bible's personalities than to have them act as those people in role play? By using drama, they can apply Bible truths in simulated situations in the classroom. The abstract concepts of love, sharing, kindness, joy, and many others can be illustrated far more clearly through drama than through mere dictionary definitions.

A teacher cannot draw the curtain on classroom drama thinking every production has to be a Broadway spectacle. Simple productions can clarify Bible truths and promote learning through involvement. Dramatic role play happens all the time in the early childhood classroom: "You be the daddy and I'll be the mommy." Children develop their own dramatic play, assigning roles and ad-libbing lines like seasoned professionals. The value of their play increases when a teacher sits in and guides their interaction: "Pretend you're the mommy, and these are your two little boys who are fighting over a toy. What can you say to them about sharing?"

Every classroom can use a few puppets. Full-scale productions are fine for older learners, but young children can succeed with a puppet and an idea. The value of the play depends on the input of the teacher.

The most familiar use of drama in Sunday school is the acting out of Bible stories. Such productions can be elaborately planned, or simple and spontaneous. A teacher can introduce the story and then use drama as a review tool. He or she may assign roles and dole out simple, Bible-times costumes kept on hand in the classroom or storage room. With the teacher narrating the play and directing the action, the players are able to ad-lib with creativity and insights. Simple props can be a great addition. (Older learners who are self-conscious may require more scene-setting and encouragement than younger children.)

Pantomime can be a nice change from the usual drama in that all action is played out without dialogue. Youngsters learn to communicate feelings and ideas through gestures. A teacher can enhance this with a sheet and a light, creating a silhouette effect. Players can move between the light and the sheet while the audience, on the other side of the sheet, sees only their shadows.

Role play helps students put themselves in other people's shoes. The teacher can assign a few roles, describe the situation in which the characters interact, and then ask a few questions to get an ad-lib dialogue going. "Mark, you be the father of the lost son. Josh, you be the son. You've run away from home and spent all the money your father gave you. Now you want to come back. Mark, how do you feel toward Josh?"

Role play is helpful in applying Bible truth to modern-day situations. In any drama, students can be asked to trade roles and articulate the other character's viewpoint. "Mary, you've been the mother of Joan, who stayed out late without permission. Now be Joan. How do you feel about coming home?"

Choral speaking and other forms of dramatic reading can involve groups or individuals. The art involved in this kind of presentation is more than simple recitation. An actor must clearly understand the meaning of the piece in order to give the right characterization.

Skits are often thought of as being just for fun, but they can have immense teaching value. Technically, a skit is a short, loosely planned or impromptu play. A group of students is given a topic and in a few minutes must come up with a skit to present its meaning. Because the skit only lasts a few minutes, the presentation must be kept simple. Teachers can use the skit format to ask learners to illustrate the application of the day's lesson. "Ann, your group is to present the meaning of the Good Samaritan. Stick to the plot, but make your story happen in today's world." Teachers can also present a group with an open-ended idea and see what develops. "Matt, your group will make up a skit that talks about forgiveness. Make the setting the school gym." Activities like these can test the learners' level of understanding. The truest assessment of whether children have grasped a concept is their ability to express it in their own words.

Students may enjoy presenting Bible characters and their stories in a TV or radio talk show format. Interviews, game shows, and commercials can all be adapted to lesson material. Scripts, tape recorders, microphones, and stage props can make the production come alive. "I'm the apostle Paul, and I'll be your guide on today's trip to the Holy Land. . . ."

You can experiment with some of these ideas—but don't get so caught up in scenery or costumes or even dialogue that the central purpose is lost. Your primary goal in using drama is to teach biblical truth. Keep the concept clear, the production simple, and your students actively involved. On with the show!

Evaluation

An important but often neglected segment of the children's ministry programming cycle is evaluation. But why is it neglected?

Sometimes the program that was such a spectacular flop was handpicked by the pastor. Perhaps the teacher you can't stand is married to the superintendent you'd hate to lose. Maybe the pews impractically nailed to the floor of the early children's room were a cherished memorial gift.

These reasons are not good enough, however, to forestall a sweeping, objective evaluation of the ministry. The job of evaluation should be done by a committee or even by an outside consultant. Evaluation is a prelude to change—and change in the church can be pretty tricky.

The approach to an evaluation should be that of rallying team spirit. A review of the ministry's goals and a rededication of effort can provide the sense of unity and objectivity needed for the task. You can use the set of goals that brought you to your current situation—they can be a great assessment tool. Ask objectively—were those goals met? Well-articulated goals and objectives are easily applied to facilities, personnel, programs, and policies. In the absence of existing goals, however, the committee must start from scratch by developing goals based on the church's philosophy of ministry, approach to education, and unique needs.

If, for example, the goal is to have a quality nursery, observers may measure the ministry's current conditions against recommended standards for nursery personnel, furnishings, and other considerations. Once the committee has established the span of the gulf between what a church has, needs, and can afford, the job of prioritizing begins. There's always money in the budget for what the majority considers vital.

If the item under scrutiny is a program, it should be evaluated in the framework of the church's overall ministry. Does the program fulfill unmet needs? Is its impact measurable in terms of changed behavior, increased attendance, or evangelistic outreach? Is it impossible to staff, hard to schedule, or too expensive to run? Is it necessary?

When evaluation forms are studied, and a list of strengths and weaknesses can be compiled, the big question becomes: "What do we tackle first?" A wise place to begin your improvements is in the nursery and early childhood division. Safety and quality programming for these children must be a priority.

Wherever a church begins its overhaul, changes should be made in terms of reachable, measurable goals; so set a realistic timetable for implementing your improvements, with mile markers along the way. Plan long-range goals, but work on them in bite-size pieces.

In a yearly review, or immediately following any special event, evaluate what has happened. If goals have been met, review the changed situation and set brand-new goals. If goals are still unmet, change your strategy accordingly—and be realistic!

Standards

Bible study

- Is the curriculum Bible-centered and evangelistic?
- Do lessons actively involve each learner?
- Are activities and concepts appropriate to the learner's age level?

- Does the lesson plan make the best use of time?
- Do all activities in a single session teach the same concept?
- Do units of lessons in the curriculum support a single aim?
- Is the curriculum unified throughout the children's program?

Organization

- Are learners divided into age-group classes?
- Is there a correct teacher-to-learner ratio at each age level?
- Is there a team to help with administration and communication?
- Are there meetings for planning and evaluation?

Recruitment

- Is there an ongoing recruitment program?
- Are there written job descriptions for each worker?
- Are recruits given time to consider their decision?
- Is every recruit given pre-service and in-service training?

Training and planning

- Is continuous training available to workers?
- Are there meetings for training and planning?

Facilities

- Do the facilities reflect the teaching-learning philosophy?
- Is floor space adequate for learners and appropriate for their age and number?
- Are furnishings provided in correct size and number?
- Do room arrangements allow large- and small-group activities?

Growth

- Is there a plan for locating and reaching new prospects?
- Is there a continuing outreach program?
- Are enrollment and attendance records accurate?
- Are new classes created to meet the demands of growth?
- Does Sunday school meet the needs of all family members?

Case Study: The Church of the Bulging Basement

Here is a "case study," or example of a typical ministry evaluation:

Evaluation

Facilities — inadequate floor space in nursery/early childhood and children's rooms.

Furnishings — children have to use adult chairs and tables, and some rooms have unused teacher desks, file cabinets, and pianos.

Floors — vinyl tile, easy to clean but cold and noisy.

Floor plan — central meeting area in children's department has miniature pews nailed to the floor, surrounded by cubbyhole rooms.

Toilet/sink — few bathrooms, all adult size; no sinks for art activities.

Statistics — toddlers and infants share same floor space under hazardous conditions, early childhood rooms all crowded.

Congregation— young families with children outnumbering adults, visitors with young children seldom return.

Teachers — good teacher-to-learner ratio, but overcrowding causes frustration and burnout.

Recommendations:

Try to switch rooms to make better use of space. If adults have large rooms that could serve the children, move the adults to the sanctuary or a nearby office building or restaurant for Sunday school (make sure you get the owner's okay first). Dispose of unused furniture, pianos, etc. Buy child-scale furniture. Use carpet squares or area rugs when children have to sit on vinyl floors. Redesign the room with the little pews. Rethink having an assembly in the beginning; you could make better use of those minutes. Provide child-scale toilet facilities. Until larger rooms are available, separate infants and toddlers using waist-high dividers.

Once needs and problems are identified, resolutions and answers come a lot easier!

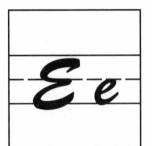

Evangelism of Children

Few adults feel they know the "correct" way to lead a child, especially a young child, to salvation through faith in Jesus Christ. Even fewer adults agree on a minimum age for decision-making. Educators agree, however, that most decisions for Christ are made in childhood rather than in the later teen and adult years. If these are the best years to present the plan of salvation to a youngster, then what are the best methods to use?

Teachers should begin with their own understanding of the process and its foundations in Scripture. Because symbolic words and abstract concepts are beyond the grasp of most children below the age of ten or twelve, the language of salvation must be made meaningful on their level. In addition, a child may have the sense to grasp the concepts involved in salvation—but that does not mean the child has the inclination to take action. Teachers must be sensitive to each child's spiritual growth and to be alert to any child who displays readiness.

If leaders present the plan of salvation to children, they should offer the youngsters a chance to speak privately with one of them, to ask questions, or to have one of the adults pray with them to accept Christ. Teachers should always avoid appeals that prey on children's emotions and their desire to please their teacher. Sometimes children raise their hands along with their classmates simply to be part of the crowd, or because of some other incentive such as a prize.

The teacher's role is simply to present God's love to each child on his or her own level of understanding, and to be sensitive to the child's readiness to respond to that love. The task of directing the child's heart toward God is not that of the teacher, but of God's Holy Spirit.

A Simplified Five-Step Presentation

Not all children come through the church doors with the same background or knowledge of God. The starting block has to be—even for some older children—awareness of God's existence. Teachers must ask thoughtful questions to ascertain how much a child does or does not already understand.

The following five steps can serve as a general guideline for a teacher's presentation of the gospel to children:

Step One "The same powerful God that made the earth and all the universe also made you. He made you very special, and He loves you very much. He would like you to love Him, too, and to be a part of His family." (Assure children this does not mean leaving their earthly family, but rather joining a special family with brothers and sisters all over the world.)

Step Two "Whenever you do bad things, or even think about doing them, that is called 'sin.' This sin keeps us from joining God's family. It keeps us from being happy." (A child should be able to list some sins applicable to his or her own life. Answers that are inapplicable to the child's experience, such as murder or adultery, may reveal a lack of understanding that he or she is a sinner and does commit sins.)

Step Three "Our Bible tells the story of the first people who sinned. They did not behave the way God told them to. Because they sinned, they would someday grow old and die. They would not be allowed to live forever in the beautiful home God had made for them. All of us sin, and someday each one of us will die. Even people who try hard to be good sin sometimes.'' (Children may need to be told, however, that death does not follow instantly on the heels of misbehavior, but rather at a time we cannot know. Death is the natural result of sin.)

"After we die, there is a special part of us that continues to live. The body we wore on earth—the one that grew up, got hurt or sick, ran, jumped, and played—will no longer be needed and will be buried in the ground. The special part that is invisible, like God, can still think and feel. In order for this part of us, which is called our soul, to go to God's wonderful home in heaven and be with Him, we must have no sins. Because if we have sins, we cannot go in.

"God has made it possible for our sins to be forgiven. He sent His Son, Jesus, to take the punishment for all of us. When Jesus died, He took the punishment for all the sins of every person in the world. God gave up His Son, Jesus, to take our punishment so that God can forgive us. It is as if we had never sinned at all. We can live with God and be part of His family.''

Step Four "We don't have to wait until we die and go to heaven to be friends with God. We can be part of His family right now. We have to tell God that we know we sin, and we are sorry. Because of what Jesus did, God can give us the free gift of forgiveness. We can tell God that we accept His gift and believe that Jesus saved us from punishment for our sins.

"Talking to God is easy. Just call His name and He will listen. He has been waiting for you to talk to Him. You don't have to be in a special place or wait for a special time of day.''

Step Five "When you trust God to forgive your sins, you become a member of His family. As His child, you will want to obey God's rules. Sometimes you will make a mistake and do something wrong. Don't worry—God will never put you out of His family. You can always talk to God in prayer. You can read His special messages to you in the Bible. People will know you are God's child if they see you obeying your parents, helping others, and being kind. You can tell your friends about Jesus, and perhaps they will want to be part of His family, too.''

References to Use (NIV):

- 1 John 4:8: "God is love."
- Romans 3:23: "All have sinned and fall short of the glory of God."
- Romans 6:23: "The wages of sin is death, but the gift of God is eternal life in Christ Jesus our Lord."
- 1 Corinthians 15:3: "Christ died for our sins according to the Scriptures."
- 1 John 4:14: "The Father has sent his Son to be the Savior of the world."
- John 1:12: "To those who believed in his name, he gave the right to become children of God."
- Psalm 119:11: "I have hidden your word in my heart that I might not sin against you."

It's a good idea to locate and read these verses using the child's own Bible. But remember—the whole point of finding these verses in the child's Bible is to reaffirm that they are true for the child personally, and that there are promises in God's Word that he or she can read and believe. God's Word will never return to Him without accomplishing the purpose for which He sent it; but a teacher who turns a discussion of salvation into a reading lesson impedes progress toward the desired goal. If the child has limited reading proficiency, or the version being used is not easily understood, it is enough for the teacher to explain the meaning of what can be found in Scripture.

Once a child has made a decision to accept Christ as his or her Savior, the work of follow-up begins. It is rare for the teacher who leads a child to Christ to personally direct that child's discipleship through the adolescent and teen years into adulthood. Yet, it is often possible for the teacher to provide follow-up Bible study material, along with encouraging notes and phone calls.

Here are some additional teaching cues:

- Provide experiences that illustrate abstract concepts. Make the most of teachable moments. "John, I heard you forgive Mark for hitting you. That is what God can do for us when we break His rules."
- Be suspicious of "pat" answers. Require answers in a child's terms and understanding—not rote, teacher-pleasing replies. If a child uses the term "Jesus in my heart," ask him to explain what he means without using the word *heart*.
- Allow children to dramatize feelings that are hard to express in words.
- Explain concepts in logical sequence.
- Remember that the growing number of absent or abusive fathers may make the term "loving, heavenly Father" difficult to understand.

Facilities: Room for Improvement

Consider the word *facilitate*. Webster defines it as "to make easier." Do your facilities make teaching easier?

Sometimes teachers overlook aspects of their classroom environment that actually hinder their efforts to impart God's Word to their students. All teachers have to realize any factor that fails to satisfy the physical needs of students influences the state of their mental, spiritual, emotional, and social characteristics.

Examine the furniture, for example. A second-grade boy with an average attention span of about ten minutes will begin wiggling in his seat after only a few moments if his chair is unsuited to his height. And adult-height tables may put the child's work surface only a few inches below his nose. (Imagine—for an adult, this would be like having to eat dinner from a table while kneeling on the floor!)

Efforts to complete activities under such conditions will only be met with frustration. Ideally, children should be able to sit with their feet on the floor and their arms at a comfortable working level. If your church is about to invest in scaled-down furnishings, consider small, round, or half-round tables to encourage small-group activities, and chairs that stack for easy storage. If tables are to be used for multiple age levels, buy ones that can be adjusted for height. Until then, you may have to sit on the floor and use lapboards for writing activities.

Implement some anti-noise strategies. Carpet absorbs noise, provides warmth, and encourages the creative use of floor space. Teachers of young children can salvage outdated carpet sample books and use the squares for the vinyl or cement floors in the classrooms. Acoustical ceiling panels also aid in controlling noise levels. Small groups of the same age level may be able to work simultaneously on different activities in the same room, but walls between departments should be soundproofed to avoid distractions.

Eyestrain and headaches can be the result of working under poor lighting conditions. You may need to shed some light on the subject. Unfortunately, many churches relegate children's classes to a windowless basement, and poor lighting fixtures have an overwhelming influence on mood and productivity. Classroom windows or fixtures should always provide adequate light for reading and writing without a harsh glare.

Do your learners have a hard time warming up to subjects? They may be too cold. A room thermostat indicates the temperature at the eye level of a standing adult—but ignores the air temperature at the floor level, where young children spend most of their time. A room that is comfortable when the teacher arrives to prepare for class can become unbearably stuffy and overheated when it fills with children, so keep your eye on the thermostat to avoid overheated tempers.

Does your room have colorful character? Dark or intense colors are inappropriate for children's classrooms. Light, sunny pastels provide an airy, cheerful atmosphere and a positive influence on the students' attitudes toward learning. Aim for a harmonious combination of colors in your room decoration.

Do your visuals need aid? Children enjoy a changing panorama of appealing visuals posted at their eye level that relate to the morning lesson or to the season. (After about a month, however, a chart or poster no longer draws attention. If walls are "busy," leave empty spaces on them.

What about creating a "help yourself" shelf? Children are eager to take responsibility for their own belongings and for the equipment and materials used in the classroom. Low, open shelves can enable them to obtain and return crayons, paper, and other items. Sections labeled with students' names can provide storage for sweaters, purses, and take-home papers until dismissal times. Some teachers use shoe boxes, wall-mounted clothespins, large milk jugs, or bags that slip over the back of each chair.

In some classrooms, especially multi-use rooms, storage areas can become a problem. Too many cabinets and shelves can serve only as clutter magnets and can gobble up valuable floor space. In some cases, arguments may arise between teachers over ownership and use of supplies, with each group insisting on its own storage area—and there is little room left for children! For many groups, the answer lies in a resource room in which all curriculum, equipment, and supplies can be stored in an organized manner. Each group can have its own box—to be loaded with the supplies for the day's lesson, carried to class, and later returned to the resource room.

Does your room suffer from "facility inability"? If your program is dictated by the arrangement of your room and its furnishings, then try a new arrangement. Remove extra furniture and partitions that inhibit easy movement from large- to small-group activities. Open up the room to offer the greatest potential for creative use of space. Sometimes a solution can be as simple as removing a door or switching a room with another class. Often, the solution comes during an evaluation of the program—when a teacher discovers that discontinuing a multi-class opening assembly will improve both teaching time and room space.

Does your room have tight spaces? Ease the squeeze by providing twenty-five to thirty square feet per student. Overcrowding can indicate a poor teacher-to-student ratio, insufficient furniture, lack of personal attention, inevitable discipline problems, and a predictable halt in growth when the number of students exceeds the comfortable maximum. When more than thirty students are regularly attending, you probably should divide the department.

When preparing to teach, do not neglect the crucial influence of the learning environment—your classroom. If the changes needed require more funds or know-how than you can provide on your own, bring those needs to the attention of the personnel in charge of facilities. Don't be bashful— you may be the only one aware of the needs concerning those too young to help themselves!

Here are several things you can do right away:

- Evaluate the use of each chair, desk, table, and cabinet. If it doesn't help your situation, it is a hindrance.
- Get down on the learners' level. Can you see the visuals? Can you sit comfortably? Are you too warm or too chilly? Do you experience eyestrain when working? Can you see out the window?
- Measure your floor space to see if you have allowed twenty-five to thirty square feet per learner. Later, count how many disruptions during class are the result of pushing, shoving, or maneuvering for space.
- Do you have to raise your voice to be heard over neighboring rooms?
- Do you spend time getting supplies and personal belongings for children who are old enough to get them for themselves?
- Check out the posters and charts on your wall. Are they outdated or faded? Can you remember when you hung them up?

Family Problems: Helping Children Cope

Research tells us that about half of all marriages in the United States end in divorce. This statistic should concern educators, because part of the teaching ministry is to understand learners and be willing to help them through difficult family situations. All children should have security, loving relationships, and both parents—but this is not always the reality. A teacher can make a vast difference in the life of a child from a fractured family.

Parents in Continuing Conflict

Continual conflict between parents is harmful to sons and daughters of any age. Children whose parents frequently argue at home are socially less competent and score lower in the classroom. They tend to have less motivation toward understanding or grasping spiritual matters. A teacher can do several things to help. He or she can:

- provide a caring relationship both within and outside of class.
- adapt to the needs of children who need to grieve.
- give individual attention, encouragement, and praise.

- remember that the child has no control over his or her home situation.

Parents in Separation

Once parents have agreed upon a trial or final separation, a child is confronted with many lingering questions: "When will Daddy leave? Where will I live? Where will I go for Christmas?" The child may not be sure of what is happening or even why. The grief process for the loss of an absent parent will take at least a year. In this case, a teacher should:

- realize that losing a parent is serious business.
- understand that the child will suffer insecurity about the future.
- reaffirm that the child is not at fault.
- be sensitive to the child's emotions.

Parents in Divorce

Many children of divorce blame themselves for the conflict, believing that if they had behaved better the divorce would not have happened. Over and over, the child must be reassured that the separation is between the parents and not between the parents and the child. Because some divorces involve an abusive parent, statements about how much both Mom and Dad still love their child may not always be appropriate. So the teacher should:

- expect the child to cry and grieve.
- understand the child's outpourings of anger and resentment.
- be available to listen.
- maintain awareness, without undue prying, of the situation at home.

During this time the child will experience shock, disbelief, sadness, and loneliness; will worry about his or her changing world; and will be ashamed at being different from classmates. The youngster will display anger and perhaps be confused about his or her loyalties to Mom and Dad. During this time, the teacher should be watchful, monitoring the child's behavior and noting depression or withdrawal from friends. Extreme mood swings and radical changes in behavior may indicate a need for professional intervention. The church's pastoral staff may be able to offer helpful counseling or referral to other resources.

Teachers who want to build a supportive relationship with the child of a fractured family would be wise to keep these few cautions in mind:

- Do not try to fill the role of the absent parent.
- Be aware that the newly divorced parent is vulnerable and insecure.
- Be on the alert for the non-custodial parent after a custody battle.
- Refer counseling needs to competent professionals.

Years ago divorce was a rare occurrence, leaving a social stigma that separated divided families from "polite society." Today, it is difficult to find a family that cannot count at least one divorce among its extended family. Because divorce has become so common, we may have become insensitive to its effects, especially upon children. The world of the child of divorce changes forever; in one stroke, the child may lose a parent, grandparents, aunts, uncles, and cousins. He may move away from friends, church, school, and home. Few experiences in life can impact a child as dramatically as the divorce of his or her parents. In times past, the church might have turned its back on such a child, but the church today must open its arms wide to embrace those youngsters who suffer through the experience.

Food

God's instructions to the Hebrews on the eve of the Passover included the eating of symbolic food. The lamb whose blood marked the doorposts of the Hebrew households, the unleavened bread, and the bitter herbs all pointed to remembrance of the Israelites' experience in Egypt, their hurried exodus from slavery, and their anticipation of God's new covenant. Today, Jewish children everywhere learn about their heritage by partaking at the seder table.

Teachers in children's ministry can also utilize food as a teaching tool—for developing social skills, as a way to help children explore God's creation, and in serving the whole needs of children.

Learning to Share

Part of the fun of a simulated home living center in a children's ministry room is the preparation and sharing of food. The sink, stove, and refrigerator may be cardboard, but the food can be real. (In fact, plastic toy food can be a serious threat to young children's safety.) In working and in playing, children can learn to serve each other and to express thanks to God for what He has provided. Performing simple tasks such as distributing napkins, counting cookies, or cleaning up spills can build confidence in a child's own skills. Being part of a food preparation team for a snack shared by everyone can demonstrate to each child the important contribution he or she can make to the group.

School teachers who use food activities know the excitement and enjoyment their learners find in making such simple things as butter, applesauce, or a fruit salad. Baking bread or cookies involves the learner in reading, measuring, and timekeeping. Children love lessons they can smell, taste, and touch. Why not include such activities in Sunday school, club, or summer ministries?

Food activities centered around the table are an ideal time to practice manners. Children can learn to help at home by setting the silverware, plates, and napkins in their proper places. Best of all, children who have worked to prepare food are better able to express genuine gratitude to God for His provision. There are many teaching resources on the market that show the journey food makes from the farm to the table, including several books written specifically for Christian education.

Food activities can also be a part of bringing a multicultural awareness and appreciation to the classroom. Ethnic grocery stores are sources of unusual foods and utensils. Teachers who want to reach beyond the Americanized versions of ethnic food traditions can seek out recipes in libraries. Granted, an unfamiliar food is not always an immediate hit with young children—but even a small taste of something different can be a learning experience. As always, the teacher should model the behavior (and sense of adventure!) expected from the learners.

Discovering God's World

Many children—especially those growing up in urban areas—have no idea where food originates. Teachers who want learners to thank God for His provision of food must first make clear that food comes from plants and animals. It may come as a complete surprise to many children that the seeds inside a fruit are God's way of promising a new crop next year. (Be aware, however, that young children may be upset by the fact that animals are killed to provide meat.)

Growing small vegetables is a great learning experience for children. This might be possible in a protected area of the playground, or in large patio pots. Even easier (although not as spectacular) would be an herb garden of small pots on a sunny window sill.

Physical Needs

Some teachers of young children provide a mid-morning snack of juice and cookies. Young children especially need to refuel. Without the lift a snack provides, learners can become cranky, restless, and have a hard time concentrating. Highly sugared snacks, however, have undesirable side effects on children—and adults who distribute sugary snacks will see a marked change in their behavior almost instantly!

Teachers should check their learners' reactions to certain foods and their allergies. Some diabetic youngsters may not have the self-discipline to resist sugary snacks offered by an unknowing adult. Artificial food coloring is a prime suspect in many cases of allergy attacks. A safer, saner alternative would be the serving of low-sugar snacks of fruits or vegetables, whole grains, and drinks that are low in sugar and caffeine-free. (It would be wise to ask parents about food allergies.)

Food activities can help young children develop large and small muscles and even practice hand-eye coordination. Successfully buttering a slice of bread can be a great source of satisfaction to a young child. By guiding conversation around the food activity, a teacher can help children observe and describe the effects of their own actions.

Teachers should be aware of children's behavior when snacks are served. Youngsters who always appear hungrier than classmates may suffer from malnutrition. Some schools, and even some churches, provide breakfast for children. (Be aware—children who appear malnourished may be victims of neglect. When there is reason to suspect child abuse or neglect, authorities must be alerted.)

Some Guidelines for Using Food

- Check policies on food preparation within the facility. Although small-scale food activities can be monitored to minimize messes, teachers still need to take precautions. Large-scale operations, such as daily food preparation at a day-care center, involve many legal restrictions designed to safeguard the health of children. Anyone considering food service at a center or school will need to contact local authorities.
- Choose projects that are interesting, tasty, and age-appropriate.
- Keep hot plates, sharp utensils, motorized appliances, and electrical cords out of the reach of small children. Carefully monitor their use by older learners. Choose child-powered tools over motor-driven appliances.
- Follow safety procedures to avoid food spoilage or contamination. (Even contaminated food can taste normal.)
- Use clear plastic containers for maximum visibility.
- Use wooden-handle utensils that don't conduct heat to little hands.
- Protect learners' clothing with aprons or old, discarded shirts.
- Be specific with instructions and words of praise.
- Give instructions one at a time, in sequential order.
- Don't do for learners what they are able to do for themselves.
- Periodic tasting should be part of the preparation experience; however, when the food is finally ready, the teacher and learners should sit down together to share the snack.

Some Food Activities

- Make peanut butter in a blender and spread it on apple slices.
- Shake cream in small containers to make into butter; serve it on crackers.

- Make food gifts for parents and friends.
- Squeeze oranges, grapefruits, or lemons to make juice.
- Roll banana slices in chopped nuts.
- Make snow cones with real snow and flavored syrups.
- Boil eggs and make egg salad. (Remember that anything containing mayonnaise will spoil quickly if not kept at a proper temperature!)
- Make gelatin or instant pudding.
- Open a coconut, chew the meat, and taste the milk.
- Have everyone bring a vegetable and make soup.
- Mix fresh fruit with plain yogurt.
- Peel, core, and slice a fresh pineapple.
- Crank up some ice cream.
- Make popcorn.

Games,
Competition,
and Prizes

Many children enjoy competition—some even thrive on it. And often youngsters can better maintain their interest in an otherwise tedious task by competing with others. Many children of all age groups, however, are not yet mature enough to handle competition; they can't withstand the temptation to flaunt a winner's prize, or they're not tough enough to hold back tears of disappointment.

So—what's a teacher to do? Shall we ban all forms of competition because some children will be poor losers? Shall we indulge in games and contests regardless, to motivate those children who respond to this kind of prompting?

"Losers, weepers," is the key phrase to remember when planning the use of games and contests in the Christian education program. Contests generally produce large numbers of losers and very few winners. No one likes to feel like a loser, and the vulnerable self-image of a young child should not become a casualty of classroom contests.

Teachers needn't excise all forms of competition from their programs, but they should examine closely the following criteria:

- Does the competition have a goal consistent with biblical teaching? Does it have a teaching aim? Is there an

attendance-building objective? Is there a review purpose?

- Is the goal of the competition worth the time, money,
  and effort?
- Will the excitement generated by the competition over-
  shadow the ultimate goal?
- Are the prizes or awards numerous enough to encourage participation, inexpensive enough to be numerous, and of sufficient quality to be worthwhile?
- Will the awarding of prizes become addictive among
  the children? Will they be taught to expect bigger and
  better awards whenever they excel?

These questions point out some of the negative aspects
of competition in the church. But we do well to ask what
positive factors there are. Youngsters enjoy the process of
competing, and they love to win at games and contests; it is
the losing they hate. Therefore, teachers should select those
forms of competition that minimize losing. For example:

1. *Let each child compete with his or her own record
of progress.* Praise the memorization whiz kid who rattles off
an entire chapter of the Bible, but also honor the reluctant
reciter of "Jesus wept," if that verse is an improvement over
his or her recitation of the past Sunday.

2. *In presenting awards, try to vary the winning categories.* The student who never gets to be the smartest, fast-
est, or strongest may, for example, be recognized as
"kindest" or "most helpful." Find enough categories for
prize-winning so that no student is ignored.

3. *Substitute team games for those games that eliminate all but a single winner or loser.* Single winners or
losers often become snubbed by their peers. Team efforts, on
the other hand, encourage cooperation and sharpen group
relational skills.

4. *Use games that have value to your teaching aim.*
Small group games, such as board games and puzzles, are
available through most Christian bookstores and curriculum
suppliers. These games can center interest on the Bible les-

son, provide recreation, stimulate interaction, and serve as useful review tools. Teachers or students can invent their own lesson-centered games, based on classic game formats with familiar rules. Game pieces for these are available through educational supply stores.

Think about the philosophy behind classic party games. A game such as musical chairs, for instance, teaches children that to succeed one must be the first to take what everyone wants. Children who smash a piñata learn to grab as much as possible before other children can.

For parties, camps, and club meetings, search out games that keep players involved round after round, instead of putting them out of the competition. Games that rotate leadership give everyone a chance to be the center of attention. Avoid games that have a lot of body contact and the possibility of bruises, scratches, and hurt feelings.

At a camp or other large facility, players can be divided into small groups and rotated to stations where they learn a new skill or complete a task. Each group needs the contributions of each of its members in order to meet the challenges of each station in a minimum of time. This kind of activity is called a "wide game." It encourages participation, builds mutual support for team members, and provides opportunities to learn and practice new skills.

Games can teach Bible content, help children learn each other's names, burn up excess energy, and build teamwork. Safe, age-appropriate games provide plain old fun. The next time you plan to use a form of competition in your class, prayerfully consider all the factors involved. Choose those methods that will promote your teaching aim, motivate your students to learn, and create an atmosphere of cooperation and fun.

Grief and Death

How can a teacher affirm the goodness of God to a child who has lost a friend or family member through death?

When the apostle Paul wrote to the church in Corinth, he answered many of their questions about death (1 Cor. 15): What happens? Where does the body go? What will the resurrection be like? Paul refers them to the example of a seed: It must die before it can produce new life. When we look at a tomato seed and compare it with the plump, juicy fruit it produces, it is hard for us to believe they are part of the same process.

Death was part of God's plan for Jesus. His resurrection provided the ultimate proof that death has no power over the Christian. The dead do not return to this life but instead proceed to a better life with God. A teacher who knows this can help children to understand that the body of the person they remember, which might have been injured or sick, is no longer needed by the one they loved. A special, invisible part of that person has gone to live with God in a beautiful, new home. That loved one will receive a brand-new body with which he or she will be happy.

Children also need to understand that death is real and final. For many, their first experience with death is the death of a pet. They may watch an expired goldfish float for hours before admitting that it will no longer need to be fed.

Then, one day "it" happens to a friend or relative. In these situations, an adult shouldn't speak of death in terms of "sleeping" or "they went away"; that only teaches children lies. They must never be taught what will need to be untaught later on. The euphemism of "sleep" might make sense to a child in the case of a peaceful death by natural causes; on the other hand, it may cause a child to be afraid to go to sleep. It leaves the youngster without answers when confronted by someone's violent death from terrible injuries.

In today's mobile society, intergenerational households are rare. Children are seldom exposed to an aging person's death by natural causes. Most of the deaths they witness are violent ones represented in movies and TV shows; few children are prepared for the real thing. Parents and teachers should discuss death with children before it happens to someone near and dear. These adults should explain the facts of physical death and share the fact of the believer's eternal life.

When death comes to someone close, an adult should comfort a grieving child without negating the child's loss. There is great joy in heaven for the dead in Christ, but those left behind must be allowed to express their sorrow. Too often, adults exclude children from grief over the death of a family member or friend, hoping to spare them unhappiness. This is an injustice. If the child shared the love of that person, then the youngster is entitled to share the loss.

A Sunday school teacher who explains death to a child may be at odds with the child's parents. Well-meaning adults, hoping to spare the child's feelings, may explain that Gramps is vacationing or just resting. This is one time when a solid teacher-parent relationship is valuable. Teachers can provide parents with biblical, age-appropriate answers to their children's questions, and direct those questions to parents who wish to discuss the topic at home. Teachers are not, however, to reinforce unbiblical teachings. It is vital that the information a child gets from parents and teachers is consistent and biblical.

The Grieving Process

Upon learning of the death of a loved one, an individual goes through these stages: shock, confusion, hope, and, finally, acceptance. Each stage is marked by predictable characteristics:

1. Shock: numbness, disorientation; physical symptoms including weakness, headaches, body aches, and possibly fainting.

2. Confusion: anger, guilt, fear, uncertainty, bargaining with God, crying, panic, preoccupation with memories of the dead one and the circumstances of the death; physical symptoms including insomnia, loss of appetite, and nervousness.

3. Hope: the beginning of positive thoughts.

4. Acceptance: adjustment, reconstruction, resumption of work, and interaction.

At each stage, those who support mourners need to accept the feelings they express and to provide positive reinforcement and spiritual insight. Almost always, however, the company of a silent listener is more therapeutic than that of a well-intentioned lecturer. We are expected to grieve, but urged not "to grieve like the rest of men, who have no hope" (1 Thess. 4:13 NIV). The work of the mourner is to grieve, and the work of the church family is to support and encourage. Because grief is part of the restoration to normalcy, it is truly "good" grief.

Teachers can support grieving children by:

- listening.
- helping them to accept the reality of their loss.
- encouraging expressions of grief.
- encouraging good eating and sleeping habits, exercise, and social interaction.
- providing gentle memories of the lost loved one.
- being alert for denials of grief, lasting anger, physical symptoms, or continued withdrawal from friends. Professional counseling may be needed.

Not all who die go to heaven. It will be hard to accept the death of a beloved unbeliever. It's one thing to know that a faceless, foreign heathen may burn in hell, but quite another to know that Grandma faces eternal torment. Sometimes the spiritual status of the loved one who has died is unknown, and mourners can hope for the best. In the case of an outspoken unbeliever, we can only provide biblical answers and sincere sympathy. God is merciful, but it is also His nature to be just.

Many adults think that children adjust faster to a loss than they; but much depends on the suddenness of the loss, the degree of preparation, and the age and sensitivity of the child. Although the stages of grief are predictable, the timetable for these varies from person to person. If a child's loss was that of a sibling, the parents may withdraw from each other and smother the surviving child with affection. This especially is a time for the church to minister to the whole family.

Growth in the Ministry: Pains and Plans

When discussing growth, church administrators like to differentiate between qualitative and quantitative growth, yet is there always so wide a chasm between the two? The same ministries that produce disciples are also likely to attract visitors who will become regular attenders. The church that wants to grow in numbers as well as in spiritual maturity needs to take a look at where it is, where it has been, and where it is going.

Where Are We Now?

As is true in other areas of children's ministry, the first step in growth is evaluation. Are the classrooms attractive? Are the activities interesting? Do the teachers relate well to the learners? Do learners run eagerly to their classrooms, or do they creep to school unwillingly like snails?

Once again, the key to the learner's attitude is the teacher's attitude. The teacher must create a stimulating learning environment and an atmosphere of love and acceptance. God's love is discovered in the context of caring relationships, and as we have stated before, children don't care what you know until they know that you care.

Here are some basic items to evaluate:

- Curriculum (Bible-based, learner-focused).
- Teaching staff (training, support, retention).

- Learning environment (safety, stimulation, participation).
- Teacher-to-learner ratio (encouragement of relationships).
- Balance of worship, fellowship, expression, and instruction.
- Teacher-parent partnership.
- Outreach and evangelism.
- Visitor and absentee follow-up.
- Church-wide and community promotion of the children's ministry.

Where Have We Been?

A look backward should include, if possible, a survey of attendance figures for the past ten years. Find out where the low points and high points are. Can those points be accounted for?

Try these effective number-crunching evaluations:

- Compare attendance figures for each program in the children's ministry. Why do children choose to participate in certain programs and not in others?
- Compare the number of first-time visitors to the number of those first-timers who actually return. Which classes or clubs have the highest and lowest retention?
- Compare the number of graduating sixth-graders to the number of seventh-graders the following September. Are junior-highers dropping out?
- What are the sizes of the age groups in the children's ministry compared to the age groups in the neighborhood? Which unchurched groups have not been contacted by outreach efforts?

It is naïve to think that non-Christian parents will get up on Sunday mornings to bring their children to church. A child's attendance may depend instead on getting a ride from a neighbor or teacher, or on the availability of public transportation. When children cannot come to church, the church may have to go to them. Plans for growth need to consider sites such as community rooms in housing projects, after-school programs in local schools, or backyard clubs.

Where Are We Going?

There is a story going around that a goldfish will grow to fit the size of its aquarium. This may not actually be true of goldfish—but it is certainly true of congregations! Once a comfortable number of learners per class has been exceeded, growth will halt. Part of planning for growth is excellence in ministry; the other part is projecting for expansion.

Here are some things to consider:

- Review the goals of the children's ministry and the overall goals of the church. Do the programs that would be held in new facilities line up with these purposes?
- Evaluate the use of the current space. Is it being used efficiently?
- Use attendance and community population figures to predict growth. Should the church build a senior-citizen center or a child-care facility? Should growth come through church-planting?
- Visit area churches. What are their perceptions and plans? Can your club program be a joint effort with theirs? Can Vacation Bible Schools be cooperative?

If building is the only option, do what carpenters are trained to do—measure twice and cut once! Consult professionals who are trained in the planning of worship, recreation, and education facilities. Tailor your facilities to programs—don't program to suit the facilities.

Many churches that expand their facilities experience a sudden increase in numbers. Then, in the months that follow, their growth levels off. Panicking, they sponsor flashy events designed to attract visitors and award prizes to children who bring their unchurched friends. (Although the winning of a prize is an undesirable motivation, bringing a friend is fine; it is certainly biblical!)

In the early church, many who were brought into the fellowship of believers arrived with their entire households. This *oikos* (the Greek word for "household") style of outreach is a natural way of bringing, evangelizing, and keeping friends and family members of regular attenders in the church. People who live in the same household or neighborhood form a network of accountability for attendance and growth. Children who play on the same team, attend the same school, or live on the same block may supply mutual encouragement to grow in Christ. In any case, the ideal set forth for us and for the community should be: "Church is a place for families!"

Guiding Conversation

Luke 2:52 tells us, "Jesus increased in wisdom and stature, and in favor with God and men." This passage suggests that God planned for children to progress through certain developmental stages. And these stages affect every area of growth—social, emotional, spiritual, physical, and mental.

Children have a wide range of interests, and as they grow they develop an increasingly varied palette of experiences to stimulate their intellect. They increase their mental abilities and develop their power to reason. Literal thinking develops into abstract thinking. Attention span and memory increase.

Teachers can help children develop this way through the use of guided conversation. By using good, directed questions, teachers can help move children from a knowledge-level to a deep understanding and practical application of God's Word in their lives.

Jesus used many teaching methods in His ministry. Among them were object lessons, parables, sermons, visual aids, illustrations, and questions. Of the 125 teaching sessions recorded in the four Gospels, more than two-thirds were initiated by a question. Jesus asked a question and let His listeners respond.

On the Emmaus road, Jesus asked the two travelers what they were talking about. Feigning ignorance, He asked them to describe the recent events in Jerusalem. Then, to help them understand the meaning of those events, He asked, "Ought not the Christ to have suffered these things and to enter into His glory?" (Luke 24:26). His questions moved them farther down the road, to a fuller understanding.

Basically, there are three levels of questions to use with children:

- Level One—knowledge questions. Ask the learner to recall facts or other objective information, such as names and places. "Where was the traveler going when he was attacked?"
- Level Two—comprehension questions. Ask the learner to show his or her understanding of the facts. To answer this kind of question, the child must comprehend the implications. "Why didn't the traveler expect the Samaritan's help?"
- Level Three—application questions. The learner must use information to solve a problem. In other words, his or her understanding must be transferred to personal experience. "If what happened to the Samaritan happened to you today, who do you think each character might be? How would it change your feelings toward the person who stopped to help?"

Implicit in asking questions is the teacher's willingness to listen carefully to answers. Listening involves accepting both the feelings and the ideas voiced by learners. If a child is hurt and angry, it does no good for the teacher to say, "You're not supposed to be mad!" Instead, the teacher should say, "I can see that you're mad—tell me why."

A child may declare that "Daniel was dumb" for going to the lions' den for his faith. When this happens, a teacher will get further with the question, "Why do you say that?" than with, "You shouldn't say that!" In correcting a child's behavior, a teacher's carefully chosen questions about alternative choices of behavior will provoke more thought than will a stern lecture. "What will you do the next time Robby pokes you?" is the type of question that takes advantage of a teaching moment. But the reply, "Don't you ever do that again!" doesn't!

When you can weave the lesson aim into the natural flow of conversation throughout your classroom session, you will multiply the minutes!

Handling the Holidays

As Christmas shopping becomes more and more a year-round event, it is easy to forget that there are other holidays on the calendar. To be sure, Easter and Thanksgiving have a religious context that make them easy to integrate into children's ministry, but what about other observances? Which ones should be celebrated—and which others should be ignored or reinterpreted?

New Year's Day

The new year is a good time for adults to put the past year in perspective and to plan for the one to come. On the other hand, young children live in the "here and now"—and the significance of the holiday is lost on them. Martin Luther King, Jr.'s birthday, which comes later in the month, presents an opportunity to teach about brotherhood and equality.

Valentine's Day

Lost among all the cards and candy of this holiday is the story of a Christian martyr. Valentine's Day presents an opportunity to teach children about the love of God and the fellowship of believers. This story is a great way to do just that. (Teachers who provide parties for their classes should remember that excess amounts of sugar and caffeine will promote misbehavior.)

President's Day

For this holiday, teachers can concentrate on the idea that our leaders have always helped keep our country free for us to worship God openly. Older children can be helped to understand this is not a freedom that all people enjoy.

Saint Patrick's Day

Apart from the business about the snakes, the story of Patrick's life is an exciting and inspiring tale of kidnapping, forgiveness, and love. This celebration from another part of the globe can help to build cultural awareness in children.

Arbor Day (or Earth Day)

Arbor Day is a "natural" for a lesson on our stewardship of God's world and the planting of trees or shrubs around the church. (Avoid references to "Mother Nature," however. Emphasize the beauty and order of creation as evidence of God's power!)

Easter

Most curricula provide Easter material. Sometimes it is no more than a one-lesson unit, sandwiched between unrelated lessons. The best use of this holiday requires that the story be set in the correct framework. A teacher can help children understand its significance by explaining all the events of Easter (using age-appropriate concepts and vocabulary). Remember that young children have little grasp of time and place; they may assume that Jesus grew from a baby into an adult in the months between Christmas and Easter!

The egg has long been a symbol of new life, and egg hunts have become an Easter tradition. Although the symbolism is lost on young children, egg hunts are fun and harmless in moderation. (Be careful, however, not to let the Easter bunny become another Santa Claus.)

Passover

This holiday and other traditional Jewish celebrations deserve more consideration from Christians. Most have roots recorded in the Old Testament and are rich with symbols of the events of the New. Many guides are available to help teachers interpret the significance of Passover and its place in Christian theology.

Mother's Day and Father's Day

Bible learning activities on these two Sundays can focus on the biblical mandates for children's behavior toward their parents, and on thankfulness for God's provision of a caring mother and father. Since many children are from divided families, teachers will need to include the roles of those nonparental adult caregivers who are involved in the lives of such children.

Memorial Day (and the Fourth of July)

Like Hanukkah, Bastille Day, and Cinco de Mayo, these holidays are patriotic celebrations of national significance. They are opportunities for children to discuss and be thankful for the freedom they enjoy.

Halloween

For theological reasons and/or safety considerations, increasing numbers of adults have become apprehensive about Halloween celebrations. Most young children perceive the day as nothing more than a chance to dress up and eat candy.

Indeed, few people consider the Druidic roots of the holiday centuries ago, when it honored Samhain, lord of the dead. Although only a small number of those who observe Halloween do so as Satan worship, their growing number includes many adolescents. Teachers should provide older children with information that will help them identify and avoid witchcraft, Satan worship, and other unbiblical practices.

Churches that sponsor Halloween parties wishing to provide a safe, supervised celebration should monitor activities, costumes, and decorations to minimize the emphasis on the supernatural. Sukkoth, the Jewish harvest festival, presents a biblical Halloween alternative. Simchas Torah, the last day of Sukkoth, honors the Scriptures. These observances can be both instructive and safe alternatives to Halloween celebrations.

Thanksgiving

This holiday was originally a harvest celebration, and two hundred years passed before it became an official national observance. Even though Thanksgiving comes only once a year, it is helpful to have this holiday which promotes gratitude to God.

Many teachers choose to reenact the first Thanksgiving event with costumes and a feast. Adults must be careful to correct Native American stereotypes. Teachers—emphasize thanksgiving as a lifestyle!

Ethnic Celebrations

Awareness of other cultures is a step toward appreciating different ideas, lifestyles, and ethnic groups. Many churches save this type of study for a missions emphasis week. It can (and should) be integrated into activities and lessons year-round by including food, games, and other aspects of differing cultures. Part of the fun can be in observing a holiday from another land.

On March 3, Japanese girls dress in kimonos and display their favorite dolls. On May 5, boys take their turn with fish-shaped kites and warrior heroes. In contrast to the largess of Christmas giving, the African-American holiday of Kwanzaa (December 26 through January 1) encourages the exchange of small, homemade gifts to family members. During the week preceding Christmas, Mexican and Hispanic children participate in the reenactment of Mary and Joseph's search for an inn by staging Las Posadas.

Holidays from America and from around the world present wonderful learning opportunities for the classroom. They help to teach about events from the Bible, to examine history with a Christian perspective, to appreciate other cultures, and to discern the context of traditional celebrations in the light of biblical truth.

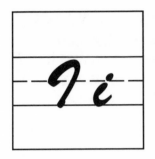

Intergenerational tional Programs: "Pardon Me, Your Generation Gap Is Showing"

The mobility of the average American family has made it common for children to grow up without knowing aunts, uncles, or grandparents. Children today have little exposure to the aging process and little opportunity for interaction with older adults. Despite the fact that our culture is extremely youth-oriented, a larger number of Americans than ever before soon will be senior adults. How can today's children form attitudes that will help them relate to older adults now—and to cope with their own aging later on?

The church can help by doing several things, such as:

- inviting older adults to participate in special activities with children.
- adopting a "grandparent" with whom the class can exchange letters and pray.
- sponsoring events to which each child should bring an older adult guest.

- including older adults among those recruited for children's work.
- arranging for children to help housebound adults with chores such as sweeping sidewalks, decorating for Christmas, or mailing letters.

Relationships between children and older adults benefit both. Most senior adults enjoy interaction with children and have the skills and leisure time to lend to the education ministry. In turn, the children receive instruction, affection, and the opportunity to be helpful. It is easy to forget that growing Christians need to serve—and that growing Christians come in all ages and stages of life.

Not all senior adults have the stamina or the inclination to minister to children. The seniors in a church could be surveyed to see who would like to participate in the children's ministry and to what extent. As is true in any recruitment process, care must be taken to match skills with job descriptions. Some older adults will go beyond the call of duty by bringing home-baked cookies to every class, while the most that some seniors will be able to do is to communicate through notes and calls from their homes. Each contribution is equally valuable.

Some Christian schools use a "class grandparent" program. Each classroom is assigned an older adult with whom the learners exchange letters, cassettes, photos, or even visits. It is sometimes possible for the same "grandparent" to maintain a relationship with a group of children as the young ones grow and mature during the elementary school years.

Other programs can be developed that involve not only children and senior adults, but all the ages in between—in intergenerational classes. For example, groups of families meet together on Sunday morning. One set of parents takes the lead in teaching their entire group of children and adults, using methods that utilize other parents as assistants. In this approach, parents learn teaching skills to use at home, and the entire family learns the same lesson. Some disadvantages, however, include the difficulty of keeping learners of widely varying ages actively involved in the same material, and keeping the biblical concepts relevant and applicable to such a wide span of ages. One approach, with similar benefits but fewer disadvantages, would be to include interested parents in teacher-training sessions, where they could learn methods to apply during any "teaching moment" at home.

Adolescents who serve with children's programs can learn while they serve. Being involved with older teachers means they can observe experienced teachers at work, receive valuable training for a lifetime, and provide the extra attention younger learners sometimes need. Assistants in this age bracket often minister with their parents. This provides learners with a model of parent-child interaction. Recruiters should take care, however, that helpers are not coerced into service; removed from instruction designed for their own age level; or excused from worship services to socialize with other helpers. Adults must not put too much authority or responsibility on young shoulders. No helper should be expected to maintain discipline over learners who are just a few years his or her junior.

One common complaint about church programs is that they divide rather than unite the family. Once a family enters the church, each member migrates to a group that shares his or her age and interests. The family may or may not reassemble for corporate worship.

This complaint would be valid if Sunday morning was a family's only opportunity to worship God together, but opportunities for spontaneous family worship (along with regularly scheduled times) occur throughout the week in the home. Anytime the family is together can be the right time to respond to God with worship. The church's education ministry to children must make the most of its time to teach God's Word on an age-appropriate level, and to encourage a worship response based on what has been learned. Parents interested in reinforcing lesson aims or planning lesson-related worship times at home usually have access to their children's take-home materials each week. The primary learning place for a child's spiritual development is the home!

Job Descriptions

Accepting a job without a written job description is like diving into waters of undetermined depth. Virtually no paid worker would consider it; why then do churches ask volunteers to take on positions of undetermined duration and parameters?

Search committees and recruiters find their work made much easier when they have detailed descriptions of the positions the church needs to fill. Workers are more likely to volunteer if they can see how a position's responsibilities stack up with their talents, interests, and schedule.

With a set of job descriptions that covers every position in the children's ministry, an administrator can discover areas of overlapping responsibility as well as important tasks for which no worker assumes responsibility. By coordinating job descriptions on an organizational chart, the administrator can determine which jobs require too broad a span of control, which require support staff, and what new roles must be created. For example, many churches relieve individual teachers of the burden of buying supplies by creating a position for a resource room director.

When a worker leaves a position, the administrator should conduct an "exit interview" to determine how the job may have changed or perhaps should be changed. Sometimes a task that a person has quietly handled for an extended period inadvertently becomes part of the job *but is not in the original job description.* If the nursery coordinator who just moved away had taken on the responsibility for supplying disposable diapers, that added task should be written into her job description before someone else takes over.

A well-written job description will list these six items:

1. The purpose of the position.
2. Personal qualifications, training, and experience required.
3. Time commitment.
4. General duties.
5. Specific duties.
6. An organizational chart indicating authority and accountability.

Sample Job Descriptions

The Teacher

Purpose:

The teacher is to model God's love, create an effective learning environment, and guide children into learning how to apply the Bible to their lives.

Qualifications:

1. A lifestyle that reflects spiritual maturity and consistent growth.
2. A faithful prayer life.
3. Agreement with the church's theological position and philosophy of education.
4. Participation in pre-service training.

Time Commitment: _____

Duties:

1. Attendance at planning meetings and training events.
2. Faithful and creative preparation of the weekly lesson.
3. Cooperation with fellow teachers and administrators.
4. Regular and punctual attendance, and advance notice of absences.
5. Personal interest in each learner.

6. Care of the classroom and good stewardship of supplies.

The Department Leader

Purpose:

To assist and supervise teachers within a particular age-level department. To act as liaison with the division coordinator.

Qualifications (in addition to teacher qualifications):

1. Leadership ability.
2. Servanthood attitude.

Time Commitment: _____

Duties:

1. Leadership of department-level teacher meetings.
2. Attendance at training events.
3. Supervision of the lesson plan.
4. Record-keeping; prompt follow-up of visitors and absentees.
5. Regular and punctual attendance.
6. Provision of substitutes.
7. Personal interest in each learner and teacher.

The Division Coordinator

Purpose:

To administrate the departments that comprise an age-level division. To act as liaison with Sunday school superintendent.

Qualifications (in addition to department leader qualifications):

1. Organizational and administrative skills.
2. Ability to communicate.

Time Commitment: _____

Duties:

1. Observation and evaluation of teachers and department leaders.
2. Staff development through modeling and mentoring.
3. Supervision of attendance and class division when needed.

4. Participation in planning and training events.
5. Responsibility for inventory and ordering of supplies for division.
6. Regular and punctual attendance.
7. Leadership of division-level department leader meetings.

Superintendent

Purpose:

To administrate the Sunday school program. To act as liaison with church board or C.E. committee.

Qualifications (in addition to those of division coordinator):

1. Comprehensive view of the church's education ministry.
2. Exceptional administrative skills.

Time Commitment: _____

Duties:

1. Observation and evaluation of the program.
2. Direction of long-range planning and goal-setting.
3. Planning of teacher-training program.
4. Directing of recruitment process.
5. Evaluation of needs for equipment, facilities, resources, personnel.
6. Supervision of the calendar of events.
7. Preparation of the budget for submission.
8. Maintenance of records.
9. Leadership of division coordinator meetings.

The Christian Education team, also called the C.E. committee, is comprised of individuals who take responsibility for:

promotion
personnel
facilities
finance
resources
outreach
curriculum

equipment
supplies
retreats
camps
special ministries

The Sunday school superintendent is a member of this administrative team. Sometimes teachers, department leaders, and division coordinators double as members of the C.E. team.

Because every church is as unique as each of its members, it is unlikely that a job description which suits one church will meet the needs of another exactly. The Christian Education Specialist who wishes to develop useful job descriptions for his or her church will benefit from visits to other churches and from the advice of colleagues in the ministry, but the CES must always keep in mind the unique needs of his or her own congregation.

For the benefit of the recruit, the following must all be spelled out for his or her prayerful consideration: the schedule of the program to which the volunteer commits, the frequency of planning meetings, and the hours of required training. The more specific the description, the less likely there will be a clash of expectations down the line. The length of the commitment must be a loophole not only for the burned-out worker, but for the administrator who needs to dislodge a worker from a position for which he or she is not suited.

If your church is currently operating without job descriptions for volunteer as well as paid positions, act now to do the following:

1. Have workers prepare detailed job descriptions of all they do, listing purpose, qualifications, and duties.
2. Have each worker meet with the person to whom he or she is accountable to discuss the first draft of the description.

3. Assemble the descriptions and compare them to the ministry's organizational chart.
4. Check for overburdened positions and overlooked tasks.
5. Keep descriptions on file for recruitment purposes. Update them yearly and/or whenever a worker leaves a position.

Learning
Centers

What's the best way to teach a young child how to ride a bicycle? Should the teacher sit the child down at her desk and lecture the youngster on how it's done? Should she show the child pictures of someone riding a bicycle correctly? Should she get on a bicycle and demonstrate the technique herself? These approaches might be of minimal help—but one could hardly expect the learner to jump onto a new two-wheeler afterward and pedal away.

The most efficient method of learning to ride a bicycle is *to get on and start pedaling.* The student might require training wheels at first and an adult with enough stamina to run alongside and hold the bike upright. But eventually the child will master the skill.

What is the difference between these teaching methods? The main difference is that learners benefit most from *sensory stimulation.* They retain greater degrees of lesson content when the teacher's methods appeal to many of their senses. Telling a child how to ride a bicycle involves only hearing; a demonstration, on the other hand, adds the visual factor. If the child can climb aboard, he or she will become actively involved and will participate fully in the learning experience. The old adage applies: "I hear and I forget; I see and I remember; I do and I understand."

This method of learning through participation is the purpose behind having a learning center in the classroom. In this approach, teachers create a setting in which carefully selected activities are made available to small groups of learners. With minimal assistance, learners can make their own discoveries. Activities are teacher-guided, but learner-focused. This technique has been employed in public schools for many years. In fact, children's teachers must be aware that youngsters who are used to participating in this way can become easily frustrated and bored by the passive role they may be forced to follow on Sunday morning.

Imagine you are a learner in your class at church. Do you get into trouble before class even starts? Do periods of sitting and listening stretch the limits of your attention span and physical needs? Do you find your eyes and thoughts wandering? Do you have the urge to poke the student sitting in front of you simply because you have nothing more interesting to do?

Now imagine that, as a learner, you walk into your classroom and are invited to choose one of several appealing activities. In one corner some students are looking at objects from nature under a microscope. At a table, students are watching a filmstrip and listening to the narration on earphones. In another area, children are busily preparing an art project that will be used as a visual aid later in the lesson. Somewhere else, a group of advanced readers are using the children's dictionaries to discover the meaning of new words they will encounter in the upcoming Bible story. Teachers and helpers stand by to assist when needed and to guide conversation toward the teaching aim. The room is filled with controlled activity.

Now, does that sound inviting—and educational—to you? Here are some suggested activities for learning centers:

- Art: drawing, painting, posters, dioramas, collages.
- Drama: role plays, skits, pantomimes, puppets, props, costumes.
- Communications: discussion groups, interviews, panel discussions.

- Writing: poetry, letters, diaries, cassette recorders.
- Music: listening to recordings, writing, using instruments.
- Research: children's dictionaries, maps, filmstrips, videos.
- God's world: nature items, magnifying glasses, teaching pictures.
- Home living: child-size furniture, dolls, food, dress-up clothes.
- Books: sufficient light, comfortable seating, book racks.
- Blocks: cardboard or wooden blocks, people figures.
- Puzzles: simple, theme-related puzzles; puzzle rack.

The two main criteria for selecting activities for learning centers is (1) that they meet students' needs and abilities and (2) that the activities are keyed to the teaching aim of the lesson. Some centers may not change for the duration of a study unit, while others may change weekly. Each center should be planned and assembled ahead of time, and each activity should be limited to a small number of learners.

Centers can be used at the beginning of a lesson to stimulate interest and at the end to reinforce and review. Teachers should be prepared with stimulating questions to guide conversation around the activity. It's good to keep in mind that the younger the learners are the more time they will spend actively participating rather than sitting and listening.

A teaching session should combine presentation of the Bible lesson with learner-focused activities that explore applications of the lesson. This will help students not only to know God's Word but also to be motivated to apply it to their everyday experience. Consider the teaching methods used by Jesus. Although He employed the lecture method, He usually paired the teaching of a concept with a related activity. As they gathered to share their last supper together, the disciples had their feet washed by their Lord and Teacher. Christ performed this menial task, usually the work of a servant, to give them "an example, that you should do as I have done to you" (John 13:15).

Let's follow Jesus' example—let's provide students with interesting activities through which they can get the most out of the learning process. Then, perhaps the "miracle" it would take to motivate some students will turn out to be as simple as a learning center.

Learning Styles

In his first letter to the Corinthians, the apostle Paul likened the interdependence of the various parts of the human body to the cooperation of believers in the church. Each member contributes according to his or her gifts and thus benefits the whole. The contributing members, however, are gifted neither equally nor identically.

The human brain functions in the same way—different segments of the brain are designed to perform different jobs. Information from the different senses and nerves is fed to the corresponding area in the brain that provides for the most efficient processing.

Long before a person is born, the brain contains a full complement of cells. As the person grows, the brain develops into a more complex structure. The first burst of brain development occurs when a fetus is about three months old and grows billions of nerve cells. Each nerve cell makes over ten thousand connections with other nerve cells. The job of "hooking up" those nerve cells begins during the third trimester and lasts until midway through the early childhood years. (The young brain is so "plastic"—that is, durable—that damage to one area will be compensated by a rerouting of the function to another area of the brain.)

Research shows that an enhanced, stimulating environment in the early childhood years can improve a child's ability to learn. The way a child learns best can be called his or her preferred "learning style." Whether this style is primarily auditory, visual, tactile, or kinesthetic depends on which part of the child's brain dominates the function of processing, storing, and utilizing information.

Why is it important for teachers to identify their students' learning styles?

Observe the learners in your classroom. Even if they are the same age and hold to the same basic age-group characteristics and needs, each learner displays differences in how he or she processes new concepts. As learners listen to the lesson, for example, one may prefer to sit upright at a desk while another squirms on the floor. One may be content to quietly pore over the illustrations, while another fires a barrage of questions and comments at you. We each learn through all of our senses—but different individuals will rely more heavily on certain ones.

The left side of the brain controls communication, logic, and analytical ability. Learners whose left-side functions dominate their thinking may excel in math, reading, and writing. The right side of the brain controls spatial ability, visual perception, creativity, rhythm, and intuition. Right-brain thinkers tend to be artistic and creative.

Because most teaching favors those who can read, write, and do arithmetic (all left-brain tasks), children who process information through right-brain avenues may be judged unfairly as learning disabled and uncooperative. (It is not only traditional teaching styles that tend to favor left-brain style learning, but also the traditional classroom itself!) Research among school children has shown that a varied curriculum of arts and standard academic subjects improved their performance in all areas.

Young children use all their senses to learn about their world. They need to touch, taste, smell, hear, and see things. The young child who says he or she is anxious to "see" an object usually wants to hold it while looking at it. As children age, they tend to rely more heavily on sound and sight for input. This may be because they have been conditioned to learn mostly through the more formal teaching methods. When a teacher uses a variety of activities to bring across a concept, however, the entire complement of senses can be brought into play. The more senses that are involved in the learning process, the greater the chance the learner will understand and apply what he or she has learned, and teachers who address the needs of children with a wide range of learning styles can speak to each learner's special "sense" while broadening the abilities of all the learners.

Here are the three basic types of input available to a teacher who wishes to fully engage students:

1. *Tactile-kinesthetic input:* Hands-on activities, such as art projects, educational games, and the use of manipulatives (beads, puzzles, objects to sort), stimulate learning for tactile-kinesthetic children. Field trips and drama are good teaching techniques for reaching children who prefer these styles of learning. When a tactile-kinesthetic learner hears a word, he or she responds with an emotional or physical feeling. To these learners, the word *joy* would mean shouting, clapping their hands, and dancing.

2. *Visual input:* Illustrations, charts, and visual aids are the tools of visual learners. These children may benefit from reading a lesson prior to listening to it. When a visual learner hears a word, he or she receives a mental impression or image.

3. *Auditory input:* This is a traditional style. The auditory processing system delivers information more efficiently when it is heard rather than read or written. The auditory learner responds to meaning in the sound of the words he or she hears.

Let's apply these three learning styles to the planning of a lesson that will teach the importance of following God's rules even when it demands courage. The Bible story used to illustrate the concept will be Daniel's interpretation of the writing on the wall (Dan. 5).

- *Auditory:* Learners listen to taped interviews with Bible characters; highly descriptive words are used in the telling of the story.
- *Visual:* Maps show the locations of sites in the story; pictures illustrate events and trace chronology.
- *Tactile-kinesthetic:* As paint is applied, a wax-resist art project dramatically reveals the message written in white crayon on white paper; props and costumes enhance the learners' dramatization of the story.

For learners who enjoy reviewing facts, objective questions will suffice. Subjective questions will be fielded by those who prefer to discuss motives and emotions. Role plays will help physically oriented learners to apply the new concept to real-life situations.

Each learner must experience the process of learning a concept, developing an attitude toward it, and making it a part of his or her behavior. In this particular lesson, the teaching aims would be to help learners (1) *know* that God helped Daniel to face the king with the truth, (2) *feel* that Daniel's faith in God gave him courage, and (3) *act* as Daniel did when called upon to do the right thing under challenging circumstances.

Brain research bears out other principles that teachers will recognize:

- Review "resets" the mind to continue learning.
- Repetition enhances memory.
- Memory tends to retain material heard at the beginning and end of a presentation.
- A change of activity "rests" the brain.
- Anything heard after the attention span ends will be forgotten.
- A learning context outside the classroom, but similar to that in which a lesson was learned, will stimulate memory (e.g., the use of dramatizations and stories of real-life application).
- Rhythm and rhyme are memory aids. (Some memory

devices involve visual imagery. This type of mnemonic device, which is often symbolic, is not recommended for use with younger, more concrete thinkers.)

In his letter to the church at Corinth, the apostle Paul went on to say he was willing to "become all things to all men, that I might by all means save some" (1 Cor. 9:22). We must teach in a variety of styles so that we may, by all possible means, reach each of our learners most effectively with the Word of God.

Lesson Planning

The effectiveness of a lesson depends on the level at which it is learned. There are three levels of learning—*knowledge*, *understanding*, and *application*. Benjamin Bloom, who did extensive research in child development during the 1930s, explained the implications of these stages and how they relate to one another.

Knowledge

At the *knowledge* level, the learner grasps the literal meaning of what is presented. In answer to the question, "What does the Bible *say?*" the learner should be able to recall or recognize specific words, phrases, and information from the Scripture lesson. The knowledge level is important as the basis on which the others are built.

Here are several knowledge-level activities:

- Involve students in activities that call for active responses, such as exercises in reading or writing. Use worksheets that accompany the curriculum, or design your own. Games—secret codes, puzzles, matchups—challenge learners and provide fun.
- Provide multisensory activities.
- Provide affirmation. Show enthusiasm, and praise and encourage effort.

- Relate all activities to the central aim of the lesson. Unity of purpose focuses the learner's thinking on one main truth and increases the likelihood of his or her retention, understanding, and application. One of the reasons camps and retreats are so productive is that activities at these events are usually planned to revolve around a unifying theme.
- Provide fresh and appealing activities. The worst activity for the current week would be the one that made a big hit last week. There are a hundred exciting, creative methods for teaching the Bible to children.
- Ask questions that require fact-based answers. With objective questions, a teacher can easily evaluate a learner's grasp of basic information.

Understanding

At the *understanding* level, the learner appreciates the meaning and consequence of the facts he or she has assimilated. In this area, the teacher must ask the question, "What does the Bible *mean?*" The learner can be expected to demonstrate an understanding of the information he has learned.

Here are a few understanding-level activities:

- Provide activities in which the learner must transform ideas into new forms. Ask a child to rephrase what he or she has heard using his or her own choice of words. This is a good way to check the learner's level of understanding. Students thus can go beyond the Bible's stated facts and into the feelings and emotions of its characters.
- Use activities in which the learner discovers the relationship between ideas. On a knowledge level, for instance, a child can know that Jesus forgave sins. He can also know that only God can forgive sins. Now, on the *understanding* level, the student can connect these concepts and know that Jesus is God in the flesh! Helping a child clarify thoughts and put them in logical order is a skill any teacher can practice. Teachers must

learn to guide conversation so that learners arrive at conclusions in logical sequence.

- Provide opportunities for learners to define and interpret biblical concepts. Listen carefully for any rote phrases that might camouflage confusion.
- Ask questions that require a child to understand what is happening in the lesson. This style of questioning requires a level of understanding beyond that of the answers expected on a simple knowledge level. Offer learners time to think about their answers.

Sometimes teachers feel satisfied when they have completed this step in teaching—that is, when the child knows and understands what Scripture is saying, but this is not the ultimate goal.

Application

On the *application* level the learner applies the concept to daily experience. Principles presented in the lesson must be made clear so the child can act on them even in situations of extreme pressure. Children should be able to use a principle to solve a problem. In other words, the child must transfer his *understanding* to a new situation—his own life. He must answer the question, "What does the Bible mean *to me*?"

Application level activities:

- Involve the learner in activities that require the use of principles from Scripture in practical ways, such as drama, interviews, role plays, and actual situations in the classroom. Simulations can be a valuable "dry run" for daily life. The teacher's skill at guiding conversation is a crucial factor.
- Ask questions that help children transfer Bible learning to a new situation. Assist them in thinking through a Christian response to a set of circumstances that presents itself at school or on the playground. Observe

learners' behavior—try to identify typical situations you could present in class as test cases.

To some adults, such run-throughs may seem elementary and unnecessary. "These are innocent children," some might reason. "They will instinctively do right." *Wrong.* Morality is a concept learned first from adults, then from peers.

David Elkind, a renowned researcher in the child development field, reported Piaget's experiments on this very subject. Children entering middle childhood were presented with two scenarios and asked to pick which was bad and which was good. The first story presented a child who by accident dropped fifteen dishes and broke them. The second scenario showed a child who broke one dish while attempting to raid the cookie jar.

The younger children involved in the testing selected as the guiltier of the two the child in the first story—*because he had done the most damage.* Older children were able to consider the *good intentions of the first boy* and picked child number two as the real culprit.

Other experiments have revealed that young children tend to identify an act as right or wrong depending on whether or not the act was punished. Older children, however, are able to judge an action independent of its consequences. In general, children gradually learn to judge actions more by intention than by result.

The vital importance of relating biblical principles to daily life becomes clear in this thought from Elkind: "It may be, in fact, that children do not have a general concept of morality but learn about it only in specific settings. Their failure to behave at their level of understanding in new situations may . . . be a consequence of not perceiving the moral significance of their action in this new situation" (*A Sympathetic Understanding of the Child*, Allyn & Bacon Press).

- Provide examples of children and adults who have obeyed God's laws. Students can be challenged not only by Bible characters but also by historical and contemporary figures who have stood up for their convictions. Acquaint your students with stories of courageous Christians through library books, films, newspapers, and missionary reports.

• Use disciplinary methods that help children develop a sense of right and wrong. When you witness a behavior that must be corrected, be sure the children involved understand why their actions are unacceptable. Always use correction appropriate to the misbehavior. Be reasonable in your expectations, consistent in your discipline, and fair in your use of correction. Model the characteristics you wish your learners to adopt.

A Life of Obedience

The traditional practice of Christian education has been to train children to sit, listen, and be passive. Students are then expected to go into the world and actively apply what they have learned, but passive learning never produces active application. Make it your goal to teach children God's Word in *content, understanding,* and *application.*

Literature for Children: Apples of Gold

Each year thousands of books are published for the children's market in America. Of those thousands, only a handful are written by Christian authors, and of that small percentage, even fewer can be considered well-written books. How are parents and teachers to select skillfully crafted books that convey a Christian perspective?

Librarians are an excellent source of information on children's publications. Magazines for Christian families often include book reviews. Parents who do not have time to preview their children's reading also can rely on Christian booksellers who have proven themselves to be discerning buyers, or on the imprint of a trustworthy publishing house. The Evangelical Christian Publishers Association awards Golden Medallions to their favorite books each year. Prizes such as the Caldecott, Newbery, and Horn Book Awards (none of which are restricted to Christian literature) are indications of excellence.

Many parents wonder whether they should expose their children to values through books other than those written by avowed Christians. On the one hand, there are many fine Christian authors whose work expresses the Christian worldview in so subtle a manner that their writing may not appear blatantly spiritual. On the other hand, there are Christian authors whose work has nothing to do with the application of Bible truth to real life. On still another hand, there are secular authors whose books do a great job at communicating good values or just telling a harmless, entertaining story. There's nothing wrong with such works.

Whatever a child is given to read, parents should discuss books with their youngster. What are the motives of the characters? Do they display Christian attitudes? As parents and children share books and discuss values, the outcome can be doubly edifying. Parents must be careful, however, not to impose a moral lesson on every page of a book. Some works are intended simply to be fun, and should remain so.

Provided they are well-crafted, all kinds of stories should be made available to young readers. Mystery, adventure, biography, drama, poetry, and fantasy should all be on a child's bookshelf. Often, however, some parents and teachers seem to fear works of fantasy. For those who would like to restrict their choices to Christian authors whose works of fantasy have stood the test of time, there are the classic writers George MacDonald, C. S. Lewis, and J. R. R. Tolkein.

Even though "fantasy" and "the supernatural" are for the most part synonymous, Christians usually associate fantasy with fairies, wishes, and talking animals, and the supernatural with witches, spells, and ghosts. Many mistakenly believe a scary book with an evil witch should be avoided, but a story of the same variety that features a pagan caterpillar who becomes a Christian butterfly would be appropriate. Reject those books that glamorize evil and stories that seek only to terrorize readers. Read a child a book that impresses him or her with the power of evil, rather than one in which an animal is endowed with a spiritual nature. A child can be reassured that Jesus will someday destroy evil, but that same child would have to be "untaught" the fiction that there is an animal heaven.

A youngster develops his or her imagination in early childhood. Books can be an important tool in that development. When a child reaches five or six years of age, he or she is ready to separate reality from fantasy and understand when something is "pretend." At no stage in a child's development should fantasies or fairy tales be considered inappropriate. Books are fuel to fire the imagination.

Another area of concern is fiction that elaborates on stories from Scripture. In most cases, the author's aim is to edify the reader and stick closely to the characters and events as they are recorded in the Bible. Yet, in some cases, the author's artistic license should be revoked for careless writing! (Bible stories for children are often told from the viewpoint of a donkey, dove, or lamb. You can let talking, singing, or dancing animals slide—but you must draw the line when one starts to pray or worship!)

The child's bookshelf should also include books that provide insight into the lives of children from diverse cultures. Role models come in all colors and with all kinds of disabilities. Impressionable readers should not be exposed to books that include stereotypes unless they can be helped to identify them as such. Missionary stories must show a sympathetic understanding of any culture unfamiliar to the reader. The heroes of missionary stories should be Christians of various nationalities and races, not just Anglo-Americans and Europeans.

Biographies of living people such as sports figures, government leaders, and scientists are valuable teaching tools. When a popular or important figure is an outspoken Christian, his or her story can inspire a young reader. The words and actions of a child's hero can, however, get out of sync with the hero's confessed faith. At such times, the child reader needs adult guidance.

Many Christian publishing houses print mystery and adventure books in series for children. While these books are probably not destined to become classics, a youngster who enjoys an exciting novel enough to want the next edition in the series will begin to read for pleasure.

Adults should also consider whether the book's concept is on the child's level of comprehension. Many fine stories are written so they can be enjoyed on several levels, such as Lewis's *The Chronicles of Narnia* fantasy series. On one level, it is simply a charmingly written fantasy. On another level, it is a reference to Christ's death and resurrection. A young child should not be expected to grasp such symbolism, and adults should not ruin a good story by insisting on explaining the higher levels of meaning at every turn. Part of the pleasure of rereading a childhood favorite at a later age is the discovery of new meanings.

An adult also must ask if the vocabulary is on the reader's level. Every children's book should include a few challenging words that send readers to the dictionary to expand their vocabulary, but too many such words become an unbearable frustration.

Are there references to other places and other times? Children begin to grasp concepts of time and space around third grade. Until that age, the phrases "a long time ago" and "far away" will have to suffice.

Is the book too long? Many young children may have a hard time sustaining interest in a book that must be read in several sittings. Stories read a chapter at a time are best for older boys and girls who can remember characters and events.

Is the book (as well as the story) appealing and attractive? Colorful illustrations add to enjoyment, especially for young readers who depend on pictures to explain the words.

After considering these criteria, one final hurdle remains —how to get the child to read the books! A common, yet avoidable barrier, is the lack of a comfortable, well-lit, quiet nook in which to curl up with a book. Adults who want children to read must set the stage by providing an atmosphere that encourages reading. Children should have their own bookshelf (complete with a dictionary handy). Bookplates and inscriptions also make books special.

As soon as a child is on the picture-book level, he or she can be taken to the public or church library. The acquisition of one's first library card can be a special event. Many public libraries have programs that can be used as well by churches, such as story hours, movie time, puppet shows, art exhibits, and even visiting animal guests. Comfortable floor-pillows and inviting nooks and crannies encourage children to sit down and read. Book displays, colorful posters, stuffed toys, and child-scale furniture all tell children they are welcome in the library.

One major barrier to developing reading children is the lack of reading adults. Children will be readers if their parents read. Toddlers can develop good attitudes toward reading if they are read stories from colorful picture books. What child does not enjoy a bedtime story, even long after he or she has memorized the words?

The biggest hurdle to reading, however, is television. The amount of reading required in school has declined, along with the percentage of students who read for pleasure. Television is not an evil in itself; even programs that present worldly lifestyles can be topics of discussion between adults and young viewers: "Are the characters acting according to God's commandments? What happened as a result of sin? What would have been a better choice of action?" The duty of parents is to monitor their child's viewing habits—and make sure the set is turned off long enough to ensure a balanced lifestyle of exercise, cultural experiences, and social interaction.

We were taught in school that our pioneer ancestors learned to read by reading the Bible, huddled next to sputtering candles in drafty log cabins. The truth is that many of our predecessors grew up illiterate. Young readers can still tackle God's Word, but they can begin by reading illustrated Bible "storybooks" specially edited for children. "Children's Bibles" intended for young readers must be written in words that children can understand, not adult-level versions simply wrapped in a pink or blue cover. Children must see that God's Word has meaning for them—and they must be encouraged to explore its pages every day.

Media:
Picture This

As we have stated in many places throughout this book, learning and retention increase with each additional human sense that can be involved in the process. A message that is bolstered by visual aids has a much better chance of being understood and remembered. Advertisers are willing to pay thousands of dollars more for television airtime than for the same time on radio—because they know the impact of a message that is both seen *and* heard is invaluable. In children's ministry, if audiovisual resources can be used in a balanced program of various teaching methods, they can greatly enhance the effectiveness of the ministry.

Types of Audiovisual Resources

- filmstrip
- slide
- opaque projectors
- overhead projectors
- movies
- videotapes
- phonograph records
- compact discs

Classroom Applications

A trip to any Christian bookstore or educational supply store will convince a reluctant teacher that audiovisuals are not only user-friendly but also lesson-enhancing. Professionally prepared filmstrips, slides, movies, overhead transparencies, videos, and audiotapes have been produced to augment lesson material for children.

The creative potential of audiovisuals comes in classroom productions. Try these suggestions:

1. Make slides, movies, or videotapes of children in biblical or modern-day clothes to illustrate scenes teaching Bible stories and concepts.

2. Tape-record songs created by students, interviews made by research groups, or poems narrated by the authors themselves. Using individual headsets, a small group can listen to recordings without disturbing others.

3. Make slides of student artwork, or let children draw directly on blank filmstrips or overhead transparencies.

Teacher Training

Professionally prepared videos and audiocassettes can be used for teacher-training meetings, or they can be sent home to be previewed at each teacher's convenience and discussed as a group at a later date. Videos or slides of a local church's ministry can help a new teacher understand education principles in application.

Promoting the Ministry

Quality slides and videos can be shown to the congregation throughout the year to publicize the work of the children's ministry. Smiling faces and happy voices are a powerful recruitment tool, both for new students and for new workers. Since many adults who attend worship services may never see a classroom session in action, or may never meet workers in children's programs, a continuous promotional program is necessary to make known the status and needs of the ministry.

Equipment Use

1. Workers must be trained in the proper use of equipment.
2. Equipment must be kept in working order.
3. Equipment must be securely stored.
4. Up-to-date records must be maintained of equipment loans and reservations.

Although audiovisual equipment is a wonderful educational resource with tremendous potential for impact on learners, it must be remembered that the most powerful teaching tool in the classroom is still the teacher who models God's love in relationships with students.

Meetings for Planning and Training

One requirement of serving in the teaching ministry is attendance at regular planning and training meetings. The basic purpose of these meetings, of course, is to strategize future lessons. Other vital purposes are met here as well: building up each teacher through continuous training, including them in decision-making, and offering them fellowship with other staff.

Many teachers dread such meetings and rarely show up for them. Some reasons for poor attendance can include:

- *Inconvenient time.* The leaders in charge of developing the teaching staff should plan meetings for days and times that will enable parents and those who work full-time to attend. One way to do this is to schedule meetings that are limited to the teachers within a single department. That way, it is easier to tailor the schedule to fit everyone's calendar.
- *No provision for child care.* When child care must be arranged, the church should provide it. If possible, plan meetings for times when children are already at church, actively involved in a program designed for their age level. At no time should adults bring their children to church and leave them unsupervised to roam the building while they attend meetings.

- *Lengthy meetings.* By planning an agenda ahead of time and sticking to it in meetings, leaders should be able to complete work in less than two hours. Avoid getting sidetracked by matters that should be discussed at another time and place. Offer reminders to each teacher about meetings, so time will not be wasted waiting for no-shows and latecomers.
- *Little time for individual age-level concerns.* If meetings can be limited to the teachers of a certain age group, the entire time can be devoted to specific concerns. Trying to address the concerns of too wide a span of groups means not satisfying any of them.
- *No "ownership" of the process.* Include each teacher in meetings by assigning readings or the leadership of a segment. Leaders must be skilled in group management and know how to make each other feel affirmed and valued for their contribution.

A Sample Agenda

1/2 hour: Bible study based on adult application of the themes in the curriculum unit. Teachers build up one another through prayer.

1/2 hour: Preview skills needed in the unit. Having observed teachers at work, the department leader predetermines skill areas that need development. Make training specific and applicable. The leader may utilize (1) a teacher who excels in this area or (2) resources available through the curriculum publisher.

1/2 hour: Teachers identify and discuss aims for the unit and the individual lessons. Teachers divide responsibility for various segments of the lesson schedule (approach activities, music, art, storytelling, etc.).

In a small church, each age division might be a single class with a single teacher. This should not preclude teacher fellowship get-togethers; but it can reduce the effectiveness of planning and training meetings. To provide the support and accountability teachers need, the person in charge of the education ministry should meet with them individually.

In a medium-to-large church, each department meets separately for monthly training and planning under the supervision of the department leader. Administrative matters are handled by department leaders at division-wide meetings under the leadership of a division coordinator. In turn, division coordinators meet with the superintendent or Christian Education Specialist. In this way, communication flows up and down the lines of authority and responsibility freely, so that each class's interests are considered in light of the ministry's overall goals.

Minutes of a Sample Meeting

(involving eight first- and second-grade teachers who follow the same curriculum in one classroom of each grade level)

7:00 P.M.   Prayer and share time. Anne Simpson presented a short devotional based on the unit theme. Prayer was offered for Mike Como's continuing struggles with two of his students. Susan brought snacks.

7:30   Department leader Ron Kessler introduced a guest speaker who led a training segment on art activities. Each teacher completed a sample of an art activity featured in the new unit.

8:00   Ron led a preview of the new unit and a discussion of the teaching aims of each lesson. Visual aids and other resources were displayed. Teacher guides, resources, and student books were distributed.

8:30   Teachers divided into classroom groups to plan each lesson of the unit and assign responsibilities for segments of the schedule. Requests for materials were compiled for the resource room director.

Ron Kessler's Notes for the Next Division-Level Meeting:

- Teachers expressed concern over hallway traffic. Discuss possibility of staggering schedules of playground and bathroom trips so that early childhood, lower, and upper elementary are not in the hallway at the same time.
- Check to see if our departmental meeting can be held the same night as another department to share child-care arrangements.
- Have division coordinator communicate to superintendent our problems due to the mess left behind by the Saturday night club meeting. Suggest the superintendent and the club director look into solutions.
- Check attendance figures before ordering curriculum for next unit. Follow-up with summer ministries participants may increase registration.

The people who have the authority to make plans are usually far removed from the people who have to carry them out, but this system should provide church administrators with the information they need and teachers with the support they deserve. At effective training-and-planning meetings, workers' valuable time is devoted to matters with special interest and practical application.

Methods and Materials: The Right Tool for the Job

It is not enough simply to have a good tool in your hand. Some people insist on driving home a screw with a hammer and pounding a nail with a screwdriver handle.

The tool must be the right one for the job, and the worker must understand the demands of the job. A nail will do for hanging a picture, but the hinges on the front door require screws. The worker determines the method to be used and selects the tools depending on his or her training and experience.

A well-trained and experienced teacher follows the same procedures when planning a lesson:

1. *Determine the lesson aim.* What can the child learn at this stage of mental development and other age-group characteristics?
2. *Select the method.* Which teaching method best suits both the lesson aim and the learner's age group?
3. *Choose the materials.* What resources support the selected method?

Two Roads for the Traveling Samaritan

For a four- and five-year-olds' lesson on "being kind," the teacher helped the youngsters act out the Samaritan's kindness to the wounded traveler. In applying this biblical concept to real life, they drew pictures to show ways they would be kind to others. To reinforce the lesson aim, the teacher took advantage of natural "teaching moments" throughout the morning to guide their conversation toward an awareness of kindness and ways to demonstrate it.

The teacher knew her students would learn best by participating, and they loved to dramatize stories, so she planned to have them act out the Bible lesson using simple costumes and props. She had them draw pictures, because they were developing the small motor skills necessary to draw. In addition, they used the art activity to organize their thoughts about the lesson.

Kindness is too abstract a concept to teach most young children without using concrete examples, so the teacher labeled the children's acts of kindness at every opportunity. "Sean needs help with his block tower. It would be a kind thing for someone to bring him some more blocks."

The fifth- and sixth-graders also studied "The Good Samaritan." To prepare them for the lesson, their teacher had a research-activity group find out why the wounded traveler would have expected help from the priest and the Levite but not from the Samaritan. During the Bible lesson, the research group shared their findings. Afterward, learners developed a skit illustrating the concept in a contemporary setting. "Whom do you consider to be your neighbor?" the teacher asked. Another group used magazine and newspaper clippings to make a poster to show the harm caused by prejudice and ignorance.

Because students of upper elementary grades have advanced reading and writing skills, their activities can include research using maps, dictionaries, and other reference resources. Since they are old enough to comprehend some analogy, the class was enlightened rather than confused by the update of the parable. The group art project stimulated a teacher-guided discussion of the lesson. The teacher knew that learners at this age level could understand the implications of the story on a different level.

The Resourceful Teacher

In every Sunday school there are certain teachers renowned for resourcefulness and originality. These individuals usually are not just gifted but also trained and experienced. They find their ideas for methods and materials in a variety of places:

1. *Curriculum:* A well-prepared lesson should include detailed instructions for methods and provide many of the materials needed.
2. *Training:* Workshops offer specific methods and displays of usable material.
3. *Observation:* Novices can observe and learn from model teachers.

A Methods Sampler

painting/drawing	puppets	skits	discussions
posters	storytelling	interviews	poetry
diary	puzzles	dioramas	songwriting
films/videos	geography	games	nature

Materials to Stock

art supplies	costumes, props	puppets	maps
writing materials	instruments	references	AV equipment
boxes, bags	teaching pictures	old magazines	cleanup supplies
tape and glue	construction paper	newsprint	posterboard

The Resource Room

Resources should be stored in a central location under the watchful eye of a volunteer who takes inventory, restocks, and chases down borrowed items. Otherwise, a ministry will incur needless expense and waste. Unused student workbooks, teachers' guides, and resources can be stored and reused. Flannel-graph sets should be identified by lesson on the back of each piece to avoid loss and confusion.

Art supplies, recyclables, and other materials can be stocked at the beginning of each semester. The resource-room manager should compile needs for each lesson and order in bulk to save money. He or she also can assemble a box for each room weekly, based on request slips from teachers. A preview of needs can avoid a Sunday morning paper-fastener famine!

Basic supplies also can be stored in each class, with occasional restocking from the resource room. AV equipment should be centrally stored. The expensive and vulnerable nature of films, projectors, and tape recorders requires that these items be secured through a reservation and checkout system, including locked storage. A volunteer should make sure repairs are made as soon as the need is reported. The church needs to establish and enforce a policy regarding the use of AV equipment. Loan requests will be made for home Bible studies, groups outside the C.E. ministry, and the showing of Uncle Frank's slides of his trip to Buffalo.

Spice It Up

Variety is the spice of lesson-planning. A variety of methods and materials ensures that each learner's interests and learning style will be addressed. A variety of activities provides each learner with the motivation of choice. An added benefit of using new methods is that teachers can be challenged to develop new skills for ministry.

Missions

Paul arrived in Athens already familiar with the Greek culture. In fact, his knowledge of Athenian philosophy was the key that opened the doors of his listeners' minds. Taking a cue from the great apostle, modern missionaries are careful to learn all they can of the culture in which they wish to minister. Only then can they serve with understanding.

Teachers can develop a natural kinship between their learners and children of different and faraway cultures by guiding their young charges to an appreciation of their distant brothers and sisters. The best way to encourage children's interest in a different culture is to introduce aspects of it through hands-on experiences in the classroom. This is especially important when children are too young to grasp geography.

Here are some aids for doing this:

- *Visitors.* Meeting a person from another country can make that country suddenly become "real" to a child. Use your church's missionaries, when they are home on furlough, to speak to your class, or check with your denominational missions board and foreign students' associations.
- *Audio-visual aids.* Research the materials available from local libraries, museums, bookstores, and educa-

tional suppliers. Films, slides, records, and tapes bring lessons to life. Colorful posters from travel bureaus add color to classrooms.

- *Art.* Display authentic art and crafts typical of the culture being explored. Select a craft for the learners to duplicate.
- *Music.* Play recordings of music from other lands. Display and demonstrate instruments. Children enjoy learning lively folk songs with rhythmic hand motions.
- *Phrases.* Teach your learners a few phrases in an unfamiliar language—or better yet, their own names, a Bible verse, or a simple song. Display Bible translations.
- *Games.* Teach your students a game enjoyed by children in distant lands. Many American games originated in other countries.
- *Food and clothing.* Ethnic cookbooks and a few items from the gourmet department of your local supermarket can provide the class with easy-to-prepare snacks. Books and dolls from other lands can provide models for costumes.

After sharing the experiences of children from other cultures, young Christians will want to share their Savior with them. To do this, regular or special offerings can be collected for missionary work. Classes or individuals can exchange letters, photos, and tapes with missionaries. Simply by bringing missions home to our classrooms, we can enable our learners to be witnesses to the ends of the earth.

Mistakes, Misunderstandings, and Mix-ups

"We're sailing on the Titanic. Meet you in New York."

Famous last words echo throughout history. Here are a few examples of famous last words that have been heard in churches across the country.

- *"We'll start off with paid nursery workers and then recruit volunteers."* Once a job is established as a paid position, it is almost impossible to recruit volunteers to perform it. The policy of hiring workers for the nursery also separated that ministry from the rest of the children's program. Nursery ministry is thereafter perceived as a nonteaching position that involves only menial tasks.

  For nursery and early childhood programs, workers should be trained volunteers who consider their work a teaching ministry. During special events, such as planning-and-training meetings or teacher appreciation dinners, child care should be arranged and paid for by the church.
- *"I'll announce the change in the bulletin and surprise everybody."* Changes in policies and programs

must be team efforts. Leaders need to be careful to establish group goals based on a shared vision. Ninety percent of the process of successful change is *communication before the fact*. Remember: A general who is too far in front of his own troops will be mistaken for the enemy and shot by his own men!

- *"Who needs attendance records?"* Teachers need attendance records to ensure not only a complete file of names and addresses of students, but to note when a follow-up call or card should go to an absentee. Programs that award prizes for consistent attendance need records to ensure fairness. Parents may need to refer to attendance records to check on suspected truants. Planners need records to project future attendance and plan for expanded facilities. Evaluation committees need records to compare figures for various programs.
- *"We'll make the teacher appreciation dinner a potluck."* This reveals an obvious case of mistaken identities. The speaker at a dinner held to honor teachers gets a free meal, a nice honorarium, and a round of applause, while the honorees get to cook dinner, find babysitters, and take home dirty dishes.

     Call the caterer!
- *"I think the first hour the teacher took these kids to the potty."* Children have a hierarchy of needs, and physical needs have to be satisfied first. Learners need a mid-morning break for snacks, juice, and a chance to use the bathroom. Churches who program an entire morning for children need to arrange for first- or second-hour staff to attend to the learners' needs.
- *"Let's ask different people to teach each week."* Recruiting is easy if a teacher's time commitment is one Sunday per month, quarter, or year. However, this makes teaching and learning almost impossible. Bible truth is learned not just by the assimilation of knowledge, but in the context of personal relationships between children and adults.
- *"We'll keep the sick toddler separated from the*

rest." Nursery and early childhood classes must have a firm policy about not accepting children who appear to be ill. There is simply no foolproof way to keep sick children and their belongings isolated from their classmates. Parents whose children become infected through exposure to sick classmates are hesitant to bring them back to church. Nursery workers should be trained to recognize the signs of contagious diseases and, in the case of AIDS, know what practices are dangerous and what are not.

- *"What's the difference? A marker is a marker."* Familiarity with classroom supplies is something that all-too-often comes through trial and error. Experienced teachers know that the dry-erase board requires dry-erase markers, the ID labels on the sports equipment require permanent markers, and the art project requires water-soluble markers that wash out of learners' Sunday best. Early childhood classes should have blunt-end scissors, chubby crayons, and fat paint brushes. Older learners can handle standard scissors and crayons and finer paint brushes. Teachers can prepare ahead by previewing all art projects before class, using the same materials the learners will use.

- *"Who needs permission slips?"* Notes signed by parents giving their children permission to participate in an off-site or extracurricular event are absolutely necessary for the protection of the children, the church, and the leaders in charge of the event. This does not guarantee immunity from a lawsuit or other prosecution, but written permission from a parent or guardian at least proves the adults were aware of the event and willing to have their child participate. Featured on the slip should be an agreement that children can be given emergency medical care.

- *"Someone else will lock up."* Churches are notorious for having doors and windows unlocked. Certain adults should be assigned security responsibilities during activity hours and also be required to perform lock-up duties. No teacher should leave until each learner in class has been retrieved by an adult. No lock-up person should leave until doors and windows are secure, and classrooms, large closets, and bathrooms have been checked. Once a thief is inside a building with crash bars on the doors or large, unbarred windows, the vandal could escape detection and strip the building of ready-cash items at his or her leisure.

- *"I don't know what the job entails, but I'm willing to give it a try."* No one should accept a responsibility without a comprehensively written job description. Jobs that have been in existence for years usually have more reliable descriptions, especially if they have varied little over the years, from worker to worker. New positions have to be allowed a certain amount of miscalculation, but corrections should be written down for the next time the position is passed along. The job description should include the duties of the worker, the church's responsibility for training and support, the length of service required, and the system of accountability.

- *"We don't use curriculum. We do our own thing."* A systematic, Bible-centered, learner-focused curriculum is an absolute necessity for children's ministry. Because very few people have training in biblical studies, child development, and educational theory, ministry leaders should consider buying a curriculum prepared by professionals. A single curriculum that is consistently applied to each grade level in the children's ministry can provide systematic coverage of all major Bible themes throughout the years. Teachers who perceive special needs in learners should be encouraged to adapt lessons to meet those needs and interests.

- *"I'm kicking you out of this class if you continue to throw things."* Discipline policies must not include threats of action that the teacher is either unwilling or unable to carry out. Once voiced, a threat is a challenge. The misbehaving student has been put in charge of the situation and can, if he wishes, force the teacher's hand. Consider the threat that has just been made: (1) The student might be told to leave the class, but he cannot be physically *kicked* out of the room; (2) Once out of the room, where does the student go? (3) The parents who left their child in the supervision of the children's ministry are left to wonder where he is now; (4) The whole point was to get the child *into* church in the first place!

Age-appropriate discipline policies should be agreed upon by ministry leaders and teachers. Procedures should be consistently followed. Correction should be designed to teach acceptable behavior.

- *"Let's skip the publicity and just concentrate on the event."* One may assume that a well-publicized event that draws high numbers each year will attract the same crowd even if publicity is cut back. But that is somewhat like assuming children will go to sleep simply because they have been put to bed. Money spent on high-quality promotional literature is an investment in the event it publicizes. People may prejudge the quality of a dinner, seminar, or camp-out based on the impression they receive from a hastily scrawled flyer or a messy poster. (Churches that wish to publicize through doorknob hangers or other door-to-door methods should check local regulations.)

- *"Nobody's going to drag children along to an adult program."* Unless a "no children" policy has been spelled out in promotional material, leaders of events for adults can be sure someone will bring kids. And while the adults are gathered in their prayer meeting, committee meeting, or training session, the children wander through the church unsupervised. Often morning-after discoveries of vandalism and misplaced items are the result of children who were left unsupervised during a time when there were no planned activities for their age group. Doors left open to admit people to the building also admit child abusers looking for victims, and unsupervised children are easy prey. For adult meetings and events, churches must either plan for supervision of children or insist that they be left at home with a responsible care-giver.

- *"Somebody else will clean it up."* Adults who insist their children learn to clean up their own messes are often the same people who leave coffee cups under their chairs and paper scraps on the floor. According to age level, learners can be held accountable for cleaning or picking up their own cups, scraps, and other trash. But ultimately, the teacher is responsible for the condition of the room. Janitors are hired to perform normal cleanup duties, but workers should be required to take precautions regularly and plan cleanup time into the lesson schedule. This sense of responsibility for facilities should be modeled by leaders and made a part of each worker's training. Usually, the mess someone assumes the janitor will clean up is instead taken care of by the next worker to use the room. If you move something, remember to put it back. If you make a mess, clean it up. In shared facilities, these rules should be considered engraved in stone.

- *"We won't be needing any new teachers for a while."* Recruitment and training of workers needs to be an ongoing process. The longer a novice has for pre-service training, the more confident and effective that worker will be. Better-qualified teachers will result in larger classes, and larger classes will require divisions to maintain a preferred teacher-to-learner ratio. Relocations, illnesses, and sabbaticals will create openings in the worker ranks, whether or not they were planned for. The best policy is to recruit and train continuously.

- *"Next fall, all you sixth-graders will be part of the youth group."* Children rushing toward adolescence are intoxicated with their newly acquired independence and status—and yet they are intimidated by unfamiliar situations and the sophistication of the eighth- and ninth-graders. The children's ministry can help a little by introducing sixth-graders to the junior high team of workers and arranging for them to join in a few of the youth group's activities during the summer. This age is the one at which many children decide they are finished with Sunday school, but a little teamwork from children's and youth workers can build a bridge for a smooth transition to the next age-level ministry of the church.

Music

In Old and New Testament times, much instruction was given through rote memory and song. In fact, all 150 Psalms were meant to be sung. Music was—and still is—meant for expression, communication, instruction, and worship. Here are a few points to consider in using music in ministry:

- *Lyrics must be meaningful on the learners' level.* Songs used with children should have literal rather than symbolic meaning. Evaluate each lyric in the mind of your own students.
- *Action songs must be content-focused.* Children need and enjoy large muscle activities. Songs that feature actions are appealing, but the motions can become the focus of the song. Motions should relate to lyrics, which should always remain the focal point.
- *Songs should be lesson-related.* Teach one concept well by directing all activities and resources toward it.
- *Lyrics must be doctrinally and scripturally correct.* Don't use catchy, "fun" songs without first evaluating the lyrics. It is almost impossible to have a child unlearn an inaccuracy taught through the persuasive medium of music. (Be alert also for songs implying that animals have a spiritual nature.)

- *The melody should be uncomplicated.* Look for songs that appeal to the age group of your learners.

Remember that the purpose of music activities in the classroom is to teach the lesson, not to develop professional quality voices. Very young learners enjoy singing even though they are not able to match the correct notes and rhythm, as they will in years to come. A children's choir can be a worthwhile program, but it should not be considered a substitute for the Sunday school session.

Teachers can use music to set a mood, give directions, or indicate that it is time to change to a new activity. Resourceful teachers often write their own lyrics to familiar tunes to fit the lesson aim. Instruments add interest and variety to music in the classroom. An upright piano still serves as a classic classroom instrument, but floor-space limitations often make it impractical. Autoharps, guitars, and tape recordings are popular with teachers.

Music activities can be used to help older learners in their exploration of the lesson. Students can write their own songs to express ideas and perform them for classmates. Ethnic songs and instruments can be used not only during missions week, but all year long. Strictly-for-fun songs are great for club meetings, camps, and retreats, but Sunday morning's time is too short to devote precious minutes to unrelated activities.

Teachers of preteens should stock up on recordings of contemporary Christian artists who keep to scriptural messages. A selection of choruses, hymns, and new songs offers junior church a variety of expression in worship. Leaders should obey copyright laws by refraining from making their own copies of legally protected lyrics and music. Inexpensive songbooks are available at Christian bookstores and music stores and from publishers of Sunday school curriculum.

Nature Activities: Science in Sunday School?

In his letter to the church at Rome, Paul stated that "since the creation of the world God's invisible qualities—his eternal power and divine nature—have been clearly seen, being understood from what has been made" (Rom. 1:20 NIV). When teachers exclude nature and science from the church's ministry to children, they neglect a teaching resource of great impact. The Master teacher Himself used nature as a teaching tool. Field lilies, sparrows, and even mustard seeds were His visual aids.

Students may think lessons on faith belong in church, lessons on creation belong in school, and that the studies are totally unrelated. When children can learn about both the Creator and His creations in the same setting, they can get a truly Christian perspective. For children who are taught in Christian schools, such integration of Bible truth into the curriculum is an everyday experience, but for most children, a biblical view has to come from parents, Sunday school teachers, or camp counselors.

Teachers who wish to bring lessons from nature into their classroom need not be scientists. Those who are most successful in inspiring a sense of wonder in their students are themselves in awe of God's creativity and impart their own excitement by simply sharing it. In all learning, a discovered truth has more impact than one that is simply handed down by a teacher who serves as the exclusive source of knowledge. A teacher's response to most questions about God's world should be, "Let's find out together!"

Lessons from Genesis exploring the theme of creation offer many opportunities to share discoveries about plants and animals. "Nature centers" in classrooms can feature seasonal, hands-on displays of leaves, shells, fossils, seeds, or live animals (supervised). Magnifying glasses or microscopes can enhance student explorations. Books and magazines can encourage further investigation. Once again we say that whenever more than one sense can be involved in the learning process, learning is increased. Compare the impact of simply hearing that God made "creeping things" (Ps. 148:10) with the experience of seeing and touching a live mouse!

Not every lesson will lend itself to nature activities, and it is best to eliminate from lesson plans any activity that does not support or reinforce the central theme. However, there are many truths to be learned about God from exploration of his creations, and many themes to be reinforced by supplementary activities.

The best presentation of nature is up-close and personal, but films and books borrowed from libraries can be effective builders of students' awareness. Field trips taken any day of the week can both expand student understanding and build student-teacher relationships. A trip to the park, nature center, museum, planetarium, or zoo can greatly enrich the Sunday morning experience. Even a guided walk around the block can be stimulating. The simple experience of watching a change in weather through the classroom window can promote appreciation of God's power. Many teachers can recall at least one lesson that literally "went out the window" at a child's first sight of a rainbow or the first snowflakes of the season. Experienced teachers use those snowflakes as "teaching moments." Temporarily abandoning the lesson, they line up the learners at the window and explain that their heavenly Father "gives snow like wool" (Ps. 147:16).

Because young children think only in concrete, literal terms, teachers should not use symbols of any kind. You can show how a mother hen cares for its chicks and then compare it to the way God wants to care for us; but using an eggshell and its white and yolk to teach the triune nature of God is asking for trouble. (One teacher who used an egg in this way wound up with a double yolk—and had a lot of explaining to do!)

Teaching awareness of God's power through the study of nature appeals to a variety of children's learning styles. Methods can involve art, drama, writing, music, and a wealth of research activities. Children who do not speak their teacher's language, who are physically or mentally disabled, or who have learning disorders all can respond to nature on their own level. Local zoos, museums, libraries, or colleges may have a collection of materials available for loan. These institutions may provide workshops for teachers who would like to learn more about nature and how to present it to children.

As awareness grows about the worldwide problem of pollution, many Christian camps are building nature studies and conservation into their outdoor education programs. A children's ministry that includes a day-camp or resident-camping experience should take advantage of the outdoor setting to educate learners.

Teachers should first rediscover their own sense of wonder at the power and majesty of the Creator. Then they can spark that same awe in the minds of their students by providing opportunities to see God at work in His world.

The Nursery Ministry: Not Just Babysitting

Which ministry offers the most responsibility and the least status to its workers? Which area of the church receives the least consideration from the building committee and the closest scrutiny from visiting families? Which room has the most hazardous environment and the most vulnerable learners? Anyone who has worked in children's ministry recognizes this description of the church nursery.

In early America, churches "ministered" to children by reviving those who dozed off during the endless sermon with whacks on the head, using a metal ball attached to the end of a stick. Most churches have evolved beyond this, of course, but in many cases primitive conditions still exist in the nursery. First of all, most churches have nurseries that are understaffed, undersized, and overfilled. In a church that is beginning to outgrow its facilities, the nursery usually feels the pinch first.

Space Exploration

In an ideal situation, two- and three-year-olds would have separate classrooms and curriculum. Younger children would be separated into rooms for (1) crib babies from birth to eight months, (2) crawlers eight to fourteen months, and (3) toddlers fifteen to twenty-four months. By separating young children according to ability, workers could keep crawlers from scurrying under rocking chairs and toddlers from riding roughshod over the crawlers. A welcome addition to the nursery would be a room for newborns with an area for nursing mothers.

In real life, however, most churches have minimal space. One, two, or three small rooms may have to hold all the children under four years of age. In the crib room, the answer may be double-decker cribs that make up for their jailhouse effect by doubling the available floor space. High, wall-mounted cabinets and open shelves can also save floor space while keeping hazards away from little hands. Crawlers and toddlers need all the elbow room they can get, so extraneous furniture (such as teachers' desks, pianos, extra folding chairs) should be removed. These "floor people" need a soft, easy-to-clean carpet on which to crawl and move. In the same room, toddlers and crawlers can be separated by a waist-high divider that permits supervision while preventing pileups of little people. Anything that stands against the wall (shelves, cabinets, etc.) must be attached so that it cannot be pulled over onto a child. Mirrors must be unbreakable.

Because of the need for frequent cleanup of children and workers, nursery rooms need to include a sink and/or child-size toilet for those who are "in training." The changing table can be designed with a storage area below, and high chairs and playpens should be the kind that fold up for closet storage when not in use. A dorm-room-size refrigerator can fit under a counter with a bottle warmer nearby.

Developmentally appropriate books and toys should be available to children, provided they are safe, stimulating, and washable. A few low, open shelves make it possible for older children to pick out and put back their own toys. Toys must not be so small that they can fit into the mouth of a child who can grab them. This is a constant challenge for churches that keep a wide range of ages in the same room. A whole puzzle, for example, may be too big to swallow—but what about the smallest piece of it?

Down Will Come Baby

To see how hazardous your church nursery can be, get down on the level of the babies, crawlers, and toddlers. First of all, the floor is much colder than the air closer to the ceiling. Next, are there electrical outlets that need to be covered? Are there staples or carpet tacks that can be nibbled? Are there rockers, sharp corners, or casters that might catch small fingers? Do the adults wear spike heels? Is there a safety zone around the swings and around the door? Are extension cords loose and exposed?

Imagine you are a crib baby. Can you reach past the crib gym you are intended to play with and grab the small, dangly things on the mobile they don't think you can reach? Do they look like they could be swallowed? How big are the spacers on your crib or playpen? Is it possible to get your head stuck? Is there a plastic bag, strap, or cord nearby you can pull over your head?

Very young children seem to divide the world into two categories—"food" and "not food"—and to place things in the proper category, children test them in their mouths. Nursery workers must take care that young children do not have access to safety pins, cleaners, plants, balloons, chipping paint, very small or breakable toys, or jewelry dropped on the floor. Never expose floor crawlers to pesticides. Aerosol sprays of any kind can cause respiratory problems in children when used in the room repeatedly.

The staff person who has responsibility for the nursery must be sure that health and safety considerations are always observed. Workers should know what to do in case of an emergency, and someone near the nursery area should have training in CPR for the very young.

Nursery Security

Child molestation and kidnapping are a fact of life. Child abusers target churches as places where children can be found in large numbers, often unsupervised. Nursery workers need to observe the following practices:

1. If there is an outside door to the nursery, keep it locked from the inside.

2. Establish a system, such as a claim check, to be sure a child is returned to the right adult. Even proof of a parent's identity would not be proof of custody rights.

3. Never leave the children unsupervised. Don't leave a child alone in a room to take a nap.

4. If children are to be cared for at church while parents leave the building, workers should have a phone number to call.

Unfortunately, administrators also need to be wary of nursery workers. Workers should be recruited and trained along strict guidelines. It is reasonable to ask prospective staff members for references and perhaps even fingerprints; but with volunteer workers, this kind of clearance is more difficult to require. A good rule of thumb is never to leave children alone with just one adult.

Standard Disease Control

Disease-control measures involve strict rules for sanitation:

1. For diaper changes, workers should use disposable gloves, wipe the changing table with a disinfectant solution (one cup bleach to one gallon of water left ten minutes before rinsing), and wash their hands. They should put dirty cloth diapers or clothing in a labeled plastic bag for the trip home.

2. Before handling food, workers should wash their hands.

3. After use, tabletops or high-chair trays should be disinfected.

4. Discourage parents from bringing sick children to church.

5. Advise parents if their child has come in contact with an infected child so they can watch for symptoms.

6. Each time the nursery has been used, crib rails, toys, smocks, and bedding should be washed and all garbage pails emptied.

7. After helping a young child use the toilet or potty chair, both the child and the adult should wash their hands thoroughly. The toilet seat should be wiped clean and the potty emptied immediately.

8. Hands should be dried with disposable towels. Taps should be shut off with a towel to avoid reinfection.

Additional Precautions

When an AIDS child comes to church, there is a need for caution, but not hysteria.

Nursery workers caring for AIDS children must take special care to avoid contact with blood or body fluids. Disposable gloves should be worn whenever a worker tends to diaper changes, toilet needs, or open cuts (workers with cuts or abrasions on their own hands must also be careful). Contaminated surfaces need to be carefully disinfected. AIDS children must be discouraged from biting other children or sharing food or toys from their own mouth to the mouth of another child. Disposable gloves, diapers, or other items contaminated by body fluids should be discarded in sealed containers. Clothes or linens contaminated by body fluids should be sealed in plastic bags until they can be washed separately in a soap-bleach solution at a high temperature.

It's a Ministry, Not an Obligation

The nursery workers' ministry suffers from low status. The most important job in the church is often taken for granted or even passed along to paid workers who may not even be Christians, yet there is more to this work than keeping children fed, rocked, and diapered. It is in the nursery that a child develops his or her first attitudes toward God and the church. Any ministry that ignores a child's emotional, social, and spiritual needs at this point fails to minister to that child's early development.

As workers care for children, they can sing to them, play with them, and help them learn new skills. Workers who come to know young children as individuals can tell when behavior indicates illness or stress, and can watch for developmental milestones as well. Young children are anxious to find a familiar face and are reassured when someone who is special to them can be trusted to appear week after week. There is an unfortunately high turnover rate among church nursery workers. In an effort to provide enough workers to meet the minimum requirement of one to every four children, churches may resort to different workers every week.

The long-range answer may lie in teaching the congregation that nursery work is more than babysitting. If workers are required to go through a training period, they may see more of the teaching potential in that ministry. If nursery staff are recognized and honored for their contribution, the ministry may no longer be viewed as less important than the children, youth, and adult departments.

Occult Concerns: Counterfeit Christianity and the New Age Movement

Jesus warned his listeners that many would come in His name, claiming, "I am the Christ" (Matt. 24:4–5). Cults were on the rise in the Mediterranean world during the first century, and they continue today on a worldwide mission to mislead the unsuspecting and uninformed.

Counterfeit Christianity

A cult may represent itself as the only true church, exclusive and hostile to its rivals. On the other hand, a cult may incorporate many of the doctrines of other belief systems, to appeal to as wide a range of people as possible. Several characteristics are common to most cults:

- An outward appearance of Christianity.
- Denial of Christ's deity.
- Leaders and writings considered equal to or greater in authority than the Bible.
- Works-related salvation.

- Nonbiblical sources of revelation.
- Control of members' lives by the organization.

Many cults recruit followers by meeting their needs for acceptance, security, and purpose. The cult becomes the member's family and mission in life. Despite the fact that some groups (especially Mormons) project an image of wholesome family life, cults can destroy families by dividing parents and children. In order to control a person, the cult isolates an individual from unbelieving family and friends. That person's destiny is decided by leaders who dictate the amount of contributions he or she will give, the work required for salvation, and whom to marry and where to live.

Teachers can help cult-proof their young learners. Here are some guidelines:

- Teach children to turn to the Bible for God's answers to questions of everyday life and doctrine. Children can *know* the Bible is our only written source of God's truth, *feel* motivated to obey God's laws, and *act* in ways that demonstrate obedience.
- The triune nature of God is too abstract a concept to be grasped by younger learners, but they can understand that no other person has the power and authority that our Father in heaven gave to His son, Jesus. The Holy Spirit must be referred to as "He," never "It."
- Children can experience the love of God through relationships with their teachers. The teacher who demonstrates God's loving care teaches children that God is personal. Many cults teach that God is an uninvolved, impersonal being or mere consciousness.
- Teachers can use presentations of the gospel that are age-appropriate in vocabulary and concept. They can impress learners with the fact that salvation is a free gift, not an earned reward. Children need the security of the truth of eternal salvation. Many cults teach that salvation can be conditional and uncertain.

It would be unusual to discover a child from a cult family attending a Bible-believing children's ministry. Nevertheless, teachers should be familiar with cult doctrines so they can recognize flaws in a child's understanding.

Here is a brief listing of the best-known cults:

Jehovah's Witnesses Witnesses interpret their version of the Scriptures—the New World Translation—according to the writings of their organization. They consider Jesus to be a "lesser god" and the Holy Spirit to be only the force of God. Witness doctrine also identifies Jesus as the Archangel Michael. Because only 144,000 people will be resurrected after Armageddon, Witnesses' salvation is conditional and uncertain. The Witness approach usually features their hope to live someday in an earthly paradise.[1]

Mormonism Mormons consider the Bible to be inerrant only in the original writings. They place more trust in the Book of Mormon and other writings of the organization. According to Mormon doctrine, God was a man who achieved godhood through a life of obedience. Souls are believed to be the spirit children of God and his many celestial wives. At birth, a spirit-child takes bodily form. As God's first spirit-child, Jesus achieved godhood through obedience. Salvation is won through good works, which include practices and rituals required by the organization. At death, a Mormon expects to stand before God, Jesus, and Joseph Smith (a "prophet" of the Mormon faith who figured in its early history).[2]

Unification Church (Moonies) The Rev. Sun Myung Moon's interpretation of the Bible is considered superior in authority to the Bible itself. God is believed to be the invisible form of man, and man the visible form of God. Jesus was a man born without original sin who was murdered before he could complete his mission. Moon believes he has been born to finish Jesus' job. Salvation is achieved through works and obedience to Moon's requirements, which include marriage.[3]

The Way International The Way considers its leader's (Victor Wierwille) interpretation of the Bible to be superior to the Scriptures themselves. Followers deny the

Trinity and the existence of Jesus prior to the incarnation. Salvation comes through confession of faith and the gift of tongues, and includes wholeness of the body. Followers also believe they go into "soul sleep" at death to await Jesus' return.[4]

Unity This group considers the Bible to be the best of many spiritual books but not divinely inspired. Similar to New Age thought, Unity considers God an impersonal power indwelling each person. Jesus is thought to be a perfect man who achieved "Christ-consciousness" through a series of incarnations that included Moses and David. Others are to follow a similar path to Christ-consciousness and to ultimate awareness of oneness with all creation. Sin, according to Unity doctrine, is an illusion, and heaven and hell do not exist.[5]

Worldwide Church of God ("Armstrongism") The Bible's authority is subject to interpretation by Herbert W. Armstrong, the organization's founder. The doctrine of the Trinity is thought to be heresy, because all people become God and will be added to the God-family at the resurrection. According to Armstrong, Jesus became God through obedience. And the Holy Spirit has neither deity nor personhood. Salvation must be earned and will be withheld until Christ's return. Sickness is considered the result of sin, and no doctors or medicine are allowed.[6]

Christian Science The writings of this cult's founder, Mary Baker Eddy, are considered higher in authority than that of the Bible. There is no Trinity, and God is considered to be an impersonal, supreme consciousness. Jesus is thought to have become the example of ideal truth through discovery of his own divinity or Christ-consciousness. The Holy Spirit is considered not a person but the "Divine Science." Christian Scientists maintain that sin, sickness, and death are all illusions of the mind and can be overcome through denial of their existence.[7]

When a teacher recognizes that a child has been taught false doctrine, the adult must begin the hard work of "unteaching" the child in earnest. If the child's knowledge is simply rote memory, it will be easier to dislodge. If it has become part of the child's behavior, the job will be more difficult. The age at which a child is indoctrinated into a cult is also a factor; ideas that have gained a foothold in a young child's impressionable mind can be firmly entrenched.

With such children, teachers should follow standard principles and procedures: teaching age-appropriate concepts and vocabulary, applying lessons to daily life, and using a variety of methods and materials to reach learners. Children's understanding of doctrinal concepts can be checked by asking them to rephrase ideas, using their own words. Art and drama projects also are windows to a learner's interpretation of a lesson.

It is important to find out if a child's parents want to leave a cult and if they would welcome help from the church's adult ministry. On the other hand, the parents may be cult members who simply do not discern the difference of the program in which their child is involved. A teacher who finds himself or herself uncomfortably between child and parents should seek the help of the church staff. Counseling should focus on correct interpretation of the Bible and not on angry incrimination of cult family members or leaders.

Combatting the New Age Movement

The New Age movement is a conglomerate of groups and individuals moving toward the same basic goals by widely varying avenues. New-Agers hope for a new world of peace and harmony and a universal oneness of spirit.[8] Although Christians share these goals, they put their hope in God and His atoning work through Jesus Christ, and pray that His will be done in their lives. New Age followers, on the other hand, believe the future is a job for do-it-yourselfers.[9]

The movement is heavily laced with Eastern mysticism, but do not be deceived—New Agers are not all saffron-robed, cymbal-banging flower peddlers. Their ranks include scientists, economists, politicians, spiritual leaders, and celebrities. Institutes and communities in America and around the world promote New Age thinking. The number of adherents is impossible to estimate. In New Age philosophy, God is not a "he" but an "it"—a presence in all people. Followers believe power to achieve the movement's goals is found in raising the god-consciousness of each person and pooling the potential of collective humanity. In the movement's tenets, all people are God, with unlimited potential waiting to be tapped. Reality is illusion, there is no difference between good and evil—all of it plays havoc with the biblical absolute of morality. After all, gods are above morals.[10]

A quick glance at the movement's principles is enough to show its appeal. Foremost, the movement's offer of divinity is tough to pass up. In ancient times, the pharaohs of Egypt and the emperors of Rome were designated as living gods and worshiped. Power trips, however, usually have crash landings. Adam and Eve were lured by the false promise they would become like God. Luke records in Acts that Herod was struck down by God's angel when the people declared his voice to be that of a god. Satan tempted Christ unsuccessfully with offers of earthly power, and in his letter to the church at Philippi, Paul reminded believers that Christ "did not consider equality with God something to be grasped" (Phil. 2:6 NIV), but, rather, voluntarily took on the likeness of humans and the role of a servant. Obviously, the New Age movement and the Bible are poles apart on the subject of power.

In New Age thought, God is a force that shares oneness with humanity and nature. He is not the Creator, but simply a "component of the whole."[11] Paul, in his letter to the Romans, clearly states that those who accept this teaching are without excuse, because God's power and divine nature are shown through His creation. The Lord is Creator and ruler over all, and not just another ingredient in a cosmic mixmaster.

In the movement, Jesus is regarded as only one of many wise teachers.[12] But the Bible states that "there is no other name under heaven . . . by which we must be saved" (Acts 4:12). New Age thought proposes that without a judge there is no sin, no condemnation, and no need for a Savior. New Age philosophy teaches that godhood is within each individual, waiting to be brought to consciousness, but Christians believe that man is reconciled to God the Father through His Son, Jesus.[13]

The Bible and New Agers are also at odds over reincarnation. Past-life regression has become a popular contemporary study, often involving hypnosis. Many people claim to remember past lives. Reincarnation, however, is a far cry from redemption. The Bible tells us that a person dies once and then faces judgment, and where that person spends eternity depends not on his or her own deeds but whether or not the person is covered by the sacrificial blood of Christ.

Paul warns his readers that Satan's servants are likely to "masquerade as servants of righteousness" (2 Cor. 11:15 NIV). Christians must be aware of New Age teachings and how they conflict with Scripture. Like many cults, the movement's use of Christ's name may lend an air of respectability to its teachings. The philosophy is often passed along in unexpected places—a doctor's office, a training seminar for business executives, a psychology course, a science lab, a popular movie or book, or an elementary school. The more bizarre aspects of the movement are easy to spot—astrology, palm reading, channeling, crystals—but we must be alert to the more subtle aspects.

Christian educators should especially be alert to the infiltration of New Age philosophy into local school curriculum. Elementary school students have already been taught the power of the "inner self." Students are given instruction in meditation techniques and directed to seek a "special friend" spirit-guide.[14]

How can we guard children against a philosophy that has clouded so many adult intellects? Here are some tips:

- *Help children understand the nature and attributes of God.* A child who learns that God made the tree will not be led into thinking that God's Spirit can be found

237

in the trees. Keep a nature center in your classroom as a constant reminder of God's role as the Creator.

- *A child who knows God as a loving Father will not mistake Him for an impersonal cosmic force.* When teaching the Bible, point out evidence of God's continued interactions with his children.
- *Help children respect the rules for daily life that are found in God's Word.* A child who bases his or her thoughts and actions on biblical absolutes will, in later years, refute the idea that a "higher consciousness" can place a person beyond the reach of morality. Short role-plays in class can help students practice their responses to ethical problems and search God's Word for themselves.
- *Help children develop a humble spirit.* A child who reveres God and has a healthy respect for His power is unlikely as an adult to risk seeking equality with Him through mind expansion. Teach lessons that emphasize God's mercy toward those who love Him, but also report biblical accounts of the destruction of individuals and nations that disobeyed God's mandates.
- *Help children understand the nature of sin and the need for a Savior.* A child who recognizes his or her own sinful nature will acknowledge the need for Jesus as Savior. An appreciation of Jesus' uniqueness in this regard will help the child discern the difference between the Lord and mere philosophers who share similar ideals. Emphasize what Jesus said about Himself: "I am the way, the truth, and the life. No one comes to the Father except through Me" (John 14:6).
- *Help children to evaluate what they see and hear.* Many cults depend on their recruits' inability to discern what is biblical and what isn't. Early in life, a child should be taught how to use God's Word to evaluate the information he or she receives. Teachers should pose problems and then ask, "What does your Bible say?" Help students find answers in Scripture.
- *Encourage children to identify truth.* When a Chris-

tian discovers deception, he or she should know how to identify the truth found in God's Word. Children as young as elementary age are exposed to teachings contrary to God's truth. They must be taught the Bible in a way that is clear and applicable, so they can verbalize their faith and glorify God by their lives.

Organization and Administration

At the foot of Mount Sinai, Moses spent all day listening to and settling disputes among the children of Israel. Finally, his father-in-law stepped in. "This thing is too much for you," Jethro warned; "you are not able to perform it by yourself" (Ex. 18:18). Acting on his elder's advice, Moses appointed judges and officials over "thousands . . . hundreds . . . fifties, and . . . tens" (verse 25). The simple cases were handled by these men; only the most difficult situations were referred to Moses. In short, the children of Israel got organized.

The apostle Paul, in writing to the churches at Corinth and Ephesus, described different types of spiritual gifts and service. He wrote to Timothy setting forth qualifications for leaders, guidelines for handling benevolence cases, and formats to use for worship. He ordered Timothy to pass along everything he had learned to reliable men who would themselves become teachers. Paul knew that he would soon be taken to Rome—and he wanted to be certain the believers got organized.

Let me say up front something with which virtually every Christian would agree: None of us wants the church to be so organization-oriented that it loses its relational quality. But let me also say, neither should the bride of Christ be a sloppy housewife! Church administrators must make sure their church operates according to biblical directives and sound management techniques.

Among a church's many programs, the children's ministry usually involves the largest number of volunteer workers. The greater the number of people who are involved in this ministry, the more desperate the need becomes for a division of labor and clear lines of authority and responsibility.

Divide and Conquer

Children need to be divided into separate groups by age or grade in order to learn on their own ability level. Learning happens in the context of personal relationships—and children should be grouped with adults at a reasonable leader-to-learner ratio. As the number of children per adult increases, and the number of children in a room exceeds capacity, learning diminishes and discipline problems abound. No child—especially a young child—should have to resort to misbehavior to get an adult's attention. No adult should be expected to maintain an unreasonable span of control.

Recruiters and trainers of workers must be on the job year-round. Overcrowded classrooms and the assigning of too many children per adult are frequent causes of worker burnout. Workers should be recruited before a need occurs, so they can be in place before a crisis erupts. Recruiting can be made easier by the availability of the detailed job descriptions that are part of every well-run operation (see the section on "Job Descriptions").

Long-range planning should include a schedule for use of facilities. In this way, additional rooms can be made available for dividing up classes that have grown beyond the learners' requirement for space. A good children's curriculum calls for active learning, and active learners need twenty-five to thirty-five square feet per child, depending on their age. (Smaller children need larger spaces.)

241

Division of Labor

No one can steer the ship and man the oars at the same time, so workers in a children's ministry must divide up responsibilities for and authority over the program. Classroom workers who have special talents or abilities can team-teach with others whose abilities can combine with theirs to provide a well-rounded program. Those who possess administrative abilities can serve as department leaders to assist and direct classroom teachers. Age-division coordinators can administrate groupings of departments. A superintendent or Christian Education Specialist (CES) can oversee the work of the coordinators. Leaders at each level should be responsible for their own area of the ministry and be empowered to make certain decisions. Special responsibilities such as resources, finances, and record-keeping can be taken on by additional workers on the Christian education team.

Anyone who has ever attended a committee meeting knows that the larger the committee is, the longer the meeting will be and the less likely that anything will be accomplished. By dividing the education ministry into class, department, and division levels, planning and training can take place on a "localized" basis. Administrative team meetings can involve the CES, the superintendent, coordinators, and resource workers.

Too often a CES hears the cry, "That's what we hired *you* for!" But the specialist can reply that he or she is only doing what Moses did and Paul advised. Dividing the responsibility and sharing the authority of the ministry with volunteer workers not only helps organization; it also helps to develop leaders. To give a person a responsibility without the accompanying authority (or the reverse) leaves workers frustrated and leaves the captain steering, rowing, and getting nowhere.

The Captain

The Greek word used in the New Testament for administrator signifies "helmsman." Likewise today, an administrator keeps an eye on landmarks, watches for dangerous reefs, and navigates the ship to its destination.

Crews on ancient ships sat at the oars with their backs to the prow, trusting the helmsman to keep them on course.

Today, the captain of the children's ministry has to determine a way for the rowers to catch sight of the distant harbor as they continue to row—because seeing the destination can speed up their rowing! To do this, the leader must direct, organize, control, and make sure the workers share the vision of the ministry. Without this sense of vision—or "ownership"—workers easily lose interest.

The Servant Leader

Organizational charts are normally viewed from the top down. In other words, the weight of the organization rests on the workers who are on the bottom row!

The Bible, however, calls for leaders to be servants. So, to view such a chart in light of the biblical model, turn it upside down. In this way, you can see how each leader supports the workers "above" him or her!

Here is how it works: Each teacher serves his or her students and fellow teachers. In turn, each department leader supports and encourages the teachers under his or her care. Each division coordinator ministers to department leaders. The superintendent or CES directs and develops the coordinators. This leader also works with leaders of other programs in the children's ministry, to ensure coordination and avoid duplication of effort. The CES works in partnership with the board and pastoral staff to develop the education ministry so that it fits into the church's overall ministry to the body of Christ.

Parachurch Organiza- tions: Our Partners in Ministry

"Two are better than one," said the Preacher, "because they have a good reward for their labor. For if they fall, one will lift up his companion. But woe to him who is alone when he falls, for he has no one to help him up" (Eccl. 4:9–10).

Even large congregations with a broad range of programs are often unequal to the task of ministering to every age group and special-need group in the congregation. Why not seek help from Christian organizations that are specifically designed to meet specific needs?

Some churches are reluctant to work hand-in-hand with parachurch groups, fearing such groups will deplete the local church's resources and attendance, but parachurch organizations should be considered partners in ministry to God's family, and not competitors.

There are six basic kinds of parachurch organizations:

1. Children/youth organizations sponsored by local churches.
2. Children/youth organizations not locally sponsored.
3. Christian day schools.
4. Mission boards.

5. Christian publishers.
6. Camping organizations.

Imagine for a moment that the task of making disciples of all the nations depended solely on churches that acted individually as mission boards. Within days, inadequate funds, training, and information would slow the Great Commission to a crawl. Each local church would be doomed to reinvent the wheel, but by sharing the task, Christians everywhere are able to pool their best efforts toward world evangelization.

The same principle holds true for other ministries of the local church. Locally sponsored parachurch groups for children and youth ministries can provide programs, materials, leadership training, and special events at a minimal cost to the church. A good example is Pioneer Ministries. This club program for children and youth calls for local leadership, facilities, and small fees for materials—but it provides invaluable training, summer camps, and curriculum designed by experts.

Other programs for children and youth provide trained leaders to work regionally, and they depend on financial and prayer support from local churches and individuals. An example of this kind is Campus Crusade for Christ. By working in cooperation with Crusade, a church can serve college students both within and beyond its own reach. Thus, the local church can reach not only its own young people wherever they study, but their classmates as well. In addition, groups of this kind encourage participation in the local church—so a congregation may find itself enlarged rather than depleted!

A few parachurch groups publish their own training, study, and supplementary materials for use by their workers. Often, though, materials are designed to facilitate independent use, such as those of the Navigators. Curriculum publishers also fit into the category of parachurch agencies. They can provide churches with materials and sometimes training but do not provide personnel.

In selecting the help of a parachurch group, a church needs to consider:

- The biblical foundations of the ministry. Does the organization agree with our doctrinal statement?
- The educational foundations of its ministry. Does the program incorporate a sound philosophy of education?
- The purpose of its ministry. Does this program advance our statement of purpose?
- Financial and administrative integrity. Will our work with this group reflect good stewardship of our resources?
- Resources. Does our church have the necessary facilities, personnel, and finances?

Consider the case of a typical large church:

Missionaries are supported through prayer and financial contributions to mission boards. Mission organizations provide specialized training and extra support, so several of the church's members are able to minister overseas. A large number of church attenders are involved as well in local missions operated by parachurch groups. The church uses study materials published by a curriculum company for Sunday school, VBS, and growth groups. Children in the locally sponsored club program attend its regional camp. The church's high school and college students benefit not only from its own programs, but from national and international organizations with whom the church's staff members cooperate. International parachurch groups monitor the quality of the Christian camps and schools the church's children attend.

Without the help of such parachurch groups, the range of a large church's ministry can be severely limited, but with such help a church can thrive!

Parent
Education

A children's ministry can serve its children well through educating their parents. How?

Parent education programs are designed to support and encourage mothers and fathers through:

- exposure to teaching methods used at church.
- partnership with the teaching staff.
- information on child development and other concerns.
- opportunities to become involved.
- fellowship with other parents.

The work of the children's ministry is to support parents in developing their sons and daughters spiritually. The Bible specifies that *parents* are to teach children the laws of God: "Teach them diligently to your children," Moses instructed (Deut. 6:7). It may be that most parents have willingly forfeited their right to teach their children by delegating so much of that role to the church. Perhaps the church has enabled such forfeiture by being too willing to do the job alone. Whatever the case may be, the church can follow biblical practice by combining ministry to children with ministry to them *through their parents*.

The easiest place to begin a parent education program is in the adult Sunday school. In medium-to-large churches, "young families" classes are made up mostly of parents who have grade-school-age children. Curriculum for this class can be geared to these parents' special needs and concerns. Curriculum publishers offer a wide selection of prepared studies that teach Christian perspectives on child-rearing. A study of this kind could be taught in any number of ways: through a continuing Sunday school class, a quarter-long elective, a home study, or a special evening series at church.

A parent education workshop can be an excellent outreach tool. The expense of speakers and/or instructional materials can be offset by charging a small fee or by making the event a cooperative effort sponsored by several churches.

In order to attract people to such activities, churches need to offer what parents would consider valuable information and practical help. Teachers regularly evaluate their youngsters' needs before planning lessons, and churches should do likewise for parents. They should ask, in what areas do parents need help?

The first step could be a survey of parents that inquires about subject interests and convenient times for classes or events. A typical survey might turn up interest in:

- moral development.
- discipline & discipleship.
- sex education.
- blended families.
- terminal illness.

When needs and interests have been established, planners must decide the format to use—class, workshop, series, or other. The most workable times probably will be when children are involved in Sunday school or club programs. A church may begin with a special-interest Sunday school class. In this way, planners can build a core group that will draw other parents into more ambitious undertakings, such as retreats or seminars. Planners can find help through the Christian education departments of local Bible colleges, seminaries, or denominational offices.

Like their younger counterparts, adult learners need active participation in the teaching-learning process. Parent programs should feature discovery learning and various opportunities to share opinions and experiences. When, for instance, one person's child has fed the VCR a peanut butter sandwich, it helps to know that his or her friend's young son has been feeding worms to his baby brother. Programs should also provide opportunities for informal sharing by including time for fellowship. Books, videos, and other valuable resources can be offered through the church library or for sale at meetings.

Visits to children's classes are an instructive way for parents to become familiar with their children's teacher, observe their children in class, and become exposed to teaching methods and themes. Such visits should never be manipulated as teacher-recruiting devices, but often parents are so intrigued by what takes place in a classroom or club that they end up becoming involved. Sunday school "room mothers" can volunteer to help in areas such as communications and special events without committing themselves to a weekly teaching position.

Curriculum for lower and upper elementary grades usually provides each learner with a take-home paper that encourages parents to reinforce the Sunday lesson with a home-based activity or discussion. (Nursery curriculum is also available for distribution to parents.) Teachers can meet with groups of parents on a regular basis to preview topics and model teaching methods. Topics can include child development, health, and ways to build attitudes toward spiritual matters.

Crucial to the success of a parent education program will be:

- involvement of parents as leaders.
- a system for communication and promotion.

- parent-teacher interaction.
- applicability of ideas and principles presented.

Parent education programs in public schools are very successful. Planners there are reaching goals of improving parent-school relationships, empowering parents in the education system, developing parenting skills, and enriching the learning environment for children whose parents and teachers work as a team. Parent training includes regular home visits from teachers who serve as teaching models and provide age-appropriate toys and tools to support learning. Teachers can also provide parents with access to social services, such as health screening and family counseling. Teachers and parents who work as partners can effectively evaluate children's progress and plan for their growth.

We have seen in this chapter both the public school model and the biblical imperative. With those before us, our children's ministry should have sufficient motivation and encouragement to get started with parents!

Play

"**Q**uit playing around and get down to business!"

That is precisely the *wrong* directive to give children. Play *is* the business of childhood. Play is expression and recreation, and it involves both pleasure and purpose, both body and mind. Play is a child's way of learning about objects and relationships. Swiss psychologist Piaget said play is a child's way of transforming the world to meet his or her own needs.

Teachers can encourage play by providing children with opportunities, materials, and space. Why should a teacher encourage play? Play actively involves the whole child—*and that is what learning must do.* By designing play opportunities with a lesson aim in mind, and occasionally intervening with a word or two of guided conversation, a teacher can direct play toward a specific goal.

Play opportunities can be applied throughout the children's ministry. By playing peek-a-boo with the care-giver, a baby learns that the adult can be trusted to reappear even though he or she disappears for a moment. A toddler can learn about God's world through sensory activities, by, for example, playing with objects that provide a variety of textures, colors, shapes, and sounds. Squeezing a duck and hearing it quack builds a child's confidence in his or her abilities.

And, in later years, children learn through dramatic play in which they imitate adults.

To provide for such opportunities, a classroom should have a home living center furnished with scaled-down appliances, a doll and doll bed, "dress up" clothes, and a small table with a few chairs. Through guided conversation, teachers can help youngsters apply the Bible lesson to everyday experiences played out in this setting. *During activity time:* "Marcus, I can see from the way you hold the baby doll that you know how to care for a real baby." *During storytelling:* "Joseph helped Mary care for Jesus. Marcus, can you show us how Joseph would hold baby Jesus?"

If a room is cramped for space, the teacher should reevaluate room devoted to the piano, teacher's desk, or unused cabinets. This space should be made available for a home living center or a revolving selection of centers, including art, music, drama, puzzles, or blocks. If outdoor space is available, the range of possibilities is greatly expanded.

When opportunities for play are provided, social skills develop more quickly. Teachers can help an isolated toddler learn to play alongside others. In later years, the child can be guided to play in cooperation with a small group of others. The child who is old enough to interact with classmates can learn skills to last through the adult years: "Wait your turn," "Play fair," "Obey the rules," "Lose gracefully."

Workers can use a wider selection of teaching games when the children in their charge have longer attention spans, literacy skills, and socialization. Isolated games for individual children can teach Bible memory, but the meaning of a verse becomes easier to understand when it is applied to a life experience. *During activity:* "Maria, you can use these alphabet blocks to spell the words in our verse: 'Be kind.' " *During the telling of the story:* "Dorcas was kind—and you were kind, Maria, when you shared the blocks with Jane."

Traditional works of art that show Jesus surrounded by children usually picture the youngsters as standing or sitting at His feet in rapt attention. This scene is not unlike those reenacted in toy departments at Christmas as youngsters dictate their desires to Santa!

The picture would be closer to reality if it showed a few children running around Jesus in a game of tag while a toddler demands a piggy-back ride and a small girl holding a doll urges Him to pretend He's the daddy of her pretend family. That is how children probably acted—because that is the way God designed children to learn! Jesus probably played along —because He understood their needs.

Equipping a Home Living Center for Dramatic Play

A home living center should include the following items:

sink, refrigerator, stove	small table, chairs
dress-up clothes	doll, doll bed
ironing board, iron	dishes
pots, pans	mirror (unbreakable)
telephone	

Furnishings should be durable, washable, and free of splinters, sharp edges, or heavy lids, all of which can injure small fingers. Such furnishings can be bought from an institutional supplier, or they can be homemade. Either way, they must be safe and scaled appropriately for children. Use small tableware and artificial "food" only with adult supervision. Use hats, wigs, or combs and brushes with caution, to prevent the spread of lice. Clothing can be changed seasonally to add interest.

You can expand the horizons of dramatic play and discover even more ways to demonstrate Bible truth in real-life situations by creating a store, hospital, school, bank, post office, library, or airport. Teachers should avoid gender-role prejudice when encouraging boys or girls to assume roles in any of these settings.

Playgrounds: Serving the Whole Child

Since the late 1800s, playgrounds have evolved from open spaces for team sports to fanciful structures that encourage imaginative, individual play. Most modern playgrounds in America feature a central structure that incorporates myriad ways to swing, slide, climb, bounce, and pretend. Designers seek to find ways that playgrounds can serve a child's physical, social, emotional, and mental needs. And a playground that is carefully planned, maintained, and utilized can greatly enhance a church's ministry to children.

In order to minister to the whole child, the church must consider the child's physical needs. Large muscles need exercise, the mind needs recreation, and blossoming social skills need the practice of cooperative play. Some churches are reluctant to develop a playground, however, fearful of injuries and lawsuits. But a safe playground can be a powerful educational tool.

Some of the same common-sense rules for safety that are maintained indoors apply in the outdoor play area:

1. Children of varying ages and abilities should use separate areas where equipment is designed for their special needs.

2. The adult-to-child ratio must provide adequate supervision.

3. Adults must be well-trained to know what to do in the event of an emergency.

4. Equipment and surroundings must be designed, situated, and maintained to enable and protect children.

5. Special-needs children must be able to participate in activities.

Design

Churches are often the recipients of donated items. Used playground equipment that is in poor condition or is not in accordance with new safety standards is simply unacceptable. Equipment purchased for a family's backyard was never intended for the wear and tear of institutional use, and a fresh coat of paint will not eliminate serious hazards. In the absence of mandatory guidelines, each church must police itself.

Suppliers offer "designer" play structures in a variety of units to suit children's needs and to fit the size of the playground area. Most structures are made of pipes and heavy timber bolted together. Slides, swings, climbing nets, ladders, and rattle bridges are usually parts of the structure. Care must be taken, however, so that safe zones surround areas such as slides and swings. "Adventure" playgrounds that are gaining popularity in Europe feature scrap building materials, tools, auto bodies, boats, animals, and cooking areas.

Special Considerations

Both older and younger children fall down at play. For that reason, the ground of any playground area must be a surface that reduces impact. The majority of playground injuries treated in hospital emergency rooms result from falls from equipment.[1] Most other serious injuries come from equipment that revolves or has exposed gears, exposed bolts, or open places in which a child's head or limbs can get stuck. Danger zones include ponds and the areas around swings (especially older swings with heavy seats). A particular hazard of playgrounds is an unsupervised child's desire to go exploring and wander off. Special-needs children who may be more prone to injury require specially designed equipment, and all playgrounds should be fenced.

The Environment

A play area should take advantage of its outdoor environs. This can include trees, flowers, and perhaps an area for water and sand play. Quiet minutes between times of active play are "teaching" moments for contemplation of God's wonders. A simple mound of earth for climbing and digging can be a favorite. Adults should be alert to hazardous plants, animals, or pesticides present in the dirt of edible plants.

Scheduling Use

Teachers can utilize the well-designed play structure in many ways:

- *Dramatic play:* Update the Good Samaritan story with a make-believe fall from a swing.
- *Nature study:* Grow a small garden.
- *Exercise:* Guide conversation toward the ways God helps children grow.
- *Applying Bible truth:* Discuss and demonstrate following rules, being kind, and helping others.
- *Art and music:* Take projects that are too messy or too boisterous outdoors.

Another time for playground use is the time slot between Sunday school and church. Traditionally this has been a time of confusion and disorganization, as children run up and down hallways and sneak doughnuts from the adults' coffee stand. A supervised playground program can relieve children and congestion.

A playground also can serve children through club programs, summer ministries, day-care, and day-school use. Rules should be posted and understood by all supervising adults so that enforcement will be consistent.

To evaluate the playground that serves your children's

ministry, or to begin planning construction of one, send for the *Handbook for Public Playground Safety* produced by the U.S. Consumer Product Safety Commission, Washington, D.C. 20207. Before designing your own, visit other playgrounds and observe children at play. Contact institutional suppliers of playground equipment to see what is available. Children can learn, play, and grow in safety and security on a church playground, and that is why the playground must be considered a priority ministry.

Prayer: The Child Talks to God

Most parents and teachers have witnessed the confusion and disappointment of a child who has been denied a prayer request for a special present, a sunny day for a picnic, or even the health of a sick pet. In young minds, God can become a killjoy, a "meanie," or someone who listens only to grown-ups.

The opposite misconception can result when a child's desires are answered through prayer. In that case, God may seem to be a celestial Santa who dispenses gifts and favors upon demand.

How can we teach children that prayer is not merely a shopping list? Here are some guidelines:

- *Encourage spontaneous, conversational prayer.* Saying only memorized prayers may inhibit a child from genuine communication. Use any "teaching moment" to pray with your learners.
- *Praise God and thank Him for His gifts.* Learners need to understand we do not use prayer only for requests.
- *Assure your students that God listens.* Children may have a difficult time gaining the full attention of busy parents, and therefore it may be hard for them to real-

ize God always has time to hear their prayers. Spend time with them, listening and answering carefully.

- *Help your children to confess sin.* Don't insist that all prayers be said aloud and before a group. Some children may feel perfectly at ease in conversation with their heavenly Father yet intimidated by an audience. A story is told of a mother who listened at her young son's bedside as he said his prayers. "Speak up," she urged, "I can't hear you." The boy replied, "I wasn't talking to you!"
- *Teach learners to submit to God's will.* One of the hardest lessons for anyone to learn about prayer is to accept whatever God sends as His reply. Assure children that God always listens and answers—but remind them that those answers may not be the ones they hoped to receive.

Most children have experienced and understood being denied a toy or privilege that might have proven harmful. Just as parents act in their children's best interests, God does what is best for them as well, although sometimes to their disappointment. Just as parents are not obligated to explain their decisions, God does not always make His purposes clear. Don't be afraid to admit that even you don't always know God's reasons.

- *Point out that God speaks to children in a variety of ways.* His answers may come through Bible verses, decisive events, loud and clear announcements from parents, or the voice of one's conscience. God knows each child as an individual and speaks to each one in a special way.

As a child in the temple at Shiloh, Samuel heard God call his name. After that, Samuel enjoyed a lifelong dialogue that guided him in service to God, but it was old Eli, the priest, who first directed the young boy to listen for God's voice and answer willingly and humbly.

All children deserve the opportunity to talk with God through prayer. A teacher should instruct them to praise God, to thank Him, and to ask for what is not just their desire but also His will. Prepare them to celebrate God's answer, whether it is "Yes," "No," or "Wait a while." Teach them how to recognize God's voice.

Promotional Pieces: Beautiful Brochure, or Flyer-by-Night?

Flyers and brochures appear in stacks on tables in church hallways. They are stuffed into bulletins and later found tucked absentmindedly into the hymnal racks. Some are kept for months inside a Bible. Why are some advertising items noticed and read while others are ignored?

Usually it is not a promotional piece's subject matter that is unappealing, but its presentation. How can a piece be appealingly presented?

Following are the basic characteristics of successful promotional pieces:

1. *Attractiveness.* Successful promotional pieces appeal through color, readability, and attractive graphics. Photos tell stories. Layout is visually interesting. Type style and spacing are clear and consistent.

2. *Clarity.* Successful promotional pieces get their messages across through carefully worded headlines, subheadings, body copy, and captions. Registration or order forms are simple. All necessary information is presented in a logical sequence.

Promotional pieces that are used to advertise an event or

program directly influence attendance. A quality event that is poorly advertised will benefit few people, because potential attenders will act on the negative impression made by the advertising. In the reader's mind, a sloppy flyer presages a sloppy program. And a registration form with a confusing format, or a return address with an incorrect zip code, will sabotage even the best-laid plans. Quality promotional pieces are worth the time and effort they take to produce.

Type and Line Art

Thanks to desktop publishing programs, quality type and graphics are within anyone's ability to produce. If such programs are not obtainable, professional typesetting is an alternative, although it is more costly. Hundreds of graphic ideas and illustrations on a wide range of subjects are available through computer programs and clip-art books. There are dozens of volumes of clip-art books on the market, and several clip-art services cater specifically to the needs of churches.

Photos

Photos should tell the story of the event or program. Using group photos of committees, clubs, or boards adds little appeal to advertising. Instead, look for action photos and close-ups of people. If a brochure is meant to promote a canoe trip, use photos of excited campers paddling canoes, rather than mug shots of individual counselors or a group portrait of the planning committee.

Whenever a photo is reproduced, it loses a small degree of its sharpness, so use only those photos that have strong contrast and sharp details. Photos can be cropped to eliminate uninteresting areas, and can be reduced or enlarged proportionate to the original. Reducing the size of a fuzzy photo will increase its sharpness, but enlarging even a sharply focused photo may cause some blur.

Improved photocopier machines may tempt amateur brochure designers to use photos in flyers, bypassing the intermediate step of *screening*. A professional printer can re-shoot a photo through a screen that breaks up the image into a dot pattern, rendering it more suitable for reproduction. Even if the church does its own printing, photos should be taken to a printer to be screened before they are pasted onto the final layout.

Paper

One's choice of paper can have a tactile and visual impact. A glossy, enamel stock improves the contrast of photos and gives them a slick appearance. A matte stock dulls photos but may be more appropriate for certain themes. Paper is gauged in pounds according to its weight. Heavier stock is more expensive and may clog photocopiers, but it lends importance to its message. Heavy stock is a distinct advantage, however, in the case of a self-mailer.

Color

Sometimes an attractive layout is marred by an unappealing or low-impact combination of ink and paper colors. Blue ink on blue paper is a common combination, but it lacks impact and hinders readability. Brown on brown or a combination of greens seems appropriate for an outdoor event, such as a camp-out, but it usually fails to excite the age group for whom it is intended. (Even so, a multicolor or full-color printing job can be complex and expensive. Each time the brochure includes an additional color, it must be run back through the press.)

Layout

A good layout makes the best use of space on a piece without cramping type and graphics. It considers the lines that will be caused by folding and positions copy and art to their best advantage. A good layout reflects the tenor of the event it advertises. The hearts-and-flowers art and flowing script that adorn a brochure for the ladies' retreat would turn off sixth-graders. A better choice for a flyer inviting them to the "Welcome to Junior High!" bash would employ high-powered graphics and bright colors.

If a map with directions is to be included in the layout, make sure it is accurate. If it is not drawn to scale, point this out. Insert-detail maps should be accompanied by wider-area maps showing the location of the insert. Be sure to indicate compass directions and mileage between landmarks.

Include the mailing address for a registration form both on the brochure and on the form itself. That way, once the form is separated from the brochure, it will still bear the information needed to mail it, and the brochure can provide the address (and/or phone number) after the form has been sent in. Also be sure to identify registration forms with the name and date of the event to prevent mix-ups over events at the church office. To avoid confusion over payment of fees, provide a place for the registrant to indicate the form and amount of payment being sent in with the registration.

Some extra considerations have little to do with aesthetics but a lot to do with practicality. For example, a self-mailer must meet post-office regulations pertaining to size, the positioning of the bulk-mailing permit and return address, and the method of sealing. Postcards must be regulation size and weight. To be mailed inside a standard-size envelope, a brochure must be designed to fit inside after it is folded.

Professional-quality promotional pieces are simple to produce, so it is unforgivable for a sloppy flyer to dampen enthusiasm for a program or event that has included months of costly preparation!

Puppetry: Give It a Hand

Back in the days of castles and crusades, puppetry was an integral part of the church's education ministry. Puppets, stained-glass windows, tapestries, paintings, and wood carvings all served to illustrate Bible stories for the benefit of the largely illiterate congregation.

The term "marionette" comes from the "little Mary" role in the nativity story presented each Christmas in cathedrals across France. This art form has always enjoyed popularity in Europe, and has an even higher status in Asia. Archaeological evidence proves that puppets have a long history—and their success in theater and film ensures their place in the future of art and drama.

Marionettes—puppets animated from above by strings—are only one type of puppet. *Hand puppets* can be made to move their mouths, heads, and arms. Large, two-man puppets make possible the movement of a puppet's head and mouth while human hands fit into the character's glove hands and provide animated gestures. *Finger puppets* fit one-to-a-finger, and a single hand can tell a whole story using a cast of characters. *Stick puppets* offer only body and arm movement. *Shadow puppets* are silhouettes to be used against a screen or on an overhead projector.

The use of puppets is as varied as their shapes and sizes. As with any dramatic form, puppets can be used solely to entertain, but in the hands of a resourceful teacher, they can be a powerful educational resource. In the hands of a learner, puppets can be a wonderful means of expression and a lot of fun.

In the teacher's hands, a puppet can:

- announce the change to a new activity, introduce the memory verse, or urge clean-up.
- help teach the Bible or application of a Bible story.
- carry on guided conversations with young learners.
- welcome reluctant preschoolers to a new room.

In the student's hands, a puppet can:

- Be constructed as an art activity, be combined with a creative writing assignment, or be presented in a drama as part of a service project.
- Act out role-play situations that dramatize the lesson concept.
- Express feelings the learner is reluctant to discuss.

In selecting methods and materials, a teacher must first consider the needs and characteristics of the learners. What do they need to learn? Which methods and materials will enable them to participate in the learning process? If puppets help to teach a lesson concept, which type of puppet will work best with that particular lesson?

Small-group Storytelling

For use with young children, finger puppets, pop-ups, and other small puppets work best. Fuzzy animal puppets are also welcome visitors, but should not be used in evangelistic lessons because children may think that an animal has a spiritual dimension. Prepared scripts and elaborate stages are useless in classrooms with young children; they prefer to hold conversations with the puppets and give them an occasional hug.

For older children, a medium-size puppet or two could be

used to present a story from behind a simple curtain or divider, while a teacher positioned in front could guide a student-puppet dialogue.

Large-scale Productions

Some churches own large collections of professionally made puppets, elaborate stages with sound systems, and teams of trained teen and adult puppeteers. These teams perform at churches, camps, schools, and evangelistic campaigns. Because they perform for large crowds, they usually employ large puppets and prerecorded scripts.

Puppets in the Learning Center

Young children enjoy having a small "stage" and a family of puppets they can use to act out spontaneous dramas. The adult who supervises such a center can use guided conversation to steer performers toward a lesson concept. It is best if the teacher uses a different set of puppets to teach than the ones children use for play.

Puppetry as an Art, Writing, and Drama Activity

When a learner creates her own puppet for a student production, she must think about the character of her puppet persona. To write the simple script, she needs a solid understanding of the story or lesson concept. Both activities promote the lesson aim. Depending on the age of the puppeteer, construction of a puppet can be as simple as using a paper bag or as complex as detailing a marionette. Scripts can be acted out, recorded, or simply narrated by an adult as puppets pantomime the action.

By working together on a project, learners practice social skills that can be part of the lesson. In performing a drama for another group, children learn to share the message of the Bible.

After centuries of not being taken seriously in this country, puppets are back on the job in schools, hospitals, and churches. They can look funny, colorful, and silly—but when it comes to teaching, puppets mean business.

Record-keeping

Some people assume that spiritual undertakings such as a children's ministry should have nothing to do with sound business practice. On the contrary—if a ministry is to be effective, it must be supported by prayer *and* managed in good and decent order. Part of good business practice is good record-keeping.

Following are some items to be considered in this area:

Financial Records

If a church has a treasurer or financial secretary who handles accounts and makes sure bills get paid on time, then leaders of the children's ministry can concentrate on being good stewards of the budget allocated for their use. Good stewardship involves not only shopping around for best buys, but also objectively evaluating expenses in view of the church's overall ministry. A children's ministry should keep records of "per participant" costs of clubs, classes, camps, and special events. From these records, workers can balance a program's expense against its results. Then they can project costs of programs that are to be continued or expanded.

Inventories

Detailed inventories should be kept of curriculum, AV equipment, camping equipment, and other resources. This is especially important if items are loaned, sent out for repair, or tucked in nooks and crannies all over the facility, rather than stored in a central resource room. Policies should be established regarding who can borrow what items—and for how long. Records must be kept of loans in order to trace overdue items. Curriculum inventories can be especially helpful in cutting costs.

Attendance

Attendance records are vital for planners to accurately project needs for future classrooms and workers. With the names and addresses of all their students, teachers can follow up on dropouts and absentees. Mailing lists can be compiled according to age group. These can be used in promoting classes, clubs, and special events for parents as well as children. Whether they're in the form of index cards filed in shoe boxes or on computerized printout lists, attendance records are a tool basic to ministry.

Previous teachers may have made special notes in these records, including information on home visits, events in the learner's life, or insights into behavior problems. If the child has accepted Christ as his or her personal Savior, that information should be noted.

Nursery

Infants and toddlers require a more extensive record than an older child does. Files available to nursery workers should list not only the child's name and address but also any allergies or special conditions to which workers should be alerted. The files should also contain names and photos of parents or guardians, as a security measure. Whenever a young child is brought to the nursery, workers need to note the child's behavior, sleeping and eating habits, diaper changes, and the whereabouts of the child's parents during his or her time in the nursery.

Parental Permission Slips

If children are to be taken on field trips, camp-outs, or any other activity away from the church site, leaders must get permission from the parents or guardian of each child. A slip should include permission for workers to obtain emergency medical care for any child who needs it. Slips should be duplicated so that one set of copies is taken along on the trip while a backup set is kept at church. Some churches seek to have permission for emergency care on file for *all* children, even if they only participate in on-site Sunday programs.

Workers

Records need to be kept of the names and addresses of all workers in the children's ministry, whether they are paid staff or volunteers. File information should include their training and qualifications, previous experience, and any references or recommendations. These kinds of records simplify recruitment and evaluation. They also are a helpful resource whenever a worker's morals or qualifications come under fire. It may not be possible for a church to require photos and fingerprints of every worker recruited, but it would be wise for leaders to scrutinize any worker's refusal to provide them.

What to Keep, What to Toss

Just as important as deciding what records to keep is determining what records to throw out. The value of attendance records, expense reports, and permission slips lies in their accessibility. Retrieval is simplified if useful items are not submerged under piles of useless ones.

Here are some guidelines in determining the usefulness of your ministry's files:

- Keep a central file of all children's ministry workers rather than separate files in each ministry department.

Many workers participate in more than one program, and information can be needlessly duplicated. Also make sure workers have the names and numbers of supervisors to call in case of an unanticipated absence.

- Keep a central file for each child who participates in the ministry. (Many will be involved in more than one program.) These files should be organized alphabetically within each separate age-grade group.
- Keep a head count of daily attendance in Sunday school, clubs, and other continuing programs according to classroom. Teachers should have forms on which to record absences and students' names and addresses for easy follow-up. Teachers also should retain absence records in case a parent wants to check on a possible truant.
- Keep a head count of attendance at special events, according to age group. After an outreach event, make sure names and addresses are processed for follow-up.
- Keep a summary evaluation in the files of programs such as camp-outs and teacher training events. Also keep records of one-time programs, even if they were flops. Without such records, new workers may try the same program without understanding the reasons for its previous failure.
- Throw away outdated material, such as catalogs and flyers advertising past events.
- Compile yearly totals before throwing away weekly or monthly attendance figures.
- Throw away registration cards and one-time permission slips after an event, but make sure relevant information has been used to update the central file on workers and participants. Keep records on anyone who was injured during the event.
- Throw away previous versions of forms, handouts, or policies that have been revised or updated, to prevent confusion.
- Build a file of suppliers, retreat sites, and speakers for future reference.

- Build a file of magazine articles, but throw away the rest of the magazine once the useful pages have been filed.
- Build a file of program ideas and recommendations from workers.
- Separate items such as audiocassettes, photographic prints, negatives, slides, and videos. These items need to be stored in special containers away from sunlight, heat, and certain kinds of plastic or chemicals. Check with a specialist on archival storage of important perishable items.

Keep routine correspondence and other items of diminishing value only long enough to be certain they will no longer be needed for reference. Active files can be kept handy in office cabinets, while inactive files can be stored in cardboard file boxes in less valuable space. Mark inactive files with a disposal date.

Keep confidential files under lock and key. These include personnel records and notes on learners that refer to sensitive issues. Access to learner names and addresses must be limited, especially so that they won't be used to compile mailing lists for unauthorized purposes.

For some churches, computerized record-keeping is standard operating procedure. For others, it may still be considered space-age technology beyond their skills and budgets. It is wise to consider the advantages of the easy storage and retrieval a computer can provide—plus the amount of office space that potentially can be freed from file cabinets. Names and addresses can be coded for the printing of a variety of mailing lists for different purposes. Professional-quality type and graphics can enhance brochures and handouts. Outdated material can be dumped at the push of a button.

Whether a children's ministry's records are on paper or on disk, and whether attendance is twelve or twelve hundred, leaders need to follow good business practices.

Recruitment: Six Steps to Securing Servants

Our Lord walked up to His disciples and said, "Follow me." And they did.

Not since the gathering of those twelve has recruitment been so simple, direct, and successful. Volunteers today seem on the verge of extinction. Why aren't people willing to serve? Where are the workers who can staff our programs? What are we going to do?

Assess Needs and Resources

The first step for many churches must be to assess their personnel needs and determine how many workers are needed in order to get a job done decently and in order. A job done with minimum personnel and minimum standards simply is not good enough. A church has to determine how many workers are needed and what characteristics and skills they should possess. A recruiter should observe these six procedures before picking up the phone or ringing a doorbell in search of a volunteer.

1. Prepare Job Descriptions Some workers burn out because they were initially misinformed or became confused about their responsibilities. A recruiter should have a written job description for each position to be filled. This is standard procedure in the business world, and is sound practice for any volunteer organization. A number of churches use the written method: In this case, the volunteer and the Christian education specialist enter into a year-long agreement—calling on the church to provide adequate training and materials, and calling on the worker to fulfill specific responsibilities toward learners and fellow workers. At the end of that period, the agreement is evaluated and, hopefully, renewed.

Once personnel needs have been determined, those needs should be made public. Newsletters, bulletin boards, and bulletins all can be utilized in an effort to match the right person to the job. Successful recruitment is more than "plugging holes"; it is, rather, a match of person and position that serves both.

Take, for example, an individual gifted in the area of administration. Suppose an insightful recruiter places that person in a position of authority where his or her gift will be developed and utilized. The result? The congregation is blessed with a competent leader—and that leader has the opportunity to honor the Lord by his or her use of a God-given talent.

2. Screen the Candidates Once the church leaders and congregation are aware of the needs, the time comes to begin "zeroing in" on potential recruits. A screening committee must be established to approve potential workers before they are contacted by recruiters. This type of committee may seem to be just an additional stretch of red tape, when empty positions are crying to be filled. In reality, it serves many important functions. Among them is the necessary elimination of individuals whose doctrinal positions may not be in agreement with that of the church. Others, especially new Christians, may not have the spiritual maturity or grasp of basic doctrine to equip them for positions of leadership.

Another committee function is to protect workers who have demonstrated their usefulness and been asked to assume too many tasks. It may take just one more job to send an already overloaded superintendent-treasurer-secretary-janitor to that nice church down the street!

3. Approach the Prospects Supplied with a list of prospective workers, armed with copies of up-to-date job descriptions, and backed by the approval of the screening committee, the recruiter is ready to approach some prospects. Here are some rules for the recruiter to follow:

- Arrange a convenient time to speak to the prospect about the job.
- Don't push for a decision at the time of first contact.
- Be able to present the responsibilities and time commitment involved in the job.
- Explain what materials and training will be provided.
- Specify the personal gifts or talents that suit this particular prospect to the job.
- If possible, offer the prospect the opportunity to observe the job.
- Give the prospect a week or so to think it over.
- Accept the prospect's answer. Don't apply pressure if the answer is no.

4. Follow Up on Volunteers The job of fitting the person to the position doesn't end when the recruit says yes. Any recruiter who drops a tenderfoot into a position and doesn't follow up on that worker might as well start looking for a replacement—because the position will be empty again within the month! A fresh recruit should be taken under the wing of a seasoned veteran and trained for the work he or she has been asked to do. Occasional checkups and performance evaluations are good morale boosters. Words of encouragement, a climate of teamwork, and a sincere interest in the growth of the new worker will greatly increase that worker's longevity.

5. Find Out Why People Quit When a worker is ready to resign from a position, it may be because the responsibilities of the job have ended. On the other hand, it may be because the worker's energy and patience have been exhausted. In either case, it is a good practice to sit down and conduct an "exit interview." This is an opportunity for both worker and supervisor to update the job description and evaluate the performance of both individuals. Were the responsibilities too much of a burden? Was the training adequate? Is there still a need for this position? This information is invaluable in planning future needs.

6. Keep the Process Active Recruitment is like membership—it's all right to have a big drive now and then, but the best method for growth is to encourage volunteerism all year long. Evaluate needs; plan; recruit; train; evaluate *new* needs; plan; recruit; train. It's a cycle. It goes around and around, and at no time is this job ever finished. Church leaders who have been successful in recruiting are those who never stop the process of ferreting out potential workers.

Leaders may feel they can back off once they think their bases are covered, but those leaders are apt to find themselves plugging holes with untrained and unwilling individuals who had to be pressured into working jobs they will drop at the earliest opportunity.

Even with these helpful principles, the leader who must recruit volunteers has no easy job. Sometimes individuals who are handpicked for their enormous potential turn out to be disappointments. An increase in church attendance that seemed to herald a boost in potential volunteers may yield none. A frustrating lack of motivation among the members may begin to discourage the recruiters themselves.

May we follow Jesus' example: He said to His disciples when their ministry was just beginning: "The harvest truly is plentiful, but the laborers are few. Therefore pray the Lord of the harvest to send out laborers into His harvest" (Matt. 9:37–38).

Rented Facilities: Making the Best of It

Your small group of believers and their families have finally outgrown the living room. The group manages to pay the salary of a part-time worker trained in church planting, but you have no fund to purchase your own facility. For now, the only alternative is to rent space.

For most congregations who meet in rented space, the experience can range from awkward to miserable. Never again, you think, will you encounter such inflexible rules and hard-hearted custodians. Never again, you believe, will you pay so much to be so ill-housed. (But wait until you build your own facility and try to keep it clean, secure, and well-maintained!)

In the meantime, you make the best of your situation. Consider these rented options that are available to church groups:

- Off-peak hours in a facility shared with another church.
- A school campus.
- An office complex.
- A restaurant.
- A group of homes in the same neighborhood.

Renting a church building has immediate benefits. The furnishings are tailored to suit an educational program that includes infants and toddlers; and large rooms are already set up for group worship and fellowship events.

A school campus offers the advantages of appropriate furnishings (except for nurseries), large rooms, recreational facilities, and a more flexible schedule, but many schools may be unavailable due to the community's interpretation of separation of church and state.

An office complex may have rooms appropriate for adult classes but not for children or youth. (This may change in the near future, however, as more corporations provide on-site child care for employees.) The same is true of a restaurant. The system of using a group of homes in the same neighborhood on Sunday is a difficult arrangement; children must be dropped off at different locations, and the whole situation may prove incomprehensible to first-time visitors.

Most groups end up sharing rooms in another church's facility. While this is a minor inconvenience for teachers of adult classes, and irritating to the youth group as well (who would prefer to have their own planet), it can cause major problems for the children's ministry. What are these problems, and how can they best be handled?

Confusion

Teachers should post signs directing learners to the correct rooms, even though the signs must be posted and taken down each week. With the host church's permission, your group can set up a sign and schedule in a prominent spot outdoors. Post a greeter to welcome visitors and provide directions.

Territorial Rights

From the start, be clear on what is "yours, mine, and ours." Keep children, youth, and adults out of restricted areas. Clean up after meetings, and don't use the host church's consumable supplies or equipment unless it is part of your rental agreement. Be especially conscientious about maintaining the condition of the nursery and kitchen. Always provide constant supervision of children and youth, and lock up when you leave.

The renting group continually walks on thin ice. If the host church's ruling body was initially divided over renting its facilities in the first place, a single errant coffee cup could be enough to sour the arrangement. If the renting group proves itself untrustworthy to one landlord, they may find themselves blacklisted by others. If yours is a renting group, keep communication open, and be prepared to bend over backward.

Mountains to Move

Storage space in such facilities is usually at a premium, so don't be surprised if there is no room available at church to store your group's supplies. If even one closet is available, organize your group's things into portable containers or wheeled carts that can all be locked away in the same place. Surprising amounts of supplies and equipment can be carted around in large baskets or cardboard storage boxes with cutout handles. Washable tote trays are great for art supplies. Plastic containers come in a range of bright colors that can be coded for use by different age groups.

Invest in carrying cases for expensive AV equipment. Use tape players instead of pianos. Use lapboards when desks are unavailable. Children in many age groups do not require chairs and desks, and some actually prefer sitting on the floor.

With the permission of the host church, let the two churches' teachers who share rooms exchange names and phone numbers. If minor misunderstandings can be cleared up between teachers, they won't eventually have to be brought up before the church board. Most misunderstandings between groups sharing facilities stem not from theft but from misplacement of items ranging from crayons to furniture.

Sometimes small churches meeting in large-church facilities have to place children of diverse ages in a room designed for one specific age group. Items have to be dragged in from other rooms to meet the needs of each learner. Sometimes such items can actually present a health hazard, such as a bite-size puzzle piece dropped by a first-grader and picked up by a toddler. When class is dismissed, workers can unwittingly put items back in the wrong place or mistake the host church's supplies for their own. A labeling system such as colored tape or stickers can be used for easy identification.

Complaints from host churches usually center on vandalism by unsupervised children. Those can be easily curtailed. Standard operating procedure dictates that a teacher should arrive before any of the learners, regardless of who owns the facility. If there is no teacher-directed activity for the learners when they arrive, they will invent one of their own—usually with disastrous results.

On the positive side, a growing church that rents a facility before building its own has the advantage of "trying on" a building design before buying it. If the facility does not lend itself to the group's philosophy of ministry and education, the group can look for another temporary home better suited to its needs. By learning firsthand what works and doesn't work for them, a young church can design its first facility based on experience. They can make certain, before moving from vision to blueprint, that the facility does not determine the program; rather, the program has determined the facility. Remember: measure twice—cut once!

Research Activities: Reading, Writing, and Research

Reading and writing activities are valuable teaching methods, but often they are overused by teachers who need more variety in their repertoire of methods. Most school-age children can process information by reading a text and writing answers to questions on a worksheet—but a large number of children with reading disabilities find these activities frustrating. When a reading or writing activity is provided as a learning activity choice, an alternate activity should be provided, such as art, music, drama, or games.

Research activities are ways to utilize literacy skills by combining them with problem-solving, communication, and socialization. Children who must seek information from reference books, maps, films, or interviews can learn on a higher level of participation than those who simply complete worksheet assignments. Even children who are not proficient in reading and writing can enjoy the challenge of a research project when they are teamed with classmates who share those skills.

Research activities are designed to be used with older elementary students. They require a few resources and about fifteen to twenty minutes of class time. Classrooms should be equipped with Bibles, a Bible dictionary, maps, pictures, and writing materials. Audiovisual resources will be needed from time to time, including slides, films, videotapes, and audio-cassettes.

Reading materials should be presented on the learners' level. Too often, Bible reading can evolve into a reading lesson instead of an exploration of the Bible's meaning and application. Valuable class time is sapped, and poor readers are reluctant to participate. Children's classrooms should be supplied with copies of a single version of the Scriptures in easy-to-read text. Confusion mounts when a child tries to read along in his or her own text while classmates read aloud from a different version. When text varies, children assume that only one version can be the "real" Bible. Teachers end up wasting precious minutes sorting through semantic trivia.

With a few resources at hand, children can be ready to dig into the Bible and make discoveries of their own. Here are some ways to guide them:

Interviews

Missionaries, church leaders, and others with lesson-related knowledge can be recruited to be interviewed by children. A few students equipped with a tape recorder or note-pad can ask questions that will provide information to be shared with the class later in the session.

When your class studies the travels of Paul, have a group of learners interview a missionary who has encountered dangers in his or her own journeys. "What was the scariest thing that happened? What did you do?"

Field Trips

Although field trips involve considerable preparation, they can be both fun and educational. A trip to a museum, park, hospital, or police station is a possibility. To make sure children get the most out of a field trip, their teacher should brief them on what to expect and should provide adequate supervision.

As part of a study on creation, for example, a trip to the

zoo can impress children with the variety and beauty of God's handiwork. The teacher can provide thoughts by asking questions such as, "How did God equip each animal to defend itself, move about, and care for its young?"

Models and Displays

A group of learners can get hands-on experience by assembling a collection of items related to the lesson or by building a model. These items should be identified and displayed for the rest of the class.

To better understand life in Bible times, a group can build a display of a typical ancient home. Again, questions arise: "How was the roof part of the living area? Why would a home be built near a well?"

Maps

Children old enough to grasp geographic concepts will enjoy locating places and events mentioned in the lesson. Colorful, poster-size maps of individual countries or regions are helpful. They can be supplemented by world maps so that children can place the smaller map in the proper perspective.

To gauge the distance the Hebrews traveled to the promised land, children can locate their stops along the way. "How many miles did they travel? Find the equivalent distance on a map of our own country."

Time Lines

Using their Bibles to review the story, a group of learners can arrange a series of pictures in the correct sequence and write descriptions of each event.

To better understand the chronology of Easter week, a group can read the story and arrange pictures of the entry into Jerusalem, the Last Supper, the trial, the crucifixion, and the resurrection. "Which happened first? How many days were there between these events?"

Media

Audiovisual aids such as recordings, films, and filmstrips can be an interesting and enjoyable way for a research group to discover information. Teachers should supply questions to help the students develop listening and observation skills. Headphones can be used with some equipment to avoid distracting nearby groups who are working on other projects.

For a lesson on David, a group could listen to several Psalms set to contemporary music and compare the sound to the ancient instruments to which the Psalms were first sung.

Dictionary

When unfamiliar words are part of the lesson, a research group can look them up beforehand and record the definitions or draw pictures to explain their meaning. When the words are encountered during the storytelling, the group can share their research.

In the story of Daniel and the writing on the wall, for example, several unfamiliar words can be researched by the group and later explained: *noble*, *astrologer*, *concubine*, and so on.

Books

Standard reference works should include a Bible dictionary, maps, and books on life in Bible times. Other books can include biography, science, fact, fiction, or any material that relates to the lesson. A few books can be designated as loan items, to encourage students in further study.

For a unit of study on missions, a research group can read biographies of some famous missionaries, summarize their lives, and locate their mission fields on the map.

Follow these guidelines for research activities:

1. Instructions must be clear.
2. Assignments must be on the learners' level.
3. Group projects must provide work for each student.

4. The lesson plan must provide a time for sharing results.
5. All necessary resources and supplies must be available.

Resignations: Handling Quitting Time

James wrote that suffering produces perseverance and, in turn, perseverance produces maturity. In children's ministry, suffering often produces job openings. Every church is blessed with a few tireless saints who serve year after year, coming out in weather that would intimidate sled dogs, but the vast majority of workers, perhaps because of inadequate recruiting or training procedures, bail out after a year or two.

Why do workers quit? Some move away to other locales, some choose to serve another area of ministry, and some simply get fed up. A worker who has neither the interest nor the characteristics to minister to children should be redirected to another avenue of service before he or she goes up in smoke. Workers who burn out are generally victims of abuse and neglect—chained, rather than trained, to an eternal task. When a letter of resignation arrives on the desk of a Christian Education Specialist, it is usually too late to salvage the situation and the volunteer. What is to be done when there is no more you can do?

- *Conduct an exit interview.* Workers leaving a position can be called into the CES's office—not to be strong-armed into staying, but to be asked their reasons for leaving. The exit interview is not a time for an argument, but an information-gathering tool. In some cases, a worker may be willing to remain in a position long enough to train a replacement. Because no one should be in ministry who doesn't want to serve, this "grace period" should be limited.

• *Review the job description.* To give recruiters an accurate picture of the position to be filled, the job description should be updated. Evaluate the importance of the position in the context of the overall program. Is the span of control too broad? Do the duties require special skills? Is this a job for two people? Or is this job already handled by overlapping positions?

Sometimes the worker who quits a position has been the heart and brains of the program, and when a person in charge has not delegated authority and responsibility to fellow workers, the program goes out the door along with the departing leader. Administrators need to guard against the practice of the "one man show," not only among volunteer workers but also among their teammates on the church staff.

Every program leader should examine himself or herself and the team. "What would happen if I stayed home today? What would happen if I quit altogether? Would the program grind to a halt? Would the staff have the interest and the know-how to keep it going?"

Another aspect of the "one man show" is the inclination to become a personality cult. This is particularly common in youth work. It can result in a mass exodus of admirers who have taken on the disgruntled attitude of their ex-leader.

The majority of CES's will spend less than five years in their first position. That means that the worker who has just decided to quit may be the person who has been in charge of the entire ministry. If he or she has done the job correctly, there is no reason for a church to panic. The successful manager makes workers successful, even after he or she is gone.

There are several steps a departing leader can take to ease the transition:

• Leave when it is no longer in the church's best interests to stay.

- For a short time, participate in the selection and training of a replacement.
- Endorse the replacement to the workers.
- Leave behind coherent records and a long-range plan.
- Hand over the reins and get out of the way.

It would be heavenly if all jobs came to an end with smiles all around, lavish recommendations, and the awarding of an engraved plaque. Unfortunately, any job can end in unresolved bitterness that leaves lives and ministries in shambles. A church staff should work to develop an atmosphere of trust and willingness, building up each other in love. Volunteer workers can observe such biblical models and strive to recreate them on their own administrative level.

Resource Rooms

Children's workers usually are pack rats at home. Their garages are crammed with cartons of baby-food jars and coffee cans. Their closets bulge with scraps of yarn and plastic meat trays. They rarely throw away anything without first wondering what their students could make with it.

At church, it's the same story. Each worker has items squirreled away in a classroom cabinet. You might find a few items that are used each week—pencils, scissors, crayons, Bibles—but most items are leftover work papers, craft supplies, and curricula from weeks, months, or years past. It's not just clutter—it's waste.

If a church wants to save space and money, it will set aside one area as a resource room. With a supervisor or two on hand to closely monitor the withdrawal and return of items, a resource room can serve as an organized pool of materials for the use of every children's worker.

How Do We Know What We've Got?

In our wildest dreams, the church budget committee would award the children's ministry carte blanche. The learners would have the best of everything simply because they deserve it. In real life, many students get only what their teachers can give from their own pockets. A partial solution to this is to gather up all the existing teaching resources scattered around the facility, put them all in one place, and loan them out as needed. Here are some steps to following this practice:

1. Gather up all teaching resources. Appoint a committee to sift through the pile and throw away what everyone agrees is unusable.
2. Make an inventory of supplies and equipment to be stored.
3. Engrave the church's name on large pieces of equipment, such as projectors or tape players.

How Can We Get What We Need?

At the beginning of each quarter, each class's teaching team should scan the curriculum for items they'll need in weeks to come. They should turn in a list of these items to the resource-room supervisor, who will make sure the items are on hand. A single purchaser should buy in bulk to supply several teachers. That way, money can be saved, and teachers will learn to plan ahead for the luxury of having all their supplies ready and waiting for them.

Here's how to get what you need:

1. Send for institutional catalogs that offer bulk prices.
2. Keep a file of current resource catalogs for teachers to peruse.
3. Limit the amount of reimbursement for unplanned expenses.
4. Solicit donations from local merchants.
5. Limit the number of acceptable signatures on local charge accounts.
6. Be willing to spend more for equipment that will last longer.
7. Publicize needs in the bulletin or newsletter.

How Can We Keep What We Buy?

A major problem for many churches is holding on to equipment that has been bought with church funds. It's always open season on VCRs, chairs, slide projectors, tables, and dishes "borrowed" by people who either return them to the wrong spot or fail to return them at all. The answer may be a firm policy against loans, deposits on borrowed items— or lots of padlocks!

Here are some tips:

1. Establish a firm policy on what can and cannot leave the facility.
2. Keep records of who borrows what items.
3. Track items that have been on loan longer than expected.
4. Don't hand out church keys liberally.
5. Assign responsible adults to make pre-lockup sweeps.

In a situation where two churches share a facility, the question of "Who's got what?" can be incendiary. If two dozen scissors can serve the second-grade Sunday schoolers, the third-grade club on Wednesday night, the children's choir on Friday night, and the Christian school's first grade every morning of the week, then a church can save the expense of having to buy another two dozen scissors for each group. If, however, one group fails to follow the system and return the scissors to the resource room, everyone is thrown into a panic. *Everybody has to cooperate to make the system work!*

How Do We Find What We Want?

The success of a resource room depends not just on whether an item is in stock, but also on how simple it is to locate. Follow these guidelines in keeping it simple for everyone involved:

1. Use see-through baskets or bins on open shelves.
2. Take the doors off cabinets.

3. Use puzzle racks, scissor racks, and other storage systems designed to prevent loss of specific items.
4. Provide small containers for assembling and carrying materials.
5. Keep posters or poster board in upright boxes or slotted storage areas.
6. Store paint brushes with bristles up.
7. Keep paint and glue tightly sealed.
8. Use sealed containers for dried pasta or other edibles used in crafts.
9. Provide thick, stubby crayons, blunt scissors, and nonpermanent markers for early childhood classes.
10. Keep paper that fades out of direct sunlight.
11. Keep crayons, filmstrips, and other transparencies out of hot spots.
12. Keep a reservation calendar for AV equipment and a reporting system for repairs that must be made.

Some churches ask the resource-room supervisor to make up supply boxes each week according to requests handed in by teachers. Then teachers can either stop by the resource room to pick up their supplies or have them delivered to their room. After class, all supplies have to be returned to the resource room. During the week, the supervisor should return the items to the shelves, restock class boxes, and preview coming needs.

The largest and biggest cost-saving job in the resource-room system may be the recycling of Sunday school curriculum. Flannel-graph figures and other visual aids can be reused, along with teachers' guides and unused student activity pages. Most curricula follow a three-year cycle and then begin the lessons again in a new three-year cycle. Even when a church changes curriculum publishers, many teaching resources can still be usable. For easy retrieval, store Bible story visuals in pocket files or in envelopes to be filed according to Bible chronology.

A teacher can receive training in maintaining the resource-room system through a simple initial tour of the room and an occasional refresher course in its use. The room is an ideal spot for files of activities, idea books, and a teacher-exchange bulletin board. If space allows, the room can include a large worktable, a few chairs, and a paper cutter. Other nice touches might be an extension phone, a coffeepot, and a steady supply of munchies. The room can also serve as a quiet haven for teachers to have a few moments for prayer and preparation before class. In this case, the room must be made strictly off-limits to all children. If the church has an extra photocopier with nowhere to go, this is the place it should be. In addition, if the room is large enough, it can be "action central" for all training and planning meetings.

Scheduling: Making the Most of Your Minutes

How often have you captured the interest of your learners just as the dismissal bell rang? How many times have handicraft projects gone home half-completed because there wasn't enough time? Take a critical look at your schedule and see where the problems lie:

- Make a list of the morning's activities and the time allotted to each. Remember that learning begins when the first child arrives.
- Review goals and evaluate each activity according to its contribution. The idea that "we've always done it that way" is not a useful criterion.
- Eliminate activities that do not contribute to teaching aims. Shorten the time devoted to activities with marginal value.
- Reshuffle the worthwhile activities to determine the best possible sequence. Look for natural transitions from one activity to the next.
- Decide which activities are better suited to a large group and which will be best for small groups of learners. Worship, for example, can be a large-group activity, while Bible story-time should be held for small groups with a small teacher-to-student ratio.
- Redistribute the minutes among the scheduled activi-

ties. The bulk of the time should be devoted to activities in which learners take an active, rather than a passive, role in learning. The average attention span of a third-grader is ten to fifteen minutes. Logically, then, the third-grade teaching session should be broken into segments of no more than fifteen minutes each.

The typical Sunday-school session of sixty minutes should begin with Bible-learning activities that lead learners into the lesson theme. Students should be able to choose from small-group activities, such as playing a verse-learning game, doing a theme-oriented art project, or participating in a role play based on the concept of that day's lesson. (The younger the learner, the more minutes should be spent on these activities.) Then, follow this introductory time by having Bible story-time told in small groups. The teacher-to-learner ratio should change according to the age group.

After the Bible story, learners can gather for group worship. This is a time for praise, songs, and prayer, all centered on the lesson theme. The remainder of the session can be spent on small-group activities that reinforce the concept.

Any radical change in programming should be a decision made by the teaching team with the Christian Education Specialist's input. People will not support decisions in which they have no voice. Discuss scheduling alternatives with every adult involved before making a break with tradition, and advise other groups that might be affected by changes in your area.

The main consideration, however, always must be the education of the children. If the schedule does not meet the physical, mental, emotional, social, and spiritual needs of the learners, then the schedule—not the children—must change. Greek mythology tells of a man named Procrustes who waylaid travelers and offered them the comfort of his bed. If the guest was too short, that person was stretched to fit. If the traveler was too tall, then his or her limbs were lopped off.

Let's not play Procrustes with our learners. We have neither the authority nor the ability to stretch their bodies or intellects beyond their God-ordained level of development. If our schedules, programs, or facilities do not meet the needs of children, it's time to reevaluate and reorganize.

Small-Church Education Programs: Is the Small Church a Big Problem?

A small church's Christian education ministry faces two major challenges: too few children, and too little space. Since the average congregation includes fewer than one hundred people, it can be assumed that most churches in America are afflicted by these problems.

Too Few Children

Numerical growth is never to be equated with spiritual growth. Nevertheless, such growth is a worthwhile goal. In a small church's children's ministry, a single classroom may hold children from preschool through junior age levels. An age difference of a few years is seen as negligible among adults, but it can make a world of difference in children's learning. A large number of children provides teachers with the opportunity to divide classes and tailor the curriculum to each age group's characteristics and needs.

With a small number of learners, the best organization for a Sunday school is to group grades as closely as possible. In the nursery, for example, teachers can separate active toddlers from vulnerable babies. School-age learners with some reading and writing skills should be separated from younger children so they can use their skills in Bible-learning activities. Divisions among older students may be dictated by differing rates of maturity or by gender.

Small churches are often pioneered by young families, and most of the children in the church can be close to the same age. In this case, children should be divided according to the number a room can accommodate and the required teacher-to-student ratio.

If there is a sufficient number of workers, they can effectively deal one-on-one with learners whose ages vary by too wide a span to be taught together. The problem with this system, however, is lack of fellowship for the children. They lose crucial contact with peers and opportunities to learn Bible truth in a context of social interaction.

With a small number of children ranging widely in age, a single-room children's church program can compound the problems of the Sunday school hour. As more children arrive, most workers are heading for the sanctuary. Children who attend the adult worship service understand little of what goes on there; they would be better off worshiping God on their own level in a children's church program. Organizers would be wise, however, to limit children's church to the largest compatible age group and the number that can be handled by workers. As outreach brings in more children and recruiters provide more workers, the program can be expanded to include additional age groups.

Too Little Space

A small congregation may have a large building, but in most cases small churches meet in buildings that include a sanctuary, a pastor's office, less than a half-dozen small rooms, a room for church dinners, and a tiny kitchen. In many small churches, *all* of these areas serve as Sunday school classrooms.

When room is scarce, the congregation must make the most of what it has. Churches should use discretion in making changes that don't include room for adaptability to long-range goals. Improvement may mean removing existing walls rather than constructing additional ones. Evaluate space devoted to unused furniture, teachers' desks, storage cupboards, and pianos. If an area is used for a children's opening assembly and then abandoned, drop the assembly from the program and use the space for Bible-learning activities throughout the Sunday school hour. Many children's activities do not require a table. If this is the case, try substituting carpet squares for chairs. For the nursery, consider double-decker cribs.

Since young children require more space to grow and learn than do teens and adults, their needs must become a priority. If the adult class meets in a large, attractive room, they should move to the back of the sanctuary and give their room to the five-year-olds crammed into the basement cubbyhole. Although it is best to keep everyone together at the church site, an adult class may need to meet at a nearby home, office, or coffee shop.

Too Little Planning

Some small churches will always be small. Limitations and influences can include local demographics, an obscure location, overcrowded facilities, or a ministry that does not meet the needs of the community. Some of these are beyond a church's control, while others are not. Most often, a church's ability to exceed limitations lies in prayer and planning.

To plan for growth in the children's ministry, teachers must keep good attendance records. With accurate records, planners can project growth in future years. Before rooms are filled to capacity, for example, extra space must be provided and classes should be divided. Crowded rooms frustrate teachers, concern parents, and drive children to undisciplined behavior. Before the need occurs, a church should recruit and train workers who will be ready when children arrive.

Many denominations can provide resource people to help churches in the process of expansion and growth. Other congregations may need a committee to seek out experts to help with long-range planning. Many major curriculum publishers provide consultants who can offer advice, and a local Bible college or seminary may have a faculty member who could evaluate a small church's program.

When a small church's congregation understands the necessity of the children's ministry, it will devote time, effort, and funding to its development. With that kind of commitment, that church will grow both in numbers and in servanthood.

Social Skills Development

Many children struggle with their transition from self-centeredness to an awareness of the group and how to contribute to its welfare. In just a short time, a preschooler's *"me!"* can become the growing child's "us."

Watch the free play in an early childhood room. The youngest children are the "lone rangers" who play either by themselves or beside one or two playmates who also are engaged in their own pursuits. At this age, competition is stiff for popular toys, snacks, and attention. Short periods of group activity have to be initiated and supervised by adults.

Observers of lower elementary classrooms, however, see learners who play and work in harmony. Having the teacher's attention is still important, but peer interaction and acceptance becomes necessary. This trend continues through the upper grades. (It sometimes develops into misbehavior designed to boost status with friends in spite of drawing disapproval from the teacher.)

As children's awareness of peers increases, they should become more accountable for the ways their behavior affects those around them. Observant teachers can help learners to develop appropriate social skills by applying correct discipline, providing encouragement, and programming opportunities for fellowship.

- Provide opportunities to practice taking turns. Early on, children develop strong feelings about fairness— but they are usually quicker to demand fairness than to dispense it. Not all children develop social skills at the same rate, and those who misbehave must be corrected firmly but lovingly.
- Praise cooperative effort. Point out incidents of harmonious and productive cooperation. Actions that receive praise will be repeated.
- Help students learn that individual abilities can benefit the group. Children need to appreciate not just their own talents but the talents of their classmates as well.
- Encourage independent thought. Guide and facilitate, but allow choices. Use guided conversation to indicate correct behavior.
- Provide fellowship opportunities. Giving children the chance to work and play with others in a Christian atmosphere is an important factor in their developing acceptable social behavior. Children involved in a club program may be able to develop leadership abilities. The democratic process and the acceptance of responsibility are important factors in learning to share.
- Develop social awareness through service. Find a service project appropriate for the age group of your learners. Every church has simple but time-consuming jobs that burden the staff. Senior adults are burdened with tasks they can no longer perform. Children can help— and might enjoy working—in many of these tasks.
- Do not encourage competition between boys and girls. Opposite-sex antagonism appears in the middle elementary years. Respect for peers should be taught to extend beyond a child's gender group. Competition is not as valuable as cooperation.

Teach children how to apply God's Word to their relationships with others. Show them by example how to demonstrate His love—and so guide them in following Christ's call to love our neighbor.

Special Needs

Approximately eight million American children can be classified in some way as disabled. This figure includes those who are physically, emotionally, or mentally impaired.[1] We see people with special needs all around us—the kind of people Jesus had abundant compassion for. How can teachers in children's ministry recognize special needs—and how can they help?

Physically Disabled Children

Physically disabled children can suffer from neurological impairments, such as cerebral palsy or epilepsy; orthopedic impairments, such as brittle bones or arthritis; or health impairments, such as heart disease or asthma.

- Don't assume that physical impairment indicates mental retardation.
- Ask parents for information on the child's strengths, weaknesses, and limitations.
- Reassure, affirm, and encourage such children, but do not overprotect them.
- Make your physically disabled learners part of the mainstream in your class, and adapt furnishings to serve their special needs.

Hearing-Impaired Children

Hearing impairments may afflict one or both ears in children. They can be the result of heredity, congenital problems, illnesses, or accidents.

- Soften the rejection frustration that can take place in your class by involving the child as much as possible in all activities.
- Allow hearing-impaired children to use every avenue of communication open to them—speech, hearing aids, gestures, signs, sign language, pantomime, lip-reading, writing, and pictures.
- Learn common phrases in sign language to use with the child.
- Remember to face a child who depends on lip-reading. Speak at a normal rate and volume. Do not shout, because it distorts the shape of your lips.

Visually Handicapped Children

Many children who are legally blind have partial vision. Blindness can be caused by prenatal influences; eye diseases, such as glaucoma, cataracts, or diabetes; poisonings; infectious diseases; and injuries.

- Capitalize on teaching visually handicapped children through other senses—smell, taste, touch, and hearing.
- Make explanations clear and concise. Remember the child's attention span.
- Make available to them Braille or recorded Scriptures and other resources.
- Use a variety of methods, including music, to teach God's Word. Encourage blind children to take part in many activities, and make it easy for them to do so.

Learning-Disabled Children

A child who has a learning disorder usually has difficulty using or understanding spoken or written words. These problems occur in listening, thinking, talking, reading, writing, spelling, and simple problem-solving. Many such children have been incorrectly labeled hyperactive or brain-injured.

- Because these children have problems in understanding sequences, give instructions one step at a time. Repeat directions several times.
- Engage all of the five senses in learning. Try to identify which ones the child depends on most.
- Emphasize and repeat the main idea of the lesson. Repetition is essential.
- Remove as many aural or visual distractions as possible from the classroom.
- Use concrete, literal terms and examples. Help children see and feel what is taking place.

Intellectually Impaired Children

A mentally retarded child is unable to function normally in society because of mental impairment or incomplete mental development. Mental retardation is the result of an injury or a disease of the brain that occurred before, during, or after birth. There are children with all ranges of mental retardation—from borderline to profound.

- Mentally retarded children learn in the same ways that non-impaired children learn—through the five senses, by active involvement, with great amounts of love and attention, and through consistent discipline.
- These children usually have short attention spans. Allow them to speak or share frequently.
- Most children who are mentally impaired can still hear and respond to the gospel. Share verses carefully and with feeling. Allow the child to ask questions, think, and respond as he or she is able. Remember that the child will respond to the Savior according to his or her degree of understanding.
- Use storytelling, role playing, puppets, music, Bible-

learning activities, and games to teach lessons. Avoid lecturing more than five minutes.

When ministering to children with special needs, remember to capitalize on their abilities. Tailor your expectations to their limitations—but challenge them to do their best. Include them in the mainstream of your class unless this jeopardizes any child's welfare. Refrain from showing pity for a child limited by a disability; pity in itself can be disabling. Instead, be patient and prayerful, and look for the potential in God's special children.

Storytelling: I Love to Tell the Story

In doing the work of the church, Christians today usually preach sermons and provide answers. Jesus, on the other hand, told stories and asked questions. To his listeners, the settings and situations he described were familiar. His probing questions led listeners to think about each lesson's application to their own lives.

Shepherds, fishing nets, and wells are unfamiliar to most children today, so the teller of Bible tales needs to work extra hard to bring stories to life and apply them to daily experience.

What are the ingredients of a good story? And how can a teacher implement them?

1. *The setting.* Use visual aids or descriptive phrases to set the scene and illustrate new words. Learners who hear the story of Peter's vision of the sheet filled with animals might miss the point of the story, focusing instead on the apostle's precarious perch. (Homes of that era usually had flat roofs that functioned as extra living space—but children today wouldn't know that.)

2. *The events.* Start at the beginning—flashbacks don't work well with children. If the story is a continuation of a previous lesson, check the learners' retention with review questions before starting. Make sure all events are told in chronological order. (A time line can be a good review tool.)

3. *The characters.* Establish the personality of the main characters. What are their motives? Some listening to the story of Laban's underhanded dealings with Jacob need to know which of Laban's daughters Jacob really wanted to marry. If dialogue is used in storytelling, give each character a different voice to help listeners distinguish between them.

Good storytellers transport their listeners to the story's locale and make the characters come to life. What are the techniques of a talented storyteller?

1. *Be expressive.* Use facial expressions and dramatic gestures. Vary the pitch, pace, and volume of your voice. And use props, costumes, or puppets if appropriate.

2. *Be simple.* Use vocabulary on the listeners' level of comprehension. Guide comments and questions to keep the lesson aim, and avoid distracting details. Make it possible for learners to relate the concept of the story to their own lives. Keep the story short enough to accommodate the age group's attention span. Include time, as well, for discussion after the telling of the story.

3. *Be active.* Choose active words. Use lots of body language. Provide visual as well as auditory stimulation.

4. *Be interactive.* Use subjective questions to help listeners identify characters' emotions. (A teacher can, however, occasionally ask a fact-based question to see if children have been listening.) Listeners can sometimes contribute sound effects or pantomime action. Be sure to keep eye contact with the children.

Obviously, few of these standards can be reached by teachers who read a Bible lesson straight from the curriculum. Teachers must be familiar enough with the story to *tell* it to their learners. An index card with the story's main points could be tucked into the teacher's Bible for ready reference.

If you want to ensure successful storytelling, then practice the story in front of a mirror, using props, pictures, or questions that will be used with the children. Tape your presentation and listen to the playback. Take advantage of any opportunity to watch talented storytellers work their trade.

Young listeners may not be able to distinguish between actual Bible stories and those that have been written to illustrate Bible truth in contemporary situations. When telling a Bible story, have a Bible open that can be closed and set aside during the application time.

Stories can be told sitting around a small table, huddled over a campfire, or sprawled on the floor. Make certain that listeners are comfortable before beginning, and that everyone has a clear line of vision to the storyteller. Younger listeners tend to creep up on the teller during the story, especially if there are interesting props or puppets, so set rules before beginning. An intimacy will be established between teller and listener by eye contact and interaction. To preserve this, keep the group small—and the smaller ones in the group up front.

If it is necessary to speak to a large group, position adults amid the listeners to maintain discipline and to model good listening skills. (Listeners are usually distracted when other teachers use the time to prepare for the next activity or clean up after the last one.)

If you are delayed by stragglers coming to the story area, plan to have each child bring something along. For the story of the lost sheep, give each learner a sheep sticker to apply to a poster in the story center. Praise by name those who come on time and are ready to listen. Use the same finger play, song, or signal each time you begin story time.

Stress in Children: Helping Youngsters Cope with It

Some parents program their child's week with meetings, lessons, teams, and clubs. This whirlwind of activities, they hope, will provide their child with new opportunities to learn and grow.

Some children thrive on this kind of approach, but others become overwhelmed and burned out by it. If parents, coaches, and teachers judge a child's worth by his or her achievement, activities meant to be beneficial can become demoralizing for the child who is deemed "just average."

Overprogramming is only one of many sources of childhood stress. One of the most common (and probably the most serious) is a broken home. Losing a parent through death or divorce can send a youngster careening back into baby talk and bed-wetting. Even in the most stable families, a move to a new neighborhood can produce emotional setbacks in a child. A newborn sibling or a new step-family calls for considerable adjustment in the emotional and social stability of a child. Life in a dangerous neighborhood or school produces anxiety, and stressed-out children can be indications of families in which one or both parents are addicts, alcoholics, or abusers.

1. How can a teacher know if stress is causing problems for a child?

- Talk informally with the child. Inquire, but do not interrogate. "What do you like to do for fun?" "What games do you play with your family?" Pay attention to gestures, expressions, and moods. Young children change moods rapidly, but a troubled child will be chronically sad or hostile.
- Be aware of conditions in the child's home life. Is he or she an only child? Is there a single parent at home? Do parents pressure the child to achieve? When parents ask, "Did Jack win the verse contest? His brother always won it when he was Jack's age"—teachers can understand that Jack is under pressure.
- Be alert to the child who does not participate in an activity for fear of failure. This youngster has a serious self-image problem. A youngster who is never satisfied with his or her own performance has been imprinted with the parents' drive for perfection. Watch for piles of crumpled paper and lots of erasing. Also watch for overaggressive or stubborn behavior. Children may vent their anxiety by being dominant, fighting, or using angry words.

2. How can a teacher help a pressured child?

- Affirm the child who has a low self-image. Assure that young person that everybody makes mistakes. Teachers who can acknowledge and laugh at their own mistakes will set a healthy example. Remind children that their heavenly Father loves them just the way they are.
- Reduce classroom tension. A good disciplinarian can maintain rules in a relaxed atmosphere. Don't set a rushed pace just to complete your lesson plan—be flexible. Set standards of behavior according to the age group.
- Ask open-ended questions that can be answered sub-

jectively. Avoid always asking the kind that has only one correct answer. Children who fear failure will respond negatively to questions or recitations that put them on the spot.

- Limit contests and competition. Children love to win, but they are devastated when they lose. Competition usually produces one winner and a whole lot of losers. To a child who already thinks of himself or herself as a loser, this could be serious.

- Never compare one child's performance to another's. This produces resentment and a feeling in the child that he or she is required to measure up to someone else's standards. Praise any effort by a child to improve his or her own performance.

- Know the signs of substance abuse. Anxiety and depression can be drug- or alcohol-induced, and elementary children are not exempt from addiction. Addictive substances may be easily available from a family member.

Psychologists tell us that three-fourths of the estimated eight million children and teens with emotional problems are not getting help.[1] About one child in four needs psychological counseling before sixth grade. Teachers must take time to be friends and counselors to their learners. When a serious problem arises, talk to church personnel who can provide assistance or refer families to the help they need.

Substance Abuse

Addiction to drugs and alcohol was once considered an adult problem. Then it became a youth problem. Now it is a problem among children in grade school. What can a children's ministry do to combat addiction?

The first step is *awareness*. Children are under peer pressure to experiment with smoking, drugs, and alcohol before junior high. Alcoholic beverages are promoted as soft drinks. Candy is made to resemble cigarettes. Drug pushers approach children on playgrounds with samples of their wares. Even children who have not yet experimented with drugs, alcohol, or cigarettes know of sources. It is unlikely that a child's source of an illegal substance is through the church. Nevertheless, we become part of the problem if we do not actively become a part of its solution.

The second step is *preventive education*. Children, parents, and workers need to know the dangers of addiction. Speakers, programs, and information are available through local and national agencies. In many churches, drug and alcohol education is part of the youth program, but statistics indicate that prevention needs to start much earlier. Parents and workers need to know the signs of addiction so users can be identified.

Step three—*identification*—is a difficult task. Few people want to believe that children are susceptible to addiction, and choose to deny the signs. Some indications are subtle; they require knowledge of a child's behavior over a period of time. Other indications are obvious, such as needle tracks or possession of drugs or paraphernalia. Parents who suspect drug abuse need to check not only for cigarette papers, razor blades, and hypodermics, but also for use of ordinary household solvents and aerosols, which can be abused as inhalants. If a youngster displays a lack of coordination, bizarre behavior, dizziness, watery eyes, itchy nose, drowsiness, or dry mouth, he or she may have a problem with some kind of substance abuse.

Children may change their appearances and their peer groups. They may drop out of sports or bring home falling grades. They may become isolated and develop an attitude of secrecy. All of these may be indications of a substance-abuse problem. A children's ministry worker would be alerted to these things if he or she has relationships with the children and their parents.

Who is likely to become an addict? Research shows that children of addicts are likely to become addicts themselves. Children who become addicted to one substance will probably "graduate" to more powerful drugs or alcohol. If children are exposed to advertising, movies, and television that promote smoking, drinking, or drugs as exciting and exotic lifestyles, they can be predisposed to turn to illegal substances as a way to become "grown up." Their young, developing bodies become more easily addicted than the body of a teen or adult who experiments with "gateway" substances that lead to more powerful ones.

When a child is suspected of being a user of an addictive substance, adults must move in quickly with intervention and treatment. A counselor who agrees to keep the child's "secret" becomes part of the child's problem. Instead, the church needs to contact parents immediately so that the child can be medically evaluated. In such a crisis, the church can offer panicked parents practical help and comfort by knowing what to do and whom to call. If parents are suspected of contributing to the child's problem, the church should treat the situation as child abuse and report it immediately to the local law enforcement or child protective agency. (The children's minister or other church administrators should know who is legally required to report child abuse and how state law protects those who report. The church should keep detailed records of the dates and nature of reports.) In addition to taking the correct legal action, the church may be able to work with official agencies to help the child and his or her family.

If suspicions are confirmed by lab results, the family will need help with professional rehabilitation. A children's education specialist should be familiar with helpful resources and keep a list of local hotlines posted near the phone. The local telephone directory provides neighborhood hotline numbers and the addresses of sources in the area for education and treatment.

Treatment centers and programs vary, and the addict and his or her family have little time or finances to waste. Before the need arises, church staff members should make inquiries and get recommendations for programs that are affordable, involve the family, and approach the situation from a biblical perspective. A nearby Bible college, seminary, or church with professional counselors should be able to provide information.

In a life-threatening emergency situation such as an overdose, church leaders should get help for the victim immediately. Look around for containers or other clues to identify the substance involved; this can help medical personnel to speed up treatment. Church workers should familiarize themselves with emergency-room admittance procedures before a crisis erupts.

What other action can the church take? Children's advocates can join organizations that work for addiction education, quality treatment, and the legislation of severe sentences for suppliers of illegal substances. Church workers can be trained to identify children with problems. Children's ministries can provide activities to keep potential victims from entering into compromising situations and destructive influences. Teachers can stress that each child is loved by the God who designed their bodies to be healthy and strong. The higher a child's self-esteem, the less likely he or she will be to develop addictive behavior in order to feel powerful, happy, and accepted.

Summer Ministries: Hot Tips

An education ministry loses valuable opportunities if it shuts down for the summer. "But," you may argue, "summertime is important for several things. Children need to play, families need to be together, and workers need a change. How are these needs to be reconciled to a ministry's purpose?"

The answer is that the church can offer programs that provide learning, recreation, family time, and spiritual refreshment.

Ground Rules

Before initiating a summer ministry, a children's worker should survey the needs of both the congregation and the community. What age group should be served? What schedule should be followed? Where should the program be held? A committee should begin evaluating needs at least one year ahead of time, then plan goals and design a program. Job descriptions must be developed, facilities prepared, budgets set, and publicity planned. Workers must be recruited and trained. Parachurch organizations can help many of these areas, including programs, resources, and even facilities.

Here are several possibilities for summer ministries to children:

Vacation Bible School

Vacation Bible School (VBS) is a church-wide program involving a few hours each day over a one- or two-week session. In this program, school-age learners can enjoy both study and recreation. Many curriculum publishers provide special programs for VBS. Some churches expand their ministry to include preschool through adult learners. VBS also can be a primary tool for neighborhood outreach.

Backyard Bible Clubs

Meetings of backyard Bible clubs are similar to VBS sessions, but they are held in neighborhood homes rather than at a central location. Children of similar ages are grouped together to meet in a home, where they are ministered to by teachers and a host. Club schedules can be highly flexible, but a curriculum should be unified.

Day Camp

Day camp is held in an outdoor setting and involves a full day of activities. The age group most attracted to this kind of program is lower elementary learners. Learners can enjoy a time of independence but can return home in the evening. Day camp also provides this age group with a transition from VBS to resident camping. Because day camps feature a day-long schedule and are less expensive than resident camps, they meet the needs of many working parents and can be used to reach unchurched families.

Family Camp

Family camp provides opportunities for parents and children to enjoy time together far away from the distractions of home. These programs generally include age-graded study times and evening child care for parents attending adult sessions. Afternoons at family camp are usually left free for family recreation.

Resident Camp

A typical resident summer camp provides school-age children with an all-day program of activities, three meals, and overnight accommodations for sessions of one week or longer. This type of program requires an established site, trained specialists, and considerable expense. During the camping period, counselors establish relationships with small groups of campers and teach them God's Word in the context of daily life. Churches can rent camp sites for summer camp or they can send children to camps run by denominational or parachurch groups.

Wilderness Experiences

This kind of program is relatively new and often involves backpacking, canoeing or rafting trips, rock climbing, and solo experiences. Often, private groups sponsor such programs and provide special leadership and equipment.

Because outdoor recreation includes additional risks of injury, churches need to know and meet health and safety standards and how to handle an emergency. Christian Camping International, a parachurch organization dedicated to excellence in camping programs, provides information on standards, procedures, and liability.

Outdoor recreation provides opportunities to program activities that are impossible to hold indoors. Planners should be sure to take advantage of these opportunities to use exploration of nature to teach new skills and make campers more aware of God's creativity.

Year-round school is gaining ground in many communities. A church's education ministry, therefore, must be resourceful and creative in its planning and scheduling. Lengthy summer vacations and the availability of college-age counselors may soon become a thing of the past. Act soon to evaluate needs, check out opportunities, and plan ahead.

Teacher Appreciation

Martyrdom is an enduring tradition among Christians. In the old days it was done by branding iron, thumbscrew, and the rack. Today, many church ministries martyr their own workers by lack of encouragement, no training, and nonexistent support.

Virtually every "Teacher Appreciation" dinner features a round of applause for a faithful teacher who has survived decades of service. The elderly soldier wears service stripes from shoulder to wrist, ambles up to the head table, receives a heartfelt reward, and heads back to the classroom for another year of chalk dust. It can be an inspiring and encouraging moment, but, through the years, how many colleagues did that faithful servant have to watch go down in the flames of burnout and neglect? For every success story, there are volumes of failures. What makes a worker quit?

1. Low Status of the Children's Ministry

One problem that many workers face is the lack of importance that a congregation attaches to the children's ministry. Even parents are inclined to view children's programs as mere babysitting; the adult classes are "where the action is" in Christian education. If the status of the children's ministry was raised in the eyes of administrators and members, it would be easier to attract and retain qualified workers.

Regular promotion of the children's ministry should take place in the pulpit. The Christian Education Specialist is usually busy elsewhere during adult worship services, so the preaching pastor must shoulder the responsibility for promoting the children's ministry. Awareness can also be raised through bulletin-board displays of students' and teachers' photos, slide or tape presentations, and video productions. Testimonies from teachers and students can be included in adult worship services, along with contributions from children's choirs and drama or choral-reading groups. In addition, teachers should be recognized before the congregation for their contributions to the overall ministry of the church. The pastor can encourage parents to express gratitude to teachers.

2. Inadequate Recruitment and Training Procedures

Other reasons for the low status of children's workers are, first, the typical recruitment procedure ("It's just for to-day—you're my last hope!") and, second, the typical training program ("It's just babysitting—anybody can do it!"). Ministry leaders need to know that a worker will perform at the same level of professionalism with which he or she was recruited. Workers need to know they are selected for a task because they have the special abilities needed to perform it.

Many workers of great potential, however, burn out quickly because they are given tasks for which they are neither suited nor prepared. Pre-service and in-service training must be provided. Training tells a recruit that his or her position requires a skilled worker. Yearly reviews tell that worker that he or she is accountable for performance of an important ministry. And continuing support and encouragement tell the worker he or she is appreciated.

Recognition

The annual "Teacher Appreciation" dinner is certainly a nice touch—but it is not enough. A church that truly appreciates its children's workers finds ways to recognize their contributions and support their efforts throughout the year:

- Training should be sponsored by the church at convenient times, complete with a meal and free child care. (That's prime time, prime rib, and prime rate!)
- "Teacher Appreciation" dinners must not be potluck meals. Honorees shouldn't be expected to bring their own casseroles.
- Awards should be tangible. Certificates, pins, and plaques are nice, but so are gift coupons for, say, a dinner at a local restaurant.
- Planning-and-training meetings should be convenient, short, and worthwhile.
- Length of service should be agreed upon at the point of recruitment. Nobody likes to feel chained to a job for life.
- Workers should be observed and evaluated regularly to demonstrate that the church takes their positions seriously.
- Curriculum materials and other resources must be provided by the church. Administrators who attest to the importance of the children's ministry must put their money where their mouths are.
- "Teacher of the Year" awards honor only one worker while neglecting the rest. A better approach is to recognize the unique contribution made by each worker.
- Recognize the valuable experience of a veteran worker by making him or her a model whom novices can observe in action.
- Include workers in decision-making.
- Use the special talents of workers as leaders in training events.

Churches that want to attract and retain qualified workers do well to offer their recruits and mainstays a helping hand, a word of encouragement, and a pat on the back. Even workers who glean tremendous satisfaction from serving children can resent being taken advantage of by a ministry that puts them in a position and forgets about them until they quit. No person should take on a ministry because of the recognition and status it will bestow; but everyone needs a little appreciation now and then.

Teacher Development

A common complaint among workers in the children's ministry is that they have few opportunities to participate in adult corporate worship or Sunday school classes. This complaint is absolutely valid. Workers serving in children's programs that operate simultaneously to those designed for adults must often choose between feeding or being fed.

Crowded churches usually run back-to-back Sunday school classes and worship services. Often these will offer adult classes at both times to solve overcrowding problems, but children's workers still face the challenge of balancing their need for instruction, fellowship, and worship. Those who commit their time and energy to developing spiritual maturity in others should not have to do so at the expense of their own growth.

Here's how a church can meet the needs of its workers:

- *Provide workers with sabbaticals for study and growth.* Teachers, especially those who work with young children, need to be consistent in their attendance. Only through regular exposure to each other can teachers and their learners build relationships. Anyone who has worked in an early-childhood division knows that young children depend on seeing familiar faces each week. A weekly or monthly rotation of workers does not meet such learners' needs.

An ideal length of commitment is a full year (six months may be adequate for a new recruit). Many churches will settle for a quarterly rotation of workers, but a time commitment of less than a quarter is virtually no commitment at all.

By having a program of continuous recruitment and training, ministry leaders can reach into a pool of qualified workers for relief teams. As one team of teachers goes "off duty" to return to adult Sunday school class or worship, relief workers can cover their next tour of a quarter, semester, or year. Recruiters will find it easier to draft workers if they can offer a specific length of service, guaranteed training, and a well-deserved sabbatical.

- *Provide workers with notes or tapes of material they miss when absent from adult classes or worship.* Many housebound adults participate in church through correspondence, books, tapes, and TV or radio broadcasts. Likewise, most churches today can use video cameras and audiocassette duplicating equipment to allow workers to catch up on what they missed.
- *Have a central committee oversee worker recruitment so that qualified workers will not be drawn and quartered by a multitude of ministries.* Willing and able workers are often exploited by recruiters who are unaware of their multiple commitments. A children's worker who serves in Sunday school, children's church, club, and nursery is going to experience an unavoidable personal devotional drought.
- *Provide alternative opportunities for spiritual growth.* Many teacher guides include a devotional for each lesson that is intended for the worker's personal use. These devotionals can form the basis for a time of personal study at department training-and-planning meetings.

Retreats specially designed for workers can be held twice a year, with room, board, and child care paid for by the church. In this way, workers can return to their ministries refreshed and refueled by a time of study, worship, and mutual encouragement.

Neighborhood "growth groups" intended for study and fellowship can allow workers to meet with other adults at a flexible time. On Sunday morning or club night, most adults collect their families and clear out long before workers have finished picking staples out of the carpet. Alternative get-togethers provide workers with a chance to socialize with other adults.

Leaders and administrators must remember that workers who minister to children need ministry, too. Workers must be developed, not merely used. Like children, adults need to develop in every area of their lives—socially, intellectually, physically, emotionally, and spiritually. Part of the church's ministry to children is ministry to the workers who teach them.

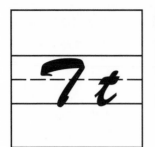

Teacher-Learner Relationships

The interpersonal relationship between a student and his or her teacher makes a deep and lasting impression. The teacher establishes in the learner's mind a standard on which the youngster consciously or unconsciously will model his or her own attitudes and actions. The teacher who builds a loving, consistent relationship with a student opens a channel through which a student may develop a lifestyle based on biblical truth and consistent obedience.

Here are some ways teachers can engender such a relationship:

- A child's favorite word is his own name. Teachers should learn the names of all students, not just the misbehaving ones, and use each one at least once during each class session.
- Teachers should express an interest in each child's activities and experiences. Children are impressed with a teacher who cheers at their soccer games, applauds at their recitals, and remembers their birthdays with a card or a call.
- Everyone likes to know when he or she has been missed. Teachers should acknowledge absences with a note or a call to the child's home. Erratic attendance often can indicate trouble in the home.

- Children need personal attention. Teachers must not allow the teacher-learner ratio to extend beyond recommended age-group limitations or their ability to interact with each child.
- Many first-time adult visitors to a church judge a congregation by the welcome they receive. Children need to be welcomed by name each time they come through the classroom door. At dismissal time, teachers should encourage each child to come back next week. Remember, the first impression you make on a child's parents may be at the classroom door—so make an effort to be pleasant and unhurried.
- Children work hard at building their self-image, and teachers who praise and encourage their learners help them realize they not only are loved but are truly lovable. This is especially significant, although more difficult, in the case of those who chronically misbehave.

Parent-Teacher Relationships

Sadly, parents have to be suspicious of adults who express an interest in their children. Part of a developing friendship between teacher and student has to be the growth of trust between the teacher and parents. Teachers can help develop this relationship in several ways:

- Home visits provide teachers with a chance to see children in their natural environment. Teachers use these opportunities to observe the parent-child relationship and to acquaint parents with teaching materials and methods.
- Teachers can invite learners' families to their homes so a child's parents can find out something about the teacher and his or her family.
- Parents can be invited to observe class. Some may have no idea what goes on in Sunday school. A few may even decide to offer their help.

- Learners' families should receive invitations to special events and information about other ministries of the church. Many unchurched parents have been reached through ministries to their children.

Teaching Aims

Imagine an archery competition: Each archer has brought his or her finest bow and arrows and has checked and rechecked the equipment to ensure optimum performance in the contest. Every possible precaution has been taken; months, even years, have gone into preparation for this moment. Shafts are checked, wrist guards are strapped into place, quivers are positioned. Yet, what if now—after all these preparations have been made—these archers look up to gauge the distance to the bull's-eye, and find that no one has set up a target?

Sound ridiculous? It happens every week in Sunday schools! The teacher arrives at church, laden with craft materials, flannel-graph figures, activity papers, songbooks, puppets, filmstrips, games, and records. He or she scurries to the classroom and assembles the students for that morning's program. With the learners finally in place, the teacher begins the lesson. Yet, what if now—after all such preparations —the teacher can't focus on what the students are to learn?

An archer is unlikely to hit a bull's-eye if he or she can't see a target, and a teacher is unlikely to impart learning if there is no learning aim.

How are teaching aims to be determined? Most reputable curricula feature learning aims that experts have found to be appropriate to the various age groups. Sometimes a situation

331

is so unique that a teacher must seek out a special unit on a particular theme, or—in extremely unusual cases—develop his or her own curriculum. Whichever the case, each teacher must understand the typical characteristics and special needs of his or her learners to be able to set goals that will be reachable, measurable, and meaningful.

Picture a class of fifth-graders who tease each other unmercifully. One child comes to church wearing the "wrong" clothes or a brand-new pair of eyeglasses, and the class erupts in ridicule. The teacher realizes this is typical behavior for the age group—but she hopes to make the class more amicable by teaching a unit on kindness and respect.

Here are the steps she writes for herself:

- Set learning aims as to what students should know, how they should feel, and what they should do when they have internalized the lesson content and understand how to apply it.
- Assemble resources of lesson material and activities on the theme. Select teaching methods.
- Evaluate the impact of the unit based on observations of the learners' behavioral change.

Following this procedure, the teacher sought the advice of the Christian Education Specialist at the church; planned a series of lessons incorporating Scripture, life-application lessons, and meaningful activities; and determined ways to measure the unit's impact on the class. Using "teaching moments" in interactions with the learners, she encouraged positive behavior and reinforced the lesson aims. After six weeks she saw enough instances of changed behavior to indicate the unit had been effective.

Why were the aims separated into "knowing, feeling, and taking action"? Learning that remains on an intellectual level alone is soon forgotten. If students grasp a concept, they should be able to articulate it in their own words. After that, they may develop an attitude about the concept. If they can see motivation for applying the concept in their own lives, it may change their behavior. Once students have acted on the new concept, it is theirs to keep.

Like the archer, a teacher has a much better chance of hitting what he or she aims at if there is a clear view of the target. With prayer, planning, and preparation, teachers can be "on target" with their teaching.

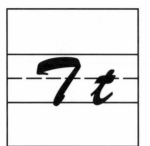

Theology for Children

Much of the stained-glass language of doctrine is incomprehensible to literal-minded youngsters. For example, the child who agrees God is invisible would say this is because He is far away in heaven, not because He is a spiritual being. A child who hears that the Holy Spirit appeared as a dove naturally thinks the Spirit *is* a bird. A young child encouraged to look forward to the return of Jesus will have a hard time keeping up the anticipation, because youngsters live only in the here and now.

How can teachers help children develop a correct theological foundation on which to build their learning in the years to come? Here are some guidelines to follow:

- Help children discover God's power through explorations in nature. Design activities that provide hands-on experiences. Guide conversations toward spontaneous worship. Engage all five senses. "Feel the soft fur on the kitten. God gave the kitten fur to keep it warm." "See how God made your fingers just right to hold your crayons? Let's thank God for our fingers." (Correct the misconception that God or some of His power is *in* any of His creations.)
- Reassure children of God's love. Children need security. Remind them of the dependability of the seasonal

cycle that God created and maintains each year. "God sent rain today to get the plants ready to grow up out of the ground. We'll see some beautiful flowers when He makes the weather warmer."

• Help children understand that when bad things happen, it is not because God is mean but because people often are. This "meanness" in people is one reason we need God's love and forgiveness. If people who do bad things appear to go unpunished, it is because God is in charge of punishments and rewards and will give them out when He is ready.

• To children, parents and teachers represent omnipotence. When adults model obedience to God's laws, children can see that God holds ultimate authority. Youngsters' prayers can include requests but never orders or bargains. Even young children can understand that nobody tells God what to do.

• In a child's understanding, the church is a building. By making use of alternative times and places of worship, teachers can help learners see that it is good, but not necessary, to be in a special building to worship and pray. Older learners can more easily be shown that "church" can mean either a building or the worldwide community of believers.

• Help children respond to God's love. Remember that a child must have an understanding of morality before he or she can acknowledge the need for forgiveness. Teachers can instill ideas of justice by being fair and consistent disciplinarians. For a child who comes from a home where discipline is lax, the consequences of misbehavior may be a new experience. For children who have never received correction for disobedience, the necessity of Christ's sacrifice may be difficult to understand. Teachers should show love for their students when youngsters must be corrected. Never give children the impression they are lovable only if they are obedient.

• Realize that a child's concept of God is largely formed

by his or her own father and other male authority figures in the household. A young child bends and shapes an abstract concept until it resembles a familiar, concrete example. Be aware that the term "heavenly Father" may have a negative meaning for children from households where the father is absent or abusive.

- Young children always have questions about God. "How tall is He?" "If we all pray at the same time, which one of us will God hear?" "Does He have a beard?" God's omnipotence may seem scary or spooky. The death or disappearance of a trusted adult may cause a child to doubt God's eternal nature.

- Go to the Bible for answers to children's questions about God: "Even from everlasting to everlasting, You are God" (Ps. 90:2). "The Father of lights, with whom there is no variation or shadow of turning" (James 1:17). "God, who made the world and everything in it, since He is Lord of heaven and earth, does not dwell in temples made with hands" (Acts 17:24).

- Encourage students' efforts at prayer. Keep track of answers to prayer so youngsters will see that God responds, even if in the negative. When children are ready to respond to God's offer of salvation, they should already be on a conversational basis with Him.

- Help children to understand God's promises about the future. Young learners are not future-oriented, which makes it hard for them to think about future events. Their chronological sense is not yet developed, as any parent can attest who has heard the incessant backseat whine, "Are we there yet?"

- Assure learners the Bible is special, personal, and true. Use an easy-to-understand version for classwork and memorization. Teach children the difference between actual Bible stories and application stories that teach Bible concepts.

- Baptism is a difficult concept for young children. They will understand it only in its most literal meaning. Youngsters must be old enough to see that the act is

336

symbolic of an inner change and evidenced by changed behavior. Some children may fear that becoming "a new creation" means becoming a stranger.

- Children can understand the application of spiritual gifts. Visits from workers in the church who are teachers, helpers, and leaders can illustrate the abilities God gives His people and how they are to be used.

Spiritual maturity develops at an unpredictable rate in children. Some will be ready to receive Christ as their Savior very early on, while others will continue to wrestle with more basic concepts. A teacher of young children has the responsibility of shaping attitudes and setting down a foundation for the basics. Another teacher may be the one to lead a young believer into the family of God—by building on that earlier foundation.

Toys, Blocks, and Puzzles

Toys are as important to learning as pencils and paper. A young child learns through play, and toys are the tools of play. They are power tools—and the power behind a toy is the imagination of a child. A young child can transform a cardboard tube into a machine gun, a telescope, a voice amplifier, a snake, and a spaceship—all in one period of play.

The most successful toys are those that provide room for imaginative play and developing skills. Each Christmas holiday brings tales of children who played for five minutes with a flashy, battery-operated toy they pleaded for, and then abandoned it only to gambol for hours in the large cardboard box in which the toy was delivered. The question for teachers is which toys stimulate children's imaginations.

Blocks

A staple of childhood, blocks provide opportunities for both isolated and group play. They come in various shapes and composition for different ages and purposes, and can be enhanced with the use of toy cars or small figures of people or animals. Toddlers enjoy brightly colored, soft blocks that can be gripped by small hands but not popped into small mouths. These young ones soon graduate to using large, cardboard blocks they love to stack and knock down. Four-

and five-year-olds are ready for wooden blocks in a variety of shapes that encourage creative arrangements. A few words of guidance from the teacher can direct learning toward the day's teaching aim.

"Sara, God gave you strong arms so you could lift up those blocks. We can say 'thank you' to God for strong arms."

"Brian, our Bible says we should be kind. Can you see a way to be kind and help Robbie put away the blocks on the block shelf?"

"Jane, our story today is about a shepherd who protected his sheep. Can you build a safe place for the shepherd to keep his sheep at night? Here are some sheep and a shepherd to include."

Puzzles

Puzzles build eye-to-hand coordination and are available to learners of every age level. The best puzzles for institutional use are those crafted of wood. They come in nature, Bible-story, and home-living themes to suit most lesson aims. Teachers should invest in a puzzle rack for storage and code the backs of individual puzzle pieces to expedite cleanup in hurried moments. By placing the pieces of a puzzle to the child's left, teachers can encourage the development of left-to-right visual skills that are used in reading.

"Charlie, here is a puzzle of an animal. Our story today is about how God created animals."

"Beth and Joanie, you can both work on this puzzle if you take turns placing the pieces."

"You did a good job on that puzzle, Tony. You worked until you got all the pieces in place."

Toys

Like many items in the home-living center, some toys are "real life" items drafted into use: pots, pans, empty cartons. Others can be recyclable items that children easily transform into playthings: cardboard tubes, plastic containers, bottles.

Commercially produced toys that are labeled "educational" are worth their investment if they are safe, durable, well-designed, and provide opportunities for imaginative play.

There are several guidelines for selecting toys that ensure usability and safety:

1. Be sure the toy will be used by children of an age for whom it was designed. Small pieces may not pose a danger to older children, but young children can choke on them. Special care should be observed in small churches where nurseries serve a wide span of ages.
2. Check toys for sharp edges, toxic paint, moving parts, and liquid or other enclosures that could fall out of a torn or broken toy. Check stuffed toys for plastic eyes and noses that could be torn off and swallowed.
3. Dolls and dress-up clothes should represent diverse cultures.
4. For indoor use, buy only indoor toys.
5. Select a classic, timeless toy, rather than one promoting a TV or movie character whose popularity may not outlive the toy.
6. For heavy-duty toys, buy from institutional suppliers.
7. Toys for use with a nature center should promote discovery learning.
8. Include toys that can be used by disabled children.
9. Provide low shelves so learners can select and put back toys.
10. Choose toys that promote cooperation over aggression.

Treat toys as you would power tools. Keep them in good working condition, replace them when necessary, use safety precautions, store them properly when not using them, buy only quality items, buy for multiple use whenever possible, and be sure to read the directions.

Toys Children Choose: The Top Ten for Classroom Use

Books, music, and art activities are favorites among children of all ages, but the methods and materials used in each must be developmentally appropriate.

Nursery:
- rattles
- crib mobiles/gyms
- unbreakable mirrors
- music boxes
- soft blocks
- teething rings/beads
- roly-poly dolls
- grip balls
- squeeze toys
- busy boxes

Toddler:
- small slide
- nesting/stacking toys
- fill & dump toys
- small cars/trucks
- dolls/stuffed toys
- push/pull/ride-on toys
- home-living toys
- sorting sets
- balls
- cardboard blocks

Preschool:
- pedal trikes
- musical instruments
- small figures/cars
- home-living toys
- dress-up clothes
- small gym
- wooden blocks
- lace/button/zip toys
- water-sand table with toys
- puzzles

First and second grade:
- home-living toys
- building sets
- magnets
- board games
- puppets
- puzzles
- tools
- magnifying glasses
- mini-communities
- printing sets

Third and fourth, fifth and sixth grade
- board games
- binoculars
- card games
- typewriter

crafts/art projects	globe
tape recorder	simple models to assemble
compass	puzzles

Training: The Continuous Process

Few teachers can launch into telling a famous Bible story without being torpedoed by a student who raises a hand and says that he or she heard the same story last year. How should a teacher respond?

"I'm going to tell some different parts of the story."

"It's time to hear it again."

"Do you want me to send for your parents?"

If not spoken aloud, these thoughts at least cross the minds of most children's teachers from time to time. Now let's change the characters in this scene. The individual now standing at the front of the room is the person in charge of the church's education ministry, and she has just asked a group of teachers to attend a training event. One teacher once attended a training event, and now he believes he's heard it all before. How should a supervisor respond to the teacher's objection?

"You'll hear something new."

Training events introduce new materials, methods, and programs. Society is changing rapidly, and curriculum publishers are responding with materials tailored to the specific needs of today's children. It is certainly true that "the word of our God stands forever" (Isa. 40:8), but stories used to illustrate the life application of Scripture need to change along with the lives of the learners. Dick, Jane, and Sally don't visit Grandma and Grandpa's farm anymore.

Technological innovations have benefited education, and Christian educators should not ignore the enormous potential of computers, audiovisual equipment, and other resources. An education ministry needs to remain open to using new resources, albeit through careful evaluation.

New research in child development offers insights to behavior problems, learning disabilities, and dysfunctional families. Knowing the typical characteristics and needs of an age group is vital for any teacher who wishes to build a relationship with children and know them as individuals.

Many large training events, such as conferences or seminars, offer specialized workshops in areas such as storytelling, organization, or puppetry. Novice teachers can benefit from generalized training at these sessions, and a teacher who needs information for a particular ministry can learn from a specialist at an in-depth session.

Not all training happens at large-scale conventions and conferences. Many churches offer periodic training as part of monthly planning-and-training meetings. Some churches, especially smaller ones, join neighboring churches to sponsor citywide or regional events.

"Listen to it again."

Many faithful teachers attend the same training event year after year—taking notes, asking questions, and examining the potential of what they hear in light of their experiences. Their insights and anecdotes can give credibility to principles, especially to novices. The experienced teacher knows instinctively what can be used in his or her own class and finds productive ways to utilize that learning.

Sometimes an experienced teacher wishes to develop his or her gifts in a particular area of ministry. In a team-teaching situation, for instance, a teacher who excels at storytelling may want extra training in that field, while other teachers may improve their skills in leading music, games, or art activities. A teacher who works alone must master every skill and needs training to shore up areas of weakness.

"You'll answer to a higher authority!"

James said in his epistle, "Let not many of you become teachers, knowing that we shall receive a stricter judgment" (James 3:1). To be sure, one day we will account for what God has invested in us and entrusted to us as teachers. The gift of teaching is like the money entrusted to a servant by the master who went on a long journey. The individual who wants to use that gift for God's glory will seek training to be able to use it wisely and productively, but the person who does not improve that skill or renew his or her motivation through continuous training is like the slave who would not invest the master's money.

The high calling of teaching is both a gift and a responsibility, and when an opportunity to attend a training event is provided, the wise teacher will dig up the talent, dust it off, and polish it up.

Guidelines for the trainer:

- Training must be continuous, both pre-service and in-service.
- Training must be made available at convenient times.
- Training must meet specific needs.
- Training must be biblically and educationally sound.

Guidelines for the teacher:

- Seek out training.
- Evaluate new techniques and materials in light of your learners' needs.
- Make changes only in cooperation with those in charge of your ministry.
- At a large-scale event, use discernment in selecting workshops.
- Learn by observing model teachers.

Guidelines for the church:

- Sponsor teachers who attend training events.
- Recruit substitutes to allow teachers time to observe models.
- Provide training materials.
- Seek out education specialists who can lead workshops.
- Be sensitive to the needs of both teachers and students.
- Encourage training as part of the teacher's commitment to ministry.

Transitions

An important but often neglected strategy in lesson planning is the transition of bodies and minds from one place or segment to another. To a novice teacher, this may seem a simple matter of moving learners through a series of activities and thought processes, but experienced workers know skills are needed to do this effectively:

- *To move from a noisy, active part of the lesson to a more subdued mood, use music.* Begin with active songs that have lively rhythms and motions, then progress to quieter melodies until the desired atmosphere has been created.
- *To change activities, signal learners with a specific song, a puppet, or a musical instrument.* (In some African cultures, storytellers attract listeners by beating a drum and beginning a ritual response chant.) If learners grow accustomed to the constant drone of their teacher's voice, it may become ineffective as a signaling device. In using signals, avoid harsh buzzers or bells that disrupt the atmosphere.
- *To move learners from one place in the classroom to another, provide incentive.* Call the names of those who are ready and in place rather than calling those who are slow in cooperating. Hide an object in the

room and direct learners to quietly go to their seats as soon as they spot its hiding place. Reinforce learning by asking children who are wearing specific colors or who have certain letters in their name to move when they are directed.

Staggering the dismissal of small groups can ease traffic congestion caused by the movements of a large assembly. Do not award prizes of "first out the door" to the most cooperative children; that can teach them that early dismissal from Sunday school is a coveted prize.

- *To move learners' thinking toward the lesson aim, use guided conversation that includes carefully planned questions.* "We learned last week that Joseph's brothers sold him into slavery. How would you feel toward the brothers if you were Joseph? Can you think of a time you wanted revenge for something that had been done to you? In today's lesson, Joseph has an opportunity to get revenge. Can you predict what he will do? What do we already know about Joseph's character?"
- *To direct learners toward the lesson, use "approach activities" coupled with guided conversation.* When children come to Sunday school or club, they do not arrive as "blank slates." They arrive filled with thoughts of what has already happened that day and anticipating what will happen after class is dismissed. You can rest assured they are not focused on the lesson theme!

Approach activities must begin as soon as the first learner arrives. This system makes the most of lesson minutes, provides incentives for punctuality, and keeps early arrivals from misbehaving. Approach activities are designed to turn attention toward the theme through drama, art, research, writing, puzzles, games, and all kinds of active participation. For example, before listening to the story of the lost sheep, young learners could:

1. Build a sheepfold with blocks and toy animals.
2. Hunt for something that has been hidden from view.
3. Care for small animals in the nature center.
4. Learn about the work of a shepherd from picture books in the book center.

- *To bridge the time gap between the end of Sunday school and the beginning of children's worship, provide supervised opportunities for snacks, trips to the bathroom, and active movement.* Workers familiar with the theme of the morning can reinforce it in their interactions with children during these minutes. Children who are left unsupervised between activities can misbehave, get into unsafe areas or situations, or perhaps fall victim to older children or criminal adults.
- *When the session is over, focus learners on individual or small-group tasks.* This will help circumvent trouble during those harrowing moments between the arrivals of the first parents to pick up their child and the last ones to retrieve their youngster. If the entire group is assembled for a story, song, or game, an early departure can be a cause of anxiety for some very young children. Before parents arrive, break up any large-group activity, and redirect learners to small-group activities that reinforce the lesson.
- *In moving from one part of the facility to another, provide close supervision for very young children.* Young ones can be directed to hold hands with a partner as they walk and look for landmarks to follow. Some teachers have success in using a long rope with evenly spaced knots for each child to hold as the group walks along. To avoid stampedes, direct young learners to pretend they are slow-moving animals.
- *To provide transition from last week's theme, a review should feature an obvious and logical tie-in with this week's lesson.* Bring back last week's teaching pictures as visual reminders. Learners old enough to remember the sequence and importance of Bible

events can be helped to see history as the fulfillment of God's promises.

- *Ease learners' transition from one age level to the next by offering youngsters a preview of things to come.* Two weeks before promotion Sunday, invite the learners' new teacher to come to class for a few minutes. During the week prior to promotion, take the learners on a short visit to the room they will be moving to. In a large church, these visits may take some engineering—but they will pay huge dividends in lowered anxiety levels. The new teacher should also send notes of welcome or make a home visit. Very young learners feel more secure when they are on their own turf during these initial encounters.

- *In early childhood and lower elementary classrooms, dismissal time should be one of order and not chaos.* This time can turn into a hectic session of identifying whose sweater, art project, boots, or take-home paper belongs to whom. Remember that arrivals and dismissals are usually the only exposure a parent has to his or her child's learning environment. So it is important that the adult's impression is not one of chaos.

To avoid this, use coat hooks that can be labeled with each child's name or photograph. Take-home materials can be stored in individual cubbyholes created by shoe boxes, baskets, or cut-out milk jugs. Some churches drape pillow-case-shaped bags over the back of each child's chair to hold his or her belongings. Such individual storage comes in handy for teachers when a child brings something to church that should have been left at home. Dropped inside a child's personal storage box, the item can remain out of sight and out of the danger of being taken or broken by another child.

Labels are a good idea for objects—but they are not a good idea for children. Children who wear name tags out of the classroom and into an unsupervised situation can be victimized by criminal adults who can use the child's name to gain the young one's trust. If young learners wear name tags in class, a teacher should hang them beside the door as a reminder of who has left the room on an errand or a bathroom trip. The teacher then can retrieve all tags at dismissal time.

Visitors

Some visitors are out-of-towners who can be counted on to turn up once or twice each year when they visit their relatives. Most visitors to church are local individuals or families looking for a new church home. If they are made to feel welcome and are favorably impressed with the staff and facilities, they may come back. If their first impression is negative, they won't likely give the church a second chance. How can a church keep visitors coming back?

First, approach your facilities as if you were a first-time visitor. Is parking set aside for visitors? Is it easy to find the building and the room for your Sunday school class? Are the hours for Sunday school and worship posted? Is someone there assigned to greet you and answer your questions? If you find yourself lost and ignored, imagine your frustration being multiplied by having to find the correct nursery or classroom for each of your children.

Some steps to follow in making visitors feel welcome:

- Mark premium parking spaces for visitors' use only. (Don't forget spaces for senior adults and the handicapped.)
- Identify buildings on outside walls facing the parking lot or main entrance ("Worship Center," "Children," "Youth," etc.).

- Post signs at entrances and classroom doors ("First Grade," "Nursery," etc.).
- Provide maps and schedules in display racks at main entrances.
- Assign friendly "greeters" to welcome and direct visitors.

Next, assuming you have found the correct building and classroom, are your children welcomed and encouraged to join their classmates in appealing activities? Does their teacher address you and ask you to provide some registration information? What is your first impression of your child's teacher and room?

Here are some tips for helping visitors feel comfortable about your ministry to children:

- Train teachers to welcome new learners in a way that is appropriate to their age level. Very young children like to ease their way into a new situation with unfamiliar adults. Older, less anxious children may be ready to dive right into an activity.
- Pinning a name tag on a visitor aids the teacher and the regular attenders, and seeing name tags on teachers and regular attenders aids the visitor. Name-learning games also are a good activity for visitor days.
- Assign one worker, such as a department leader or secretary, to greet visitors and record registration information.
- Begin each class with an approach activity that starts with the arrival of the first learner.
- Encourage teachers to keep their classrooms attractive and clean. The condition of the nursery is of primary importance. Don't overcrowd.
- Require teachers to be prepared and on time. A rushed teacher makes a poor impression on parents and children alike.
- Provide forms on which to record a visitor's name, address, and birth date. Registration cards also should in-

clude parents' names and the name of the church that the family currently attends, if any. Nursery registration forms should include more details regarding habits, health concerns, etc.

Now, on the way home from church, debrief your children. Did they have fun? Yeah. Did they meet some new friends? Yeah. Did they learn something new? Yeah.

On Tuesday, you receive a personal letter from the church with a packet of information on classes, fellowship groups, and special events. On Thursday you receive a phone call from someone in your adult Sunday school class, and the children receive notes from their teachers encouraging their return.

Here are some further steps on how to help visiting families come back:

- Have detailed policies for follow-up so visitors do not fall through the cracks in the attendance-record system. Make sure each family receives at least two contacts soon after their visit.
- Encourage teachers to use visitors' names often.
- Post photos of visitors on bulletin boards.
- Write young visitors' names on coat hooks, boxes for take-home papers, and other items bearing the names of their classmates.
- Encourage visitors to participate in other ministries for their age group.
- After a third or fourth visit, add the visitor information to the mailing list so the family will receive newsletters and other announcements.

Most churches like to provide classes designed for new members, offering the basics in doctrine and encouraging service in some ministry of the church. (In general, though, it is not good to rush new people into service. They should have a "honeymoon" period during which they and the church can get to know each other. As new people experience social acceptance and spiritual growth, they naturally will want to become more involved.)

Most of these concerns seem to pertain only to large churches where visitors might go unnoticed. Sometimes a small church has to work harder at welcoming visitors because of the "exclusive" character of many small congregations. Large or small, however, the church that wants to welcome visitors must be willing to work at it.

Worship

Before teachers can lead children in a worship experience, they must understand all that worship involves. Worship is one of the four main functions of any church, alongside instruction, fellowship, and expression.

- *Worship* means "worth-ship"; it refers to God's worth. He is the only One worthy of our praise, honor, and adoration.
- *Instruction* means proper teaching or the giving of knowledge. A teacher instructs by the Word of God and by example.
- *Fellowship* means friendship. Children develop friendships in Sunday school, clubs, and camps. Most of all, though, they need friendship with God.
- *Expression* has two parts—expression to non-Christians through evangelism, and expression to Christians through service and mutual encouragement. Children require a balanced program that helps them participate in both of these areas.

There are several principles involved in children's worship experiences:

- Worship must be *active* as opposed to *passive*. Children need to be involved in the worship experience, and activities can bring meaning to the worship. In a careful study of Psalm 119—which emphasizes the Word of God—*doing* the Word is mentioned most often, *feeling* the Word is next, and *knowing* the Word is mentioned least often. Knowledge comes first—but children must also be doers of the Word.

- Worship must be on the learner's level. Words, terms, phrases, and concepts used during worship need to be understandable. The words "born again," "justification," and "providential," if used, must be explained on an appropriate vocabulary level. Remember that young children usually cannot understand symbolism.
- Worship must become involved in building relationships. Teaching children requires knowledge, understanding, *and* strong teacher-student relationships. Children need to see that their teachers live the truths they teach. A teacher's example of Christ-like behavior can carry a learner's Bible knowledge into the emotional and behavioral levels.
- Worship must be focused on who God is. It must turn children's attention toward God. This is best accomplished when each activity of the worship time—music, prayer, Scripture reading—points to a single, specific worship aim.

How Should Worship Be Programmed for Children?

In most churches, the Sunday school lesson is followed by a separate hour devoted to worship. Children should be helped to realize worship is appropriate at any time and anywhere, but this hour is a special time set aside for that purpose.

Under ideal circumstances, children can remain in their classrooms while the first hour's team of teachers is replaced by the second hour's team, who lead a time of worship directly related to the lesson theme. In most churches, however, fewer workers are available during the second hour.

Children are therefore herded together into large groups, and a special effort must be made to relate worship to the first-hour themes and the needs of each age group.

Another typical problem is the transition time between Sunday school and church. During this time, some children leave, others arrive, and some remain. Chaos reigns for anywhere from ten minutes to a half hour. By the time children's worship begins, the children are no longer focused on spiritual matters.

Each church must work out its own solution, but children cannot be unsupervised or uncontrolled at any time. Those children who attended the first hour must have their needs met for recreation, refreshment, and restroom trips. Young children have to be occupied with activities, or they will panic when other children's parents pick up their classmates and their own parents are nowhere in sight.

Follow these guidelines in maximizing your learners' worship experience:

1. The second-hour worship experience begins with this period of transition. During this time, activities can lead children's thoughts to the theme of the hour. Memory-verse games are a good staple.
2. Preparation for worship should involve the children. They should be allowed to plan aspects of the worship. Groups can be assigned the tasks of selecting verses to be read, practicing a song, or discussing requests to be included in prayer.
3. Praise time gathers the learners together to worship God. Music, Bible memory, sharing, and a time of prayer can all be elements of this part of the session. Worship is easily enhanced by the atmosphere of the room: Posters, flowers, mood-setting music, and special lighting can all add to a feeling of reverence.
4. Dismissal time should involve a five-to-ten-minute segment of the session so that the praise time can come to an orderly close without the ringing of a bell or the arrival of parents to pick up children. Games, puzzles,

and books can be available to the children until parents arrive. Very young children become anxious and upset if they are the last to be picked up. Having individual and small-group activities to close the session can keep these "leftovers" occupied.

The key to having any meaningful worship experience is not to try to impose an attitude of reverence at a specific time and place, but rather to use experiences as opportunities for praise and prayer. Teachers must remember that a child's authentic worship of the Lord may sound more like, "Yay, God!" than, "Hallelujah, Amen." The Psalms encourage not only silence before God, but also shouting and playing all kinds of musical instruments. Even King David danced! Worship can be quiet and reflective, but it can also be noisy and celebratory. Reverence for the Lord comes in many acceptable forms.

Writing Activities

One particular writing activity is overused in Sunday school, while dozens of others go untried. The typical lesson plan involving this category requires learners to listen to a story and then use a worksheet to fill in answers to review questions. Much effort is devoted to correct spelling, neat handwriting, and finding the correct line on which to print.

A creative writing activity, on the other hand, challenges a learner to think about the meaning of the lesson and its application to daily life. Poems, stories, journals, and scripts are projects that can actively involve a student in the process of learning. Using inexpensive supplies, teachers can generate interest in a lesson while helping students practice and develop their communication skills.

Teachers who use such creative writing projects must consider the abilities and interests of their students. Those who wish to participate but do not have the required writing skills may, for instance, dictate their ideas to a classmate or the teacher. Alternative activities should be provided for those who prefer drama, music, or art.

Sentence Descriptions

Students can be asked to write sentence descriptions of lesson-related pictures that are displayed in the classroom.

As a review, the rest of the class can match the sentences with correct scenes.

For a lesson on creation, students can write descriptions of animals to be matched to photographs of the creatures.

Prayers

Written prayers should not be used to formalize the way a child communicates with God. Teachers should encourage spontaneous, conversational prayer. Writing down a prayer can, however, help children understand and organize their ideas. Written prayers also can help children keep track of how God answers their requests.

Children usually have to wait a long time for letters from the mission field; they can forget what they prayed for on the missionaries' behalf. Requests made in a written prayer can be compared with newly arrived reports—and these can provide an important lesson on how God answers prayer.

Newspaper

A favorite project among older elementary children is to create a newspaper reporting an event in Bible history. Students who prefer art activities can supply the "photographs." The succinct nature of journalism requires a reporter to isolate important events, know the roles of the characters involved, and write so that readers will understand. A typewriter or computer and a copy machine are all that a "staff" of students needs to produce a Sunday-morning edition.

To better understand the scope and sequence of the events of the Exodus, students can print a newspaper reviewing the plagues and advising the Hebrews to pack up and get ready to move. Columns can include interviews with Pharaoh and Moses.

Poetry

Some children enjoy writing poems because of the rhyming patterns, while others are reluctant to tackle poetry of any kind. Teachers can provide models of various poetry styles, including Japanese haiku, to show learners that poetry can be a fun and easy way to express feelings and ideas.

To express their feelings about God's creation of the seasons, a group can assign each season to a different writer and assemble the results in a notebook to share with the rest of the class.

Skits and Plays

Scripts can be written to dramatize either events from the Scriptures or modern-day experiences that illustrate Bible truth. Such scripts can be written for people or puppets. In order to create a script, writers must have a solid understanding of the story to be dramatized and be able to imagine themselves in the characters' roles.

A group of students may be encouraged to rewrite the events of the Bible in a contemporary setting. This practice can help them to better understand, for example, the social status of the Samaritan in the story of "The Good Samaritan." Each of the passersby can be recast in a modern-day parallel character.

Journal

There are two ways to approach a journal project. One method is to encourage students to keep a record of their thoughts about what they have learned from the Bible and how they apply its lessons to their daily life. Another technique is to write a journal entry as an "eyewitness" who has experienced an event recorded in the Bible. Reports from Bible events can also be written as letters or postcards.

Students can imagine, for example, that they have been present at the feeding of the multitude. Have them write postcards describing the event, complete with a "picture scene" on the other side.

Too much of the writing done by learners in Sunday school is no more than tedious copying and borders on busywork. Students need to write creatively and to use this medium to express their ideas and feelings about what they are learning.

Notes

Chapter One

1. Martha Farnsworth Riche, "All Mixed Up," *American Demographics*, vii (Nov. 1989), 15 (i).
2. Arthur Winter, *Build Your Brain Power* (Martin's, N.Y.: M. D. & Winter, 1986), 1. Also, "Nerves and Nervous System," *Britannia*, Macropedia Vol. 24 (Chicago: Encyclopedia Britannica, Inc.) CHI, 838. And V. H. Brix, *You Are a Computer* (New York: Emerson Book, Inc., 1970), 33.
3. Donald Ratcliff, reviewing *Godly Play* by Jerome Berryman and *Young Children and Worship* by Jerome Berryman and Sonja M. Stewart, *Christian Education Journal* (Wheaton, Ill.: Scripture Press Ministries, 1992), Autumn, 1992 Vol. xiii, Number 1.
4. Alfred Edersheim, *The Temple: Its Ministry and Services* (Grand Rapids, Mich.: Wm. B. Eerdmans, 1969).
5. Among Protestants, the church-sponsored Christian school serves a similar function. Protestant parents, however, generally retain more control.
6. Carl F. George, *Prepare Your Church for the Future* (Tarrytown, N.Y.: Fleming H. Revell Company, 1990), 104.
7. Ibid, 116.
8. Ibid.
9. Churches using good Sunday school curricula and monitoring attendance probably have the best chance of meeting this criterion, of these four mentioned areas.
10. It is generally recognized how important peer groups are for teenagers, but few adults or churches organize themselves to help teenagers begin those friendships in childhood.
11. We are not in favor of putting guilt on children about their lack of evangelism when adults fail in this same area. Basically, children ought to observe adults' lead in evangelism by example. Children will pick up the message and follow adult modeling. However, it is unrealistic to expect children to succeed where adults fail.

12. Matthew 21:15 also notes that children were present at Christ's triumphal entry. The singing of the children to Jesus was spontaneous, but it blossomed out of their understanding of the events and belief in who Jesus appeared to be. These children hoped Jesus would be their King and Messiah.

13. Compare James 1:27 with John 14:18. Also, see *The International Bible Encyclopedia* (Grand Rapids, Mich.: Wm. B. Eerdmans, 1939), Vol. II, 1101.

Chapter Five

1. Barry J. Wadsworth, *Piaget's Theory of Cognitive Development* (New York: Longman, 1979), 160.

Children's Ministry A-Z

Abuse and Advocacy

1. *Victim Services Resource Manual* (Dallas: Child Protection Program Foundation, 1991), 9.

2. *Child Protection Guide, 3rd ed.* (Santa Rosa, Calif.: Christian Action Network Foundation, 1989), 5.

3. *Victim Services Resource Manual*, 3.

4. *Child Protection Guide*, 10.

5. *Safety Tips on a Sensitive Subject: Child Sexual Abuse* (Merrill, Wis.: Church Mutual Insurance Co., 1991), 2.

6. *Victim Services Resource Manual*, 27.

7. William Katz, *Protecting Your Children from Sexual Assault* (Young America, Minn.: Little Ones Books, 1983), 14.

8. *Safety Tips on a Sensitive Subject*, 3.

9. *Child Protection Guide*, 14.

Active Learning

1. *Teacher Training Packet*. Presented during workshops at the International Center for Learning, Ventura, Calif., 1976.

Cultural Diversity

1. *USA Today*, December 4, 5, 6, 1992.

Occult Concerns

1. Unpublished material from Pat Zukeran, Probe Ministries, Dallas, Tex.
2. Ibid.
3. Ibid.
4. Ibid.
5. Ibid.
6. Ibid.
7. Ibid.
8. Neil T. Anderson and Steve Russo, *The Seduction of Our Children* (Eugene, Ore.: Harvest House Publishers, 1991), 53–54.
9. Berit Kjos, *Your Child and the New Age* (Wheaton, Ill.: Victor Books; Division of Scripture Press Publishers, 1990), 23.
10. Anderson and Russo, *The Seduction of Our Children*, 55–56.
11. Ibid, 57.
12. Ibid, 54.
13. Ibid, 56.
14. Kjos, *Your Child and the New Age*, 15–27.

Playgrounds

1. *Handbook for Public Playground Safety* (Washington, D.C.: U.S. Consumer Product Safety Commission), 1.

Special Needs

1. Gaston E. Bloom, Bruce D. Cheney, and James E. Snoddy, *Stress in Childhood* (New York: Teachers College Press, 1986), 129.

Stress in Children

1. *The State of America's Children* (Washington, D. C.: Children's Defense Fund, 1991).

Bibliography

Leadership and Administration

Brown, Carolyn C. *Developing Christian Education in the Small Church*, Nashville: Abingdon, 1982.

Brown, Lowell D. *Sunday School Standards*, Ventura, Calif.: Gospel Light, 1986.

Cionca, John R. *Solving Church Education's Ten Toughest Problems*, Wheaton, Ill.: Victor, 1990.

Clark, Joanne Brubaker and Roy B. Zuck. *Childhood Education in the Church*, Chicago: Moody, 1986.

Clark, Robert E., Lin Johnson, and Allyn K. Sloat. *Christian Education, Foundations for the Future*, Chicago: Moody, 1991.

Gangel, Kenneth O. *Building Leaders for Christian Education*, Chicago: Moody, 1981.

Gangel, Kenneth O. and Howard G. Hendricks. *The Christian Educator's Handbook on Teaching*, Wheaton, Ill.: Victor, 1988.

Gangel, Kenneth O. and Warren S. Benson. *Christian Education: Its History and Philosophy*, Chicago: Moody, 1983.

Habermas, Ronald and Klaus Issler. *Teaching for Reconciliation*, Grand Rapids: Baker, 1986.

Lawson, Michael S. and Robert J. Choun. *Directing Christian Education*, Chicago: Moody, 1992.

Richards, Lawrence O. *A Theology of Christian Education*, Grand Rapids: Zondervan, 1975.

Senter, Mark III. *The Art of Recruiting Volunteers*, Wheaton, Ill.: Victor, 1985.

Wilhoit, Jim. *Christian Education and the Search for Meaning*, Grand Rapids: Baker, 1986.

Teaching and Child Development

Bolton, Barbara J. *How to Do Bible Learning Activities Grades 1-6*, Ventura, Calif.: Gospel Light, 1982

Bolton, Barbara J., Charles Smith and Wesley Haystead. *Everything You Want to Know About Teaching Children Grades 1-6*, Ventura, Calif.: Gospel Light, 1987.

Capehart, Jody. *Becoming a Treasured Teacher*, Wheaton, Ill.: Victor, 1992.

Haystead, Wesley. *Everything You Want to Know About Teaching Young Children Birth-6 Years*, Ventura, Calif.: Gospel Light, 1989.

Ketterman, Grace H., M.D. and Herbert L. Ketterman, M.D. *The Complete Book of Baby and Child Care for Christian Parents*, Old Tappan, N.J.: Fleming H. Revell, 1982.

Klein, Karen. *How to Do Bible Learning Activities Ages 2-5*, Ventura, Calif.: Gospel Light, 1982.

LeBar, Lois. *Education That Is Christian*, Wheaton, Ill.: Victor, 1989.

Family Ministry

Sell, Charles M. *The Enrichment of Family Life Through the Church*, Grand Rapids: Zondervan, 1981.

Children in Crisis

Anderson, Bill. *When Child Abuse Comes to Church*, Minneapolis: Bethany, 1992.

Lester, Andrew D. *When Children Suffer*, Philadelphia: Westminster, 1987.

Special Ministries
Morris, Lisa Rappaport and Linda Schulz. *Creative Play Activities for Children with Disabilities*, Champaign, Ill.: Human Kinetics Books, 1989.

Schuster, Clara Shaw. *Jesus Loves Me, Too*, Kansas City, Mo.: Beacon Hill, 1985.

Schools
Schimmels, Cliff, Ph.D. *Parents' Most Asked Questions About Kids and Schools*, Wheaton, Ill.: Victor, 1989.

Camping
Graendorf, Werner and Lloyd Mattson. *An Introduction to Christian Camping*, Chicago: Moody, 1979.

Intergenerational
White, James W. *Intergenerational Religious Education*, Birmingham: Religious Education Press, 1988.

Puppets
Rottman, Fran. *Easy to Make Puppets and How to Use Them*, Vol. 1: Early Childhood; Vol. 2: Children and Youth. Ventura, Calif.: Regal Books, 1978.

Missions
Branson, Mary. *Fun Around the World*, Birmingham: New Hope, 1992.

Games
Group Books. *Fun Group Games for Children's Ministry*, Loveland, Colo.: Group, 1992.

State Conventions and Conferences

Alaska

Alaska Christian Education Convention Association
2440 East Tudor Road, Box 150
Anchorage, AK 99507
(907) 272-8760

Arizona

Greater Arizona Christian Education Association
P O Box 12686
Tucson, AZ 85732-2218
(602) 297-7238

Leaders in Growing, Helping, Training
P O Box 5161
Glendale, AZ 85312-5161
(602) 974-5321

California

Bay Area Sunday School Association
Box 2829
Castro Valley, CA 94546
(510) 537-2041

San Bernardino, Riverside Area Sunday School Association
1787 Prince Albert Drive
Riverside, CA 92507
(714) 683-1009

Central Valley Christian Education Convention
4750 North Blackstone
Fresno, CA 93726
(209) 226-0541

Church Leadership and Sunday School Convention of
Sacramento
4400 58th Street
Sacramento, CA 95820
(916) 344-7966

Greater Los Angeles Sunday School Association
(G.L.A.S.S.)
P O Box 296
Rosemead, CA 91770-0296
(818) 288-8720/(800) 282-2338
(G.L.A.S.S. also holds a Spanish convention):
(818) 288-1914

Greater Redding Area Christian Education
Shasta Bible College
2980 Hartnell Avenue
Redding, CA 96002
(916) 221-4275

Kern County Sunday School Association
P O Box 275
Bakersfield, CA 93302
(805) 327-5921/(805) 589-9733

San Diego Sunday School Association
P O Box 1776
Spring Valley, CA 91977
(691) 670-6657

Colorado

Mountain Area Sunday School Association
P O Box 5881
Denver, CO 80217
(303) 696-6277

Christian Ministries Convention
P O Box 471091
Aurora, CO 80047
(303) 696-6277

Illinois

Central Illinois Sunday School Convention
4100 War Memorial Drive
Peoria, IL 61614
(309) 688-0625

Greater Chicago Sunday School Association
44 Lake Street
Oak Park, IL 60302
(708) 383-7550

Greater Rockford Area Sunday School Association
P O Box 4005
Rockford, IL 61110
(815) 877-5769

Indiana

Three Rivers Sunday School Association
Summit Christian College
1025 West Rudisill Blvd.
Fort Wayne, IN 46807
(219) 456-2111

Iowa

Iowa State Sunday School Association
First Assembly of God
2725 Merle Hay Road
Des Moines, IA 50310
(515) 279-9766

Iowa Christian Ministries Conference
2922 54th Street
Des Moines, IA 50310
(515) 279-1538

Kansas

Kansas Leadership and Sunday School Association
6100 West Maple
Wichita, KS 67209
(316) 943-1800

Kentucky

Good News
308 East Main Street
Wilmore, KY 40390
(606) 858-4661

Maine

Maine Association of Christian Educators
RFD 1 Box 995
Clinton, ME 04927
(207) 453-6120

Maryland

Baltimore Area Sunday School Association
P O Box 24008
Baltimore, MD 21227
(301) 789-1438

Greater Washington Christian Education Association
2130 East Randolph Road
Silver Spring, MD 20904
(301) 431-4141

Massachusetts

Evangelistic Association of New England
279 Cambridge Street
Burlington, MA 01803
(617) 229-1990

New England Association for Christian Education
279 Cambridge Street
Burlington, MA 01803
(617) 229-1990

Michigan

International Christian Education Association
13165 Cloverdale, Suite #1
Oak Park, MI 48237
(313) 399-6500

Midwest Sunday School Association
3725 Grant Street
Hudsonville, MI 49426
(616) 669-3675

Minnesota

Minnesota Sunday School Association
3745 26th Avenue S.
Minneapolis, MN 55406
(612) 729-4384

Nebraska

Central Nebraska Sunday School Association
Rt. 2 Box 152
Broken Bow, NE 68822
(308) 872-2781

New Jersey

Northern New Jersey Sunday School Association
212 Westervelt Avenue
North Plainfield, NJ 07060-4108
(908) 754-3069/(908) 754-6363

New York

Greater New York Sunday School Association
3015 Morgan Drive
Wantagh, NY 11793
(516) 221-0231

New York State Sunday School Association
P O Box 1848
Williamsville, NY 14231
(716) 839-2396

North Carolina

Mid-Atlantic Christian Education Association
(North and South Carolina, Virginia, Tennessee, and
Georgia)
P O Box 29045
Charlotte, NC 28229-9045
(704) 536-6259/(800) 321-7495

North Dakota

North Dakota State Sunday School Association
P O Box 1093
Minot, ND 58701
(701) 839-1544

Ohio

Central Ohio Christian Education Conference
Heritage Christian Books and Supply
173 Cline Avenue
Mansfield, OH 44907
(419) 529-3166

North American Christian Convention
P O Box 11326
Cincinnati, OH 45211
(513) 385-2470
(sponsored by Christian Churches and Churches of Christ)

Ohio Christian Education Association
187 Casterton Avenue
Akron, OH 44303
(216) 869-5832

Oklahoma

Oklahoma Christian Education Association
c/o KQCY Radio
1919 North Broadway
Oklahoma City, OK 73103
(405) 521-1414

Oregon

Greater Eugene Christian Educators Association
P O Box 23023
Eugene, OR 97402
(503) 995-6723/(503) 689-2127

Greater Salem Association of Christian Educators
P O Box 17831
Salem, OR 97305
(503) 581-2129

Portland Christian Education Convention
Western Evangelical Seminary
4200 SE Jennings Avenue
Portland, OR 97267
(503) 654-5466

Willamette Valley Christian Education Convention
P O Box 17831
Salem, OR 97305
(503) 393-3141

Pennsylvania

Central Pennsylvania Christian Education Conference
901 Eden Road
Lancaster, PA 17601
(717) 569-7071

Delaware Valley Christian Education Convention
c/o Philadelphia College of the Bible
200 Manor Avenue
Langhorne, PA 19047-2992
(215) 752-5800 ext. 286

Greater Philadelphia Area Sunday School Association
P O Box 28882
Philadelphia, PA 19151
(215) 748-8568

Pennsylvania State Sunday School Association
5915 Fox Street
Harrisburg, PA 17112
(717) 652-1930

Susquehanna Valley Christian Education Association
321 Gettysburg Pike
Mechanicsburg, PA 17055
(717) 697-0226

South Dakota

South Dakota Sunday School Association
Crossroads Book and Music Store
3817 South Western
Sioux Falls, SD 57105
(605) 338-5951

Texas

Texas State Sunday School Convention
P O Box 2676
Grapevine, TX 76099
(817) 481-4949

Washington

Christian Growth Conference
Greater Yakima Association of Evangelicals
P O Box 989
Yakima, WA 98907

Greater Seattle Christian Education Conference
Northwest District Council, Attn: C. E. Dept.
P. O. Box 699
Kirkland, WA 98083
(206) 827-3013

Northwest Christian Education Conference
P O Box 110548
Tacoma, WA 98411-0548
(206) 352-9044

Spokane Christian Workers Conference
5302 East Sprague
Spokane, WA 99202
(509) 534-8575

National Professional Organizations

Professional Association of Christian Educators
8405 North Rockwell
5 Plaza Square, Suite 222
Oklahoma City, OK 73162
(214) 824-3094

Children's Pastors Conference
P O Box 2398
Littleton, CO 80161
(303) 799-6751

Children's Ministry Organizations

Club Programs

AWANA
One East Bode Road
Streamwood, IL 60107

Bible Memory Association
P O Box 12000
Ringgold, AL 71068

Christian Education Publishers
P O Box 261129
San Diego, CA 92126

Christian Service Brigade
Box 150
Wheaton, IL 60189

Friendship Ministries
(for people with mental impairment)
2850 Kalamazoo Avenue SE
Grand Rapids, MI 49560

Olympian Program
Word of Life Fellowship
Schroon Lake, NY 12870

Pioneer Ministries
Box 788
Wheaton, IL 60189

Schools

Association for Christian Schools International
P O Box 4097
Whittier, CA 90607

Camps

Christian Camping International
P O Box 646
Wheaton, IL 60187

Curriculum Publishers

Child Evangelism Fellowship Press
P O Box 348
Warrenton, MO 63383

Concordia Publishing House
3558 South Jefferson Street
St. Louis, MO 63188

David C. Cook
850 North Grove Avenue
Elgin, IL 60120

Gospel Light Publications
2300 Knoll Drive
Ventura, CA 93003

Radiant Life
1445 Boonville Avenue
Springfield, MO 65802

Scripture Press
1825 College Avenue
Wheaton, IL 60187

Standard Publishing
8121 Hamilton Avenue
Cincinnati, OH 45231

Missions Education

Kids Can Make a Difference
4445 Webster Drive
York, PA 17402

Sudan Interior Mission
Box 7900
Charlotte, NC 28217

The Bible League
16801 Van Dam Road
South Holland, IL 60473

Wycliffe
P O Box 2727
Huntington Beach, CA 92647

Crisis Information

American Cancer Society
777 Third Avenue
New York, NY 10017
(212) 371-2900

"Just Say No!" Clubs
1777 N. California Blvd. Suite 200
Walnut Creek, CA 94595

National AIDS Hotline
(800) 342-AIDS

National Clearinghouse for Alcohol Information
Box 2345
Rockville, MD 20852
(301) 468-2600

National Clearinghouse for Drug Abuse Information
Box 1635
Rockville, MD 20852
(301) 443-6500

National Committee for the Prevention of Child Abuse
332 South Michigan Avenue Suite 1600
Chicago, Il 60604
(312) 663-3520

Dr. Robert Choun is a professor of Christian Education at Dallas Theological Seminary in Dallas, Texas. His experience includes youth ministry in Chicago and ten years as a Christian Education Specialist in the Dallas area. Now completing doctoral studies at the University of North Texas, Dr. Choun also holds degrees from Gustavus Adolphus, Trinity Evangelical Divinity School, Wheaton Graduate School, and Faith Evangelical Lutheran Seminary.

Dr. Choun travels nationwide presenting seminars on Christian education administration and teacher-training. He has co-edited the "Young Explorer" and "General Reference" editions of *What the Bible Is All About* (Regal Books) and co-authored *Directing Christian Education* (Moody Press). He resides in Arlington, Texas, with his wife and co-worker, Jane.

Dr. Michael S. Lawson is Professor of Christian Education and chairman of the department at Dallas Theological Seminary. He was a pastor of Christian Education for more than seventeen years and has co-authored the book *Directing Christian Education* with his colleague, Bob Choun.

Dr. Lawson travels and teaches internationally in the field of Christian education. He has been President of The Professional Association of Christian Educators since 1986. Mike lives in Mesquite, Texas, with his partner in life and ministry, Tish.